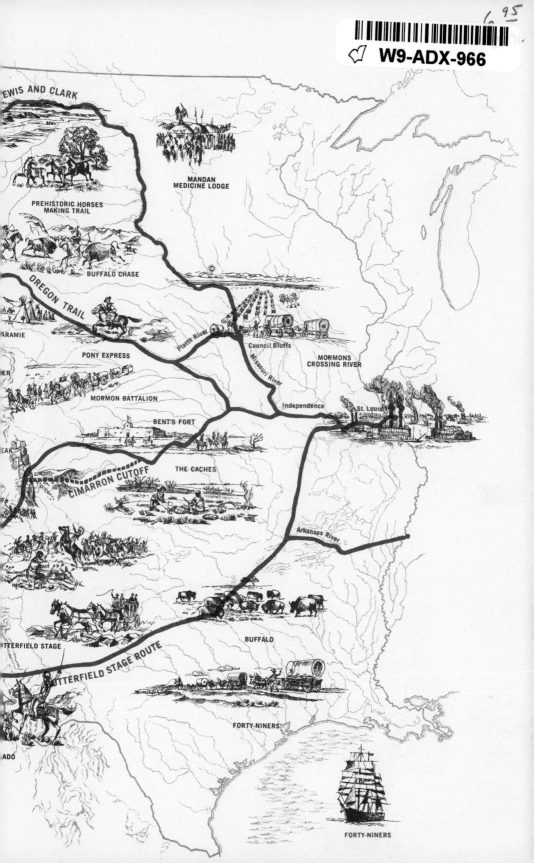

The Old Trails West

THE
OLD TRAILS
WEST

By RALPH MOODY

Thomas Y. Crowell Company

ESTABLISHED 1834

NEW YORK

TO EDNA

my beloved trailmate

Foreword

MORE THAN half a century ago, I was water boy on a large cattle ranch. Our range was on the rolling prairies along the foothills of the Rockies in northern Colorado. In summer the cattle were allowed to scatter for a considerable distance, with four or five cowhands spread out to keep them from drifting too far. My job was to ride the circuit morning and afternoon, carrying any orders the foreman wanted to send the men, and supplying them with water from a dogskin bag slung to the back of my saddle.

When the herd had grazed northward nearly to the Wyoming line I discovered a set of deep-worn old wheel ruts. Having little to do that day, I followed the overgrown trail for several miles, wondering: Why is it out here on the prairie, seemingly leading from nowhere to nowhere? Who first broke this trail, and what reason did he have for doing it? Why did he go this way instead of some other, and where was he going? Why were so many wagons driven over a road that did not seem to lead anywhere, and what were they hauling that made such deep wheel ruts?

The next man on my circuit was Hank Bevin, an oldtime cowhand, probably well along in his sixties, so I asked him the same questions I had asked myself.

"Anglin' off towards the nor'west, betwixt the Laramie and Medicine Bow ranges?" he asked.

[v]

"I don't know about the ranges, but the tracks were angling toward the foothills northwest, not in the direction of Cheyenne."

"Wouldn't be," he said. "Cheyenne's a railroad town, and there wasn't no railroads when them ruts was wore. What you stumbled onto was the trace of the old Overland Stagecoach Line. I recollect when it run clean through from Missouri to Californy. Main trail of the Overland followed the North Platte and Sweetwater, but Ben Holladay, he swung his stage line south'ard from Julesburg to pick up the Denver trade. This here's the way he went back north to get through the mountains at the end of the Medicine Bows."

"How did he know where to get through the mountains?" I asked. "There doesn't appear to be any break in them along here."

"No, but there's lots of old buffalo trails. Didn't ever you take note how the deepest buffalo and wild horse trails always leads by the easiest way to the nearest water, the best grass, and the lowest mountain passes? Remember that if you aim to be a cattleman, and it'll save you a heap of trouble. That's all Ben, or whoever laid out the old stage line, had to know. Like as not he followed the trail of buffalo headin' for grass on the west side of the range."

"I wonder how he happened to come through this way," I said.

"Didn't happen to; needed to," Hank told me, "else he'd had to go three, four hundred miles out of his way. Don't no man nor no wild critter wear a trail where he happens to go; only where he needs to go. Find where a trail changed course and you'll find where the need of them passing over it changed. It's all wrote down for them that can read, just like it is with a man. An old man's story is wrote in lines on his face; an old trail's story is wrote in lines on the face of the earth."

Ever since that day I have tried to find out as much as I could about the early trails—from oldtimers, from riding considerable portions of them while the old ruts were still traceable, and from reading —but my search has always been for the why: Why was this trail blazed in the first place, by whom, and what were the needs that changed its course? There are many excellent books available regarding the history of individual western trails and the more important events which took place upon them. The purpose of this book is not to provide a comprehensive history of any trail, but to tell the story, from origin to obliteration of the ancient character lines that once seamed the face of the American West.—R. M.

Contents

[vii]

[ix]

Maps

Illustrations

[xiii]

The Old Trails West

1

The Original Pathfinders

THE HISTORY of the United States is replete with the names of famous pioneers and pathfinders who are credited with blazing the old trails of the old West. Yet few of them blazed a trail that had not been traveled for countless generations. It is probable that most of the more important western trails had been worn deep long before the first human foot was planted on the North American continent.

Some sixty million years ago, the western portion of the North American continent lay beneath the sea, and southern Arizona was a tropical swamp. Then the Sierra Nevada and Cascade mountains were heaved up, forming a great peninsula and leaving a shallow inland sea to the eastward. The sea was roughly four hundred miles wide and a thousand long, stretching from the Gulf of California to southern Idaho. When the mountains rose they blocked the course of rain clouds blown in from the Pacific, and the inland sea evaporated until its only remaining vestige is Great Salt Lake. During millions of years the evaporating moisture was blown eastward in rain clouds, watering lush forests and grasslands that covered the high plateaus of Arizona, New Mexico, eastern Utah, and western Colorado. When the evaporation was completed Nevada, western Utah, southeastern California, and western Arizona were left desolate salt-impregnated deserts, and the high plateaus became arid wastelands.

Long before the rising of the Sierra Nevada, the Rocky Mountains had formed a solid bulwark, robbing rain clouds borne by the prevailing westerly winds, and leaving the high, rolling plains that stretched five hundred miles to the eastward a semiarid wilderness. Thus, for millions of years before there was human habitation, the western half of what is now the United States was arid or semiarid, except for the mountainous regions. But in the high altitudes snow fell deep in winter and the summer rains were abundant.

Since the summits of the Sierra Nevada and Cascade mountains are on the eastern side of the ranges, most of the water from melting snow and rainfall flows westward into the Pacific. What little flows to the east is swallowed by the parched sands of the Great American Desert. On the other hand, the Rocky Mountains and their satellites are drained to almost every point of the compass: to the northwest by tributaries of the Columbia, to the northeast and east by tributaries of the Missouri, to the south by the Rio Grande, and to the southwest by the Colorado and its various branches.

With the exception of the Rio Grande, all these great river systems rise in the vicinity of Yellowstone National Park. The Green River, an extension of the Colorado, has its source a few miles to the south, and drains the entire area between the Rocky and Wasatch mountains. The Clark's Fork and Snake tributaries of the Columbia River reach eastward toward the park as if it were a block of ice and they were the jaws of a great pair of tongs open to seize it. The headwaters of the Missouri River rise a hundred and fifty miles inside the jaws of the tongs, while its largest tributary, the Yellowstone, reaches out to touch the lower jaw just outside the southeastern corner of the park. There Two Ocean Creek flows sluggishly along a flat, heavily wooded plateau on the exact line of the Continental Divide. Its waters diverge in a swampy area to form Atlantic Creek and Pacific Creek, making it possible for a trout to swim from one ocean to the other. The water turning to the west flows 1353 miles to the Pacific Ocean by way of the Snake and Columbia rivers. That turning to the east flows 3488 miles to the Gulf of Mexico by way of the Yellowstone, Missouri, and Mississippi rivers.

Since water is a necessity of life to all creatures, these rivers and their tributaries have marked the main routes of travel throughout the western half of this country for countless centuries, but man has done this traveling only in recent times. Before the Indians came, the horse was doubtlessly the greatest American traveler. It is believed that soon after the rising of the Sierra Nevada, horses originated in what is now the central United States. They were then toed creatures no larger than a greyhound, but more than a million years ago they evolved into a single-hoofed animal very much like the horses we know today. From fossil discoveries it is known that horses traveled to every part of this hemisphere, from the tip of South America to the Arctic Circle, and wherever horses travel they wear trails along the main routes of migration.

Horses can travel only a relatively short distance without water, so it is certain that their main routes lay along river courses. This does not mean that they confined their range to the close vicinity of streams. Being grazers, with speed their chief means of defense, they, like the antelope and buffalo, preferred the open prairies, and roamed far from streams, but wild grazing animals have the ability to smell water for incredible distances. As they grazed across high, semiarid divides they traveled from stream to stream, or sought out springs, ponds, and other natural watering places to which they returned frequently, wearing well-defined trails.

In migrating from summer to winter pasturage, elk often travel hundreds of miles through seemingly impassable mountains, returning year after year to the same locality and by the same route. As innumerable generations of elk passed over these routes they were worn into trails, each following the most direct course that offered necessary grazing and water. Deer, though seldom migrating so far, have for countless centuries worn equally direct trails through practically all the mountainous regions of this continent, always taking advantage of the lowest passes and the most accessible approaches. Anyone doubting the depth to which these animal trails were worn need only observe any steep grassy hill in grazing country. Each steep slope appears to have been evenly terraced at intervals of three or four feet, and so they were, by the hoofs of grazing animals following trails and cropping grass they could reach on the hillside above them.

No one knows why, but horses disappeared entirely from this hemisphere about twenty-five thousand years ago. Scientists believe they crossed a land bridge, then connecting Alaska with Siberia at Bering Strait, to spread throughout Asia and Europe. If this is true, it is probable that most of the horses from the Great Plains migrated westward by way of a route the Indians called the Big Medicine Trail. The basis for this supposition is that migrating horses will follow the most direct route that provides ease of travel, a wide range of view, and abundant grass and water.

[3]

Old Indian Trails West. The routes of explorers were influenced by these three major water routes. They determined the course of

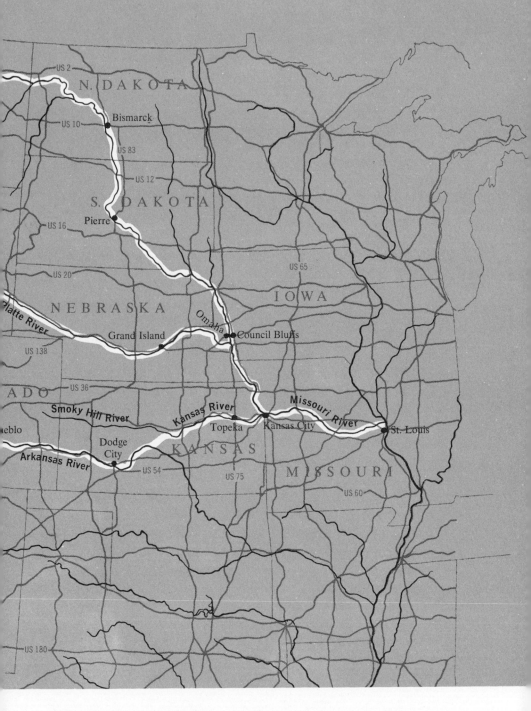

the Lewis and Clark expedition, the Oregon Trail, and the Gila Trail.

The Rocky Mountains form an almost impassable barrier to horses, stretching from the arid deserts of New Mexico to northern Canada, but in southern Wyoming there is a break in the high rampart of the range. From the Great Plains the land along the North Platte River and its tributary, the Sweetwater, rises gently to the Continental Divide, then slopes away to the Green River Valley in the southwestern corner of Wyoming. There the Wasatch Mountains form a barrier, but their northern end is circled by the looping Bear River, supplying a natural route to Snake River—the lower jaw of the tongs reaching eastward to Yellowstone Park from the Columbia. At the Idaho-Oregon boundary the curving tong of Snake River turns abruptly northward through awesome Hell's Canyon, but a series of grassy plateaus and valleys leads on to the northwest, reaching the broad valley of the Columbia north of Pendleton. This is the route by which the horses of the Great Plains are believed to have traveled in leaving the continent.

Many ethnologists believe that, at about the time the horses left, Asiatics, the ancestors of the Indians, crossed the land bridge in the opposite direction and eventually spread throughout the Western Hemisphere. How these people migrated to the various areas of North America can only be conjectured by the regions in which different linguistic groups were originally discovered. It is, however, probable that, being hunters and fishermen, they followed animal trails and watercourses in their dispersal throughout the newly discovered land. There can be little doubt that many who settled on the Great Plains, and farther to the east, followed horse trails from the Columbia River through the break in the rampart of the Rockies, for long before the white men came this route was known to the Indians as the Big Medicine Trail.

As the Indians scattered throughout the area that is now the United States, rivers became their highways, whether they traveled afoot or by canoe, for streams could be followed great distances with assurance that the traveler would be able to find his way back to the starting point. It is not probable that any Indian made a continuous transcontinental journey. The Indians did, however, have definite transcontinental routes, and are known to have traveled great distances over them. The routes lay across the country like a great cable, tightly wound at the center, its eastern quarter frazzled into innumerable cords and fibers, and its western half unwound into three widely separated strands. The main cable, kinked and twisting,

[6]

looped between Kansas City and Cincinnati along the Missouri, Mississippi, and Ohio rivers. By way of the Ohio, its chief branches—the Tennessee, Cumberland, and Allegheny—and their hundreds of tributaries, the entire region west of the Appalachian and Allegheny mountains could be reached by direct watercourses, as far south as Alabama and northward into New York.

The old trails of the old West were influenced only by the three strands that lay across the prairies, mountains, and deserts between Kansas City and the Pacific Ocean. Two of these remained tightly wound as they followed the course of the Missouri River between Kansas City and Omaha. There they separated. One continued far northward up the Missouri to its headwaters in the vicinity of Yellowstone Park, crossed the Continental Divide, and descended to the Pacific by way of the northern tong of the Columbia River. The other was the Big Medicine Trail; its course lay westward along the Platte and Sweetwater rivers to the Continental Divide at South Pass, across the Green River Valley, along the Bear, and on to the Pacific by way of the southern tong of the Columbia.

The third strand of the great cable looped far to the south, and followed four separate watercourses to reach the Pacific. From as far east as the Allegheny Mountains, the Indians could travel to the northern and central Rockies by continuous and direct watercourses. But to reach the southern Rockies by a continuous water route they must travel far down the Mississippi, then back to the northwest along the Arkansas River, lengthening the direct distance by several hundred miles. To avoid this long detour, they learned to follow the Missouri to the point where it turns northward at Kansas City, paddle up the Kansas River and its tributary, the Smoky Hill, then portage thirty miles overland to the Arkansas at the point where it makes its great northern bend in central Kansas.

In all probability the Indians discovered this more direct route because of buffalo and other animal trails that skirted the rivers and led from one to another where the overland distance was shortest. In any event, the route continued westward along the Arkansas to the foothills of the Rockies, descended the Rio Grande to southern New Mexico, then turned westward along the Gila (pronounced Heela) River to the Colorado, a few miles above the Gulf of California. This southern strand of the cable was known as the Gila Route and, together with the Big Medicine Trail, became the main line of many old trails of the West.

[7]

	Gila Trail	El Camino Real	Old Spanish Trail	Santa Fe Trail
1538	Esteban looks for Seven Cities			
1539	Diaz follows Esteban			
1540	Coronado's march			
1542		Cabrillo sails California coast		
1577		Drake sails California coast		
1602		Vizcaíno sails California coast		
1686	Kino to Pimería Alta			
1768	Garcés to Pimería Alta			
1769		Portolá at San Francisco Bay		
1774	Anza reaches Pacific	Anza to Monterey		
1775	Anza's colonizing party			
1776		Anza founds San Francisco	Escalante expedition	
1778				
1792				
1804				
1810				
1812				McKnight to Santa Fe
1821				Becknell opens Santa Fe trade
1822				Wagon party on Cimarron Cutoff

Big Medicine Trail	Oregon Trail	California Trail	—and meanwhile	
			Henry VIII reigns in England	1538
			De Soto explores Florida	1539
			Henry VIII marries Anne of Cleves	1540
			Russians trap in Alaska	1542
			Search for North-west Passage	1577
			First Englishman in New England	1602
			Connecticut Char-ter Oak incident	1686
			Methodist church in New World	1768
			Daniel Boone sees Kentucky	1769
			First Continental Congress	1774
			Revolutionary War	1775
			Declaration of Independence	1776
Cook at Nootka Sound			Franklin nego-tiates French treaty	1778
Gray finds Columbia R.			Cotton gin in-vented	1792
Lewis and Clark to Columbia R.			Jefferson re-elected President	1804
Hunt to Ft. Astoria			West Florida annexed	1810
Stuart's return to St. Louis			War with England	1812
			Missouri admitted to Union	1821
			Brazil gains in-dependence	1822

	Gila Trail	El Camino Real	Old Spanish Trail	Santa Fe Trail
1823				
1824	Patties trap Gila			
1826			Smith looks for Buena Ventura	
1827			Smith to San Gabriel again	Ft. Leavenworth built
1829	E. Young traps Gila		Armijo cutoff route	Bent caravan
1830	E. Young reaches San Gabriel		Wolfskill-Yount trapping party	Bent and St. Vrain caravan
1832				
1833				
1834				Bent's Ft. built
1836				
1841–42				
1843				
1846	Kearny's march			Kearny takes Santa Fe
1847				
1848				
1849	Duval gold-rush party			
1858	Butterfield Mail started			
1860				
1861				
1862	Apache Pass Battle			
1869				
1880				First train to Santa Fe

Big Medicine Trail	Oregon Trail	California Trail	—and meanwhile	
Smith-Fitz-patrick trapping party			Monroe Doctrine	1823
			John Q. Adams elected President	1824
			First U.S. locomotive	1826
			Barbed wire invented	1827
			Andrew Jackson inaugurated	1829
			Indian Removal Act	1830
	Wyeth, settlers to Oregon		Black Hawk War	1832
		Walker to San Francisco Bay	Steel plow introduced	1833
	Wyeth's 2nd trip	Carson traps Humboldt R.	McCormick reaper patented	1834
Whitman mission			Battle of the Alamo	1836
De Smet to Columbia R.		Bidwell party to California	W. H. Harrison inaugurated; died	1841–42
		Frémont to Sutter's Ft.	Mormons adopt polygamy	1843
		Donner tragedy	Mexican War	1846
		B. Young to Utah	Scott in Mexico	1847
		Mormon handcarts to Utah	Gold found in California	1848
			Minnesota becomes a Territory	1849
			First Atlantic-cable message	1858
		Pony Express	Lincoln elected	1860
		Telegraph line	Civil War	1861
			Homestead Act	1862
		Transcontinental railroad	Powell navigates Grand Canyon	1869
			Major Alaskan gold strike	1880

2

The Gila Trail

From artifacts discovered in New Mexico it is known that humans have lived in the region of the Gila River for at least fifteen thousand years, though their history prior to the beginning of the Christian Era is purely conjectural. Due to the extreme dryness of the climate which has preserved some of their cliff dwellings, ancient irrigation canals, and an enormous quantity of pottery shards, the past two thousand years of their history can be deciphered more accurately than that of almost any other aboriginal people.

It is believed that Indian pottery was not made until the beginning of the Christian Era or before the aborigines had gathered into communal settlement, and that none was decorated with painted designs until about the year A.D. 300. Along the lower reaches of the Gila, quantities of pottery shards have been discovered at various locations, some crudely made and undecorated, others beautifully decorated with painted designs. These are indications that primitive civilization had begun taking shape there well over two thousand years ago. The existence of traceable irrigation canals on land that is now barren desert shows that these early community dwellers were successful farmers.

Closely related to these farmers and pottery makers were the cliff dwellers who lived along the upper reaches of the Gila and its tributaries. No one knows when the first cliff dwellings were built, but those that still remain date from A.D. 1000, and they must have been of an advanced type, for the builders had considerable knowledge of architecture. Montezuma Castle is a five-story cliff dwelling of twenty-five rooms. Tuzigoot is composed of three large pueblos and probably housed about three hundred people. The discovery of ancient corncobs proves the dwellers to have been farmers as well as skillful artisans.

What became of the cliff dwellers is as much a mystery as the beginning and development of their culture. All that is known is that, probably late in the thirteenth century or early in the fourteenth, they abandoned their dwellings and disappeared. No skeletons have been found, and no indications of panic, strife, or warfare. Famine seems the most logical answer, for it is known from tree rings that a great drought struck the Southwest, lasting from 1277 until 1299. It has been suggested that when the cliff dwellers' crops failed in successive years, and when because of the drought game became scarce, these people moved down the rivers to join their pottery-making cousins who had irrigated farms. This theory is further borne out by the building of Casa Grande in the early 1300's.

Archeological discoveries show that at the time of the great drought there were at least two hundred Indian communities in the watershed of the Gila River, and that the culture of these people was further advanced than that of any other Indians in North America. The heaviest concentration of population was along the main stream, for sixty or seventy miles southeast of the point where it is joined by the Salt River—near Phoenix. There the river was then about a half mile wide, with a broad, fertile valley along its southern bank. Along the outer edge of the valley small communities were strung like beads on a rosary. Between them and the river were irrigated farms, where abundant crops of corn, beans, pumpkins, melons, and cotton were raised.

Until the drought, all the dwellings in these communities were one-story adobe huts, but about the year 1325 Casa Grande was built, showing clearly the cliff dwellers' engineering skill and architectural knowledge. It is certain that the builders also had some knowledge of astronomy. A hole about an inch and a half in diameter was pierced through the adobe high in the east and central walls. These holes were so lined up that, at 6:53 A.M. on March 6 and October 6, the sun's rays passed through both. The builders' calcula-

[13]

The ruins of Casa Grande, southeast of present-day Phoenix, Arizona. From Notes of a Military Reconnaissance, *Lieutenant Colonel W. H. Emory.* Courtesy of The New York Public Library, Rare Book Division.

tions were not far off, for March 6 is two weeks before the spring equinox, and October 6 two weeks after the fall equinox.

These Indians had developed metallurgy to some extent and were very fond of ornaments, for among the ruins have been found small copper bells, pendants and trinkets made of turquoise, bone and blue shells brought from the Pacific. They made pottery figurines in human form, and beautifully shaped vessels of all sorts, which they decorated with imaginative symbolic designs.

What happened to these highly intelligent people—called Hohokam, the ancient ones, by the Pimas who now live in the area—is one of the great mysteries of the recent past, for they practiced cremation and left no skeletons for scientific study. There is some belief that they were the ancestors of the Pimas, but if so they passed on none of their arts, skills, and knowledge, with the exceptions of agriculture and cotton cloth weaving. All that is actually known is that they disappeared about a century after the building of Casa Grande, and that before their passing they had worn deep trails along the Gila and its tributaries.

At about the time the peaceful and cultured Hohokam disappeared, the most savage and ruthless tribe of Indians on this continent invaded the headwaters of the Gila. They were hunters and raiders, overran what is now southeastern Arizona, and were so fierce in their warfare that they were called *Apache*, meaning "enemy" in the Papago tongue. The name fitted so well that it has never been changed.

These people, though nomadic savages, had a very definite religion, based on many rituals and eleven divine commandments, but it was strictly for Apaches. In their belief, they were *The People*, and for them—and them alone—Usen had made the sun, the moon and the stars, the earth, and everything upon it. To them it was a sin to kill or steal from another Apache, but it was a virtue to kill and rob anyone else, for all others were trespassers upon the earth, and whatever they possessed had been stolen from the supply Usen made for *His People*. In the Apache rituals and religious ceremonies sea-shell and turtle-shell rattles were of great importance, and runners were sent long distances to gather the shells. It is probable that the first other humans to follow the trails the Hohokam had trodden along the Gila and its tributaries were Apache runners, on their way to the Gulf of California or the Pacific for shells.

THE CONQUISTADORES

It is certain that the first human other than an Indian to tread the ancient trails along the Gila was a Negro. In 1527, barely a century after the Hohokam had abandoned Casa Grande and disappeared, Charles V of Spain sent out an expedition of five ships and six hundred men to conquer and colonize the province in North America called Florida. The Florida Indians were not in favor of the conquest, and showed their displeasure by wrecking the ships and killing most of the conquistadores. A few escaped and, on improvised rafts, made their way along the Gulf coast to what is now Galveston, Texas. There they were captured and enslaved by other Indians, but in 1528 four of them again escaped: Cabeza de Vaca, Castillo de Maldonado, Dorantes de Carranza, and Esteban, a giant Negro slave owned by Dorantes.

Incredible though it seems, they existed for eight years in the wild and semiarid region between the Gulf of Mexico and the Gulf of

California, largely because Cabeza de Vaca convinced the Indians that he was a potent medicine man. How they communicated with Indians having scores of different languages is as amazing as their survival, but this they also did, always seeking directions to the City of Mexico. Communication must, at best, have been sketchy, and just enough to lead the Spanish away from their intended objective. When they escaped at Galveston they followed the gulf in the general direction of Mexico City until reaching the Rio Grande. There, the natives very evidently directed them toward the only cities they knew; the Pueblo Indian villages near present-day Santa Fe. In any event, the Spaniards turned back to the northwest, and followed the general course of the Rio Grande to a point near El Paso, where they turned westward along what is now the International Boundary.

In the general area of Bisbee, Arizona, the completely lost little party picked up more confusing information. Indians who had traveled to the north told them of great cities there, doubtlessly Casa Grande and the Hohokam villages along the Gila. Other Indians, probably those who had been to the Gulf of California for shells, told them of a city far to the south that was inhabited by bearded white men. That was the information for which Cabeza de Vaca and his followers had been searching. They turned southward, up the headwaters of the San Pedro River, and after eight years of wandering reached Culiacán, the most northerly Spanish settlement, opposite the tip of Lower California.

The weary Spaniards' only interest was in returning to Spain as quickly as possible, but when, after months of delay, they reached Mexico City, their tales of great cities far to the north stirred up a storm of interest. These must be the fabulously wealthy cities of Cíbola, the prime object of Spanish explorations in the New World.

When the ancient Spanish city of Mérida was captured by the Moors, seven bishops of the Catholic Church had fled to avoid being killed by the infidels. Each had gathered all the wealth he could lay his hands on, taken a group of followers, and set sail to establish a new civilization in a new land. Over the centuries a legend had sprung up that each bishop had founded a great city which had become fabulously wealthy; the streets paved with gold, and the houses all of silver, studded with precious stones. At first it was only

the masses who believed the legend, but in time it was accepted as fact by the nobility and rulers.

Don Antonio de Mendoza, Viceroy of New Spain, was one of the believers. But Mendoza was an astute man—and probably a bit greedy. To head off any possibility of a gold rush, he publicly scoffed at the idea that the reported cities could be those of the legend. But before the homesick wanderers sailed back to Spain, he insisted on buying from Dorantes de Carranza the giant Negro slave, Esteban.

Mendoza gave the excitement time to die out. Then, in the fall of 1538, he sent Marcos de Niza, a Franciscan monk, on a secret mission. With Esteban to guide him, he was to make a pilgrimage to the north, ostensibly to seek out and convert the heathen, but actually to discover and map a route to the Seven Cities of Cíbola.

Fray Marcos de Niza fully understood the purpose of his mission, but was not a particularly avid explorer. Soon after he and Esteban, with a Mexican-Indian interpreter, set off from Culiacán the monk made a deal with the giant. Esteban and the interpreter were to go ahead and do the hunting for the seven fabulous cities, while he

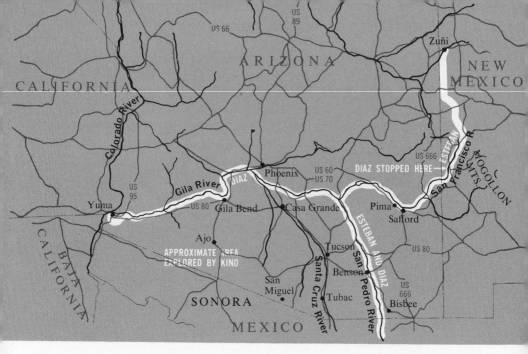

The Gila Trail: routes of Esteban and Melchior Diaz, and the approximate area explored by Father Kino. The Spanish first explored the Gila River region in search of the Seven Cities of Cíbola. Later they established missions in a colonization effort.

himself would follow in a more leisurely manner. But in order that he be kept posted at all times, the slave was to send back Indian runners at frequent intervals with reports of his success.

At first, this presented something of a problem, since Esteban could neither read nor write, and it was hardly safe to send secret information by word of mouth. But finally the good monk hit upon a happy solution: Esteban was to send back crosses, proportionate in size to the importance of his discoveries—of white wood if he found the heathen friendly, of black if he found them hostile.

Nothing could have pleased Esteban more. During eight years of wandering in the wilderness he had learned the superstitions of the Indians, and from Cabeza de Vaca he had learned the art of being a convincing medicine man. But Esteban went Cabeza one better. He decked his huge body with feathers and beads, made himself a noisy rattle, fixed up a medicine bag filled with trinkets of civilization, and proclaimed that he was a god, invulnerable to man or beast.

The giant towering more than a foot above the average Indian, and with a native flare for histrionics, must indeed have appeared godlike to the simple aborigines whose religious ceremonies were replete with magic and legends of giant spirits from another world. Esteban had no sooner left Fray Marcos behind than he began acquiring a retinue of worshipful followers, laying before him their richest gifts and bowing down to him as a great spirit. But Esteban was much more interested in the flesh than the spirit. As he made his triumphant way northward he left behind a four-hundred-mile wake of potential descendants, and the crosses he sent back to the lagging monk were of the whitest wood he could find.

At the headwaters of the San Pedro Esteban again picked up rumors of great cities to the north, so continued along the river to its confluence with the Gila. There he made contact with the Pima Indians, and was as overwhelmed by the affluence and hospitality of these gentle farmers as they were by his magnificence. Their corn, beans, and roast dog were delicious, their melons the sweetest he had even known, and their maidens the most voluptuous. Convinced that he had discovered the Promised Land, he hurried off a runner to take a cross back to Fray Marcos—a foot high and very white.

Though Esteban lingered for some time among the Pimas it is doubtful that he went as far west as Casa Grande, and it is certain that he was disappointed at finding the Hohokam villages deserted, but his Pima friends soon overcame his disappointment by telling him of inhabited cities beyond the headwaters of the Gila. These were the Zuñi pueblos, but to Esteban they could be no other than the Seven Cities of Cíbola. He immediately sent runners back to Marcos, carrying a white cross as tall as himself.

With Pima guides who knew the ancient trails along the Gila and its tributaries, and with a retinue of thirty ardent worshipers, Esteban set off for his conquest of the golden cities. But his conquesting was confined to cities, for no damsels were taken along, since the upper reaches of the Gila flowed through the Mogollon Mountains, dangerous Apache territory and the most rugged country in the Southwest.

It is not improbable that Esteban was somewhat out of sorts when, after three hundred miles of rugged mountain trails and a month of enforced chastity, he reached the Zuñi pueblo of Hawikuh and found it to be nothing but a few adobe dwellings in the center of a desert. What he said or did is simply a matter of conjecture. But it is known that the Zuñi have always been a peaceful people, highly religious, and extremely jealous of their women's virtue. Quite possibly to test the divinity of the black god, they shot a few arrows through him, which he failed to survive. His entourage beat a hasty retreat, and Opata runners hurried the sad tidings to Fray Marcos, still wending his way leisurely along the San Pedro Valley toward the Gila.

Poor Fray Marcos! He was in a terrible fix. Mendoza would not take kindly to his having lingered behind while he sent his slave ahead to discover the seven golden cities. In fact, the Viceroy might be unreasonably disappointed if he returned without tangible evidence of having visited those cities himself. But the monk had no stomach for getting any closer to the kind of people who would test a man's divinity with arrows. He turned back toward the City of Mexico with all speed, and on the way he gave his imagination free rein. Certainly Esteban must have discovered the Seven Cities of Cíbola before evil overtook him, or he would not have sent back the gigantic cross. It would be no very great sin to report that he himself had seen those cities.

By June, 1539, Fray Marcos reached Compostela, capital of the province of New Galicia, to which Francisco Vásquez de Coronado had recently been appointed governor. As soon as the monk had sent off a note to Mendoza, he announced to the governor that he was on his way back from a mission on which he had indeed discovered the Seven Cities of Cíbola. Coronado was elated. Here was the chance for conquest that would outshine Cortez's achievements. But Niza was tight lipped about details and locations; those secrets could be whispered only into the ear of the Viceroy. Immediately Coronado put his score or so of armored troops to horse, and led the triumphal procession to Mexico City.

No one knows what Fray Marcos de Niza whispered into Mendoza's ear, but he later made a written report of his mission. In it he told of Esteban's being brutally killed by the heathen, one day's journey before reaching the goal, but that with two friendly Indian chiefs as guides, "I pursued my journey until within sight of Cíbola. . . . The city is larger than the city of Mexico . . . all made of stone,

Coronado reaches the Platte River on his search for the Seven Cities of Cíbola. From The American Continent and Its Inhabitants, *Annie C. Cady.*

with stories and terraces. . . . The chiefs who had accompanied me told me it was the poorest of the seven cities, and that Totonteac is much larger, and better than all the seven, and that it has so many houses and citizens that it has no end. . . .

"I made a great heap of stones, and on top of it I placed a cross, and I declared that I erected that cross and monument in the name of Don Antonio de Mendoza, Viceroy of New Spain, for the Emperor, our lord, as a sign of possession, conforming to my instruction, and by which possession I proclaimed that I took all of the seven cities and the kingdoms of Totonteac and of Acus and of Marata, and that the reason I did not go to the latter places was in order to return to give an account of all I did and saw."

Evidently Mendoza was somewhat skeptical of the report, for he secretly sent Melchior Diaz with fifteen men to investigate and report back to him as quickly as possible. They were the first white men to travel the Gila Trail. Esteban had made enough impression on the Indians along the way that Diaz had no trouble in following his route to the Gila. There he explored far to the westward, following the ancient Hohokam trails nearly to the Colorado River. Then he turned back and, in the winter of 1539-40, followed Esteban's route toward the Zuñi villages. Stopped by heavy snows in the mountains, he decided to make camp, continuing his investigation in the spring.

In the meantime the news of Niza's fabulous discovery had set New Spain ablaze. In Compostela, Coronado was beating the drums for an immediate conquest, and in Mexico City everyone with a particle of influence was putting pressure on Mendoza. He delayed as long as possible, hoping for a confidential report from Diaz. When no word was received by the end of the year he concluded that his investigating force had been killed by the heathen in order to protect their enormous wealth. The conquest must be made at once, and it must be powerful enough to crush a mighty enemy.

On February 23, 1540, Coronado led his glorious army of conquistadores out of Compostela. At the front rode some four hundred armored Spaniards, while behind trailed seven hundred Indian slaves, bearing packs and driving pigs, sheep, oxen, and beef cattle. Although Coronado is believed to have explored as far as Nebraska, his only real discovery was that there were no golden cities, but in passing, his legion wore deeper the trails along the Gila.

The Gila region was known to the Spaniards as Pimería Alta—the upper frontier—but they became thoroughly disenchanted when Coronado discovered that it contained no cities of gold. The first to again penetrate it was Father Eusebio Francisco Kino, an extremely brilliant and talented Jesuit priest. He was thirty-six years of age when, in 1681, he was sent to New Spain to begin his foreign service.

Ever since its discovery Spain tried to colonize Lower California—then believed to be an island—for exploitation of its supposed mineral wealth, but all attempts had failed. This was partly because the peninsula was barren, but more particularly because the Indians became belligerent when the early Spaniards had tried to enslave them. In spite of the previous failures, another attempt was made in 1683, and Father Kino was assigned as priest, astronomer, and map maker. The expedition sailed two hundred miles up the Gulf of California and built a makeshift fort near the present site of Loreto. Father Kino established two small missions, learned the Indians' language, made many friends and converts among them, crossed the mountains to the Pacific, and carefully mapped the area. But in time the usual warfare broke out between the soldiers and natives, and in 1685 the colonization attempt was abandoned. Father Kino returned to Mexico City and requested permission to go into the frontier as a missionary.

During the hundred and forty years since Coronado's expedition, the frontiers of New Spain had been pushed northward into Chihuahua and eastern Sonora, but the expansion had been stopped below the present International Boundary by Apache raids. To the northwest the country was entirely unknown and unexplored, its farthest outpost having been a long-abandoned missionary station two hundred miles south of Tucson, Arizona. It was to this unexplored region, Pimería Alta, that Father Kino was assigned. He left Mexico City late in November, 1686, made the two-thousand-mile journey on horseback, explored and mapped the country surrounding the abandoned station, made friends of the Indians, and began to build his headquarters mission—Nuestra Señora de los Dolores—on March 13, 1687. Incredible as it seems, this was only a foretaste of his amazing endurance, efficiency, and determination.

Father Kino made his first exploration on the headwaters of the Sonora and Magdalena rivers, below the International Boundary, and along the Santa Cruz and San Pedro valleys of Arizona. In each valley he found upward of three thousand Pima Indians, living in primitive villages and raising corn, beans, wheat, cotton, pumpkins, and melons in irrigated patches along the stream. From them he learned of many more Pimas living along the Gila, of the fierce Apaches to the eastward, and of the Yumas and Maricopas at the Colorado River. On the Sonora and Magdalena there were about forty villages of Papagos, also farmers, but with little knowledge of irrigation. Father Kino was at once enchanted with the Pimería and its prospects. Here were Indians far more intelligent than those of Baja California, and here there would be no overbearing Spanish soldiers to start trouble and destroy his work before it was fairly begun.

From the outset Father Kino believed that Indians could successfully be taught Christianity and the fundamentals of civilization only when convinced that they would profit by it. No missionary was ever so well qualified for the task, for though conversion of the heathen was his sole aim, he was a highly gifted administrator, military strategist, cartographer, doctor, architect, artisan, and husbandman.

For his headquarters mission, Kino chose a location just beyond the farthest outposts of the Spanish frontier. It was near the source of the San Miguel River, about two hundred miles south of Tucson. There the river breaks through a narrow canyon with sheer rock walls several hundred feet high, but on either side there is a large fertile valley, ideally graded for irrigation and hemmed in by rugged mountains. At the canyon a promontory juts out, allowing a magnificent view of the valleys and approachable only from the west. On the point of the easily defensible promontory Father Kino built Mission Dolores—at first only a little log chapel and a hut to sleep in.

From this tiny headquarters Kino rode constantly among the Indians of the surrounding area, making friends, baptizing, and teaching them better methods of irrigation and farming. It was not only among the Indians that Father Kino rode. He visited the nearest settlements and ranches on the frontier, begging from the settlers tools for his people, and from the ranchers a mare, cow, goat, sheep, or hog. He sent off letters to the Church at Mexico City demanding bells, chalices, statues, and holy pictures for his mission.

To the Indians domesticated animals and the mission paraphernalia, particularly the bells, were a source of wonder and amazement. From far and near they came to see and hear, many of them staying to farm in the valleys, or to help with the construction of the permanent mission buildings; baking adobe bricks, or dragging stone and pine logs from the mountains. And as they came the padre taught them the tenets of the Christian faith, together with the skills of carpentry, masonry, agriculture, and animal husbandry. From the most intelligent of his converts he built a well-organized corps of Indian colleagues; governors, captains, justices, and neophytes. These, after long and careful training, he sent back to their native villages, to teach the gospel and the advantages of civilization.

For six years Father Kino was the only white man in Pimería Alta, but his accomplishments during those years are almost unbelievable. He rode untold thousands of miles over deserts and mountains, baptized thousands of converts, established scores of chapels, and built three major missions, each surrounded by irrigated ranches and large herds of livestock. Beyond that, his neophytes had carried his teachings throughout the Gila watershed and to the tribes along the Colorado.

It was only the Apaches that Father Kino could never reach with his Christian teachings; they would have no part in a religion which required sharing the world Usen had made exclusively for them. But though he could not convert them, he soon proved that he could control them. For a century before his coming to Pimería Alta the Apaches had raided the Pima villages at will; murdering, pillaging, and stealing women and children. As soon as Padre Kino had built up his corps of governors, captains, and justices, he organized them into a defensive force against the Apaches. At the first warning of a raid his runners were on the trails, carrying to the captains tactical instructions and word that "Nuestra Padre" would furnish beef for the fighting men. The Apaches soon learned that Pimería Alta was not a happy hunting ground, and after fifty-four were killed in a single skirmish they left it strictly alone.

By 1693 Father Kino's success in converting and keeping peace among the Indians had become too great to be ignored by either Church or State. The Church sent two black-robed Jesuit colleagues to work with him, and the Viceroy posted a company of soldiers at Mission Dolores. The soldiers were useless, for they caused the only trouble Kino ever experienced with his people, and he preferred to make his journeys alone or with an Indian guide. But the colleagues were of inestimable value in establishing his mission system.

In twenty-four years, and with never more than ten white colleagues, Father Kino established in northern Sonora and southern Arizona twenty-nine major missions and seventy-two *visitas*. The major missions were well equipped and surrounded by irrigated gardens, fields of wheat, cotton, corn, and beans; vineyards, and orchards of figs, pomegranates, quince, pears, peaches, and apricots. Each had its drove of horses, mules, oxen, cattle, sheep, and hogs. At its height Mission Dolores, alone, had a herd of fourteen hundred cattle.

These major missions were not only self-supporting but, with their throngs of devoted Indian neophytes, raised grains, fruits, and produce to be bartered for the goods of civilization necessary to the expansion. All were linked together by a system of well-worn trails, where neophytes with heavily loaded mule trains carried on the commerce of the Pimería. There was seldom a day when a pack train was not on the trails between the missions and the Spanish cities and settlements to the south.

The visitas, little chapels of sun-baked adobe, were scattered far and wide throughout the Gila watershed and deep into Sonora. These were maintained entirely by neophytes, and were generally supplied from the major missions. In them no regular services were held, but when not saying Mass in one major mission or building another, the black-robed priests were constantly on the trails, riding from one visita to another; holding services, baptizing babies and converts, ministering to the sick, and giving absolution to the dying. Father Kino himself made more than fifty journeys through the Pimería, some of them more than a thousand miles in length, and often rode sixty miles in a single day.

The blue shells which the Indians near the mouth of the Gila used as ornaments had long been of great interest to Father Kino. While on Baja California he had discovered similar shells along the western shore, but none along the eastern. This had led him to believe that he was not on an island, as the Spanish supposed, but on a peninsula. So, on finding the blue shells among the Indians on the lower Gila, he was convinced that there was a practicable overland route to the Pacific, and that it was not far distant beyond the Colorado River. Obtaining permission from Mexico City, he accomplished what the Spanish Government had been unable to do in nearly two centuries:

with his colleague Father Salvatierra, he established the first permanent mission in Lower California. This he supplied and stocked from his Pimería missions, sending a single herd of seven hundred cattle overland from Mission Dolores. These were the first, but far from the last, cattle to reach California by way of the Gila Trail.

After establishing the Lower California mission, Father Kino's greatest ambition was to go there and push the expansion northward, as he had done in Pimería Alta. But there the Church, the State, and his beloved Pimas balked: the peace and welfare of the frontier required that he remain east of the Colorado.

Father Kino died in 1711 without realizing his ambition to extend his mission system northward into Upper California. But he had planted the seed for that expansion, and spent the last ten years of his life opening the gateway for it. During those years he made repeated journeys to the west, mapping the Gila Valley, the lower Colorado River, and the northern end of the Gulf of California. At his passing he left behind a Christian people, estimated to have been nearly thirty thousand, and the trails along the Gila worn infinitely deeper. San Xavier del Bac, the joy of his old age, and one of the most magnificent mission cathedrals in the United States, stands nine miles south of Tucson.

With Father Kino's death the Church's influence in Pimería Alta disintegrated rapidly. He was followed by a succession of priests who lacked his affection for the Indians, courage, endurance, or administrative brilliance. Numerous of the larger Sonora missions, and those along the San Pedro and Santa Cruz valleys were maintained, but the Gila Valley and outlying visitas were completely abandoned. Without an organized force to oppose them the Apaches ran rampant. Worse still, the new priests looked upon the neophytes as slaves, and did little or nothing for the people. Forty years after Kino's death a generation of Pimas and Papagos who had never known him rebelled against the Church, sacked the missions in the San Pedro and Santa Cruz valleys, and drove the Spaniards out of the Gila watershed.

For two years there was no white man in Arizona. Then, in 1752, the Spanish posted a company of fifty soldiers at Tubac, a little Pima settlement near Mission Tumacacori in the Santa Cruz Valley. With soldiers to protect them the Jesuit priests came back to reopen Missions San Xavier del Bac and Tumacacori, but their tenure was short and unsuccessful. In 1767 the Jesuit Order was expelled from New

Spain, and Franciscans sent to replace them. The following year the Apaches swooped down on the Santa Cruz Valley, bottled up the frightened Spanish soldiers in their fort at Tubac, and burned San Xavier del Bac, leaving nothing standing but the charred walls of the church.

WESTWARD THE GILA TRAIL

The ashes of San Xavier del Bac were barely cold when the new Franciscan priest, Father Francisco Tomás Garcés, was sent to take over Pimería Alta. Three months earlier, Father Junípero Serra had been appointed Prefect of Lower California and sent to Loreto, the mission established by Kino and Salvatierra. These two Franciscans were, in almost every way, counterparts of Father Kino, and carried out his dream of extending the Catholic missions into Upper California.

Father Garcés is said to have looked very much like an Indian, and had nearly as great success as Padre Kino in making friends and neophytes among them, though he was never able to organize them sufficiently to repulse Apache raids. In spite of occasional raids he carried forward the rebuilding of San Xavier del Bac, and during his first six years made four journeys to the Gila, explored its tributaries far to the east, followed the mainstream to the Colorado, and crossed deserts to the California mountains. In these journeys he made thousands of converts, and became as well loved by the new generation of Pimas as Kino had been by their fathers and grandfathers.

Meanwhile Father Serra had been pushing northward from Loreto, but had run into difficulty. To survive, his missions had to be supplied, but shipping from New Spain proved undependable and the cost exorbitant. Late in 1773 Viceroy Bucareli instructed Juan Bautista de Anza, commander of the garrison at Tubac, to pioneer an overland route for supplying the Upper California missions from Pimería Alta. Anza was an excellent man for the undertaking. Having been born on the frontier, he knew how to cope with the hardships of desert and mountain travel, but only Father Garcés had crossed the California deserts and knew the trails along the Gila, so Anza wisely looked to him as pathfinder.

In January, 1774, Anza set out from Tubac with Fathers Garcés and Diaz, taking thirty-four soldiers, a pack train of a hundred and

[28]

forty horses, and sixty-five cattle. By early February they reached the Colorado, spent several days with Father Garcés's friends, the Yumas, and were helped by the Indians in crossing the river. After nearly dying of thirst in the deserts, the little expedition reached Mission San Gabriel, near Los Angeles, on March 22, opening for the first time the Gila Trail between the Colorado and the Pacific. Anza and Diaz continued northward, while Father Garcés returned to the Yumas. He stayed with them until Anza's return in late May, then guided him back to Tubac along the route that would become the mainline of the Gila Trail from Tucson to California.

For seven more years Padre Garcés worked among the Pimas, the Papagos, and Maricopas; exploring the tributaries of the Gila, teaching Christianity, baptizing converts, and tending the sick. His greatest affection, however, was for the Yumas, and he spent much time among them following Anza's first expedition to Upper California.

Not only were the Yumas intelligent, honest, industrious, and tractable, but Garcés realized that their friendship would be vital to the success of the overland route. Their villages surrounded the confluence of the Gila and Colorado rivers, the only gateway between New Spain and California. Moreover, except in time of extremely low water, the Colorado with its tricky currents could be crossed only with help from the Indians. Humans, baggage, and equipment had to be ferried on rafts poled by expert Yuma river men. Horses and cattle could be driven across only by strong Yuma swimmers who knew how to take advantage of every trick of the currents.

Even though the Gila Trail from the east followed the river, its last hundred miles or more were through an arid desert, with almost no grazing for animals. To the west of the Colorado it was even worse, for there were ninety miles of waterless, grassless desert to be crossed before reaching the California mountains. But at the confluence there was rich land that could easily be irrigated and made to produce abundant crops. Here Father Garcés envisaged a great oasis between the two deserts; a Spanish-Indian mission settlement on each side of the Colorado, with well-stocked and irrigated ranches surrounding them. At such settlements travelers to and from California could rest, recuperate their jaded animals, and replenish their provisions.

To carry out his dream Father Garcés founded Mission Purísima Concepción and Mission San Pedro y San Pablo. With help from the

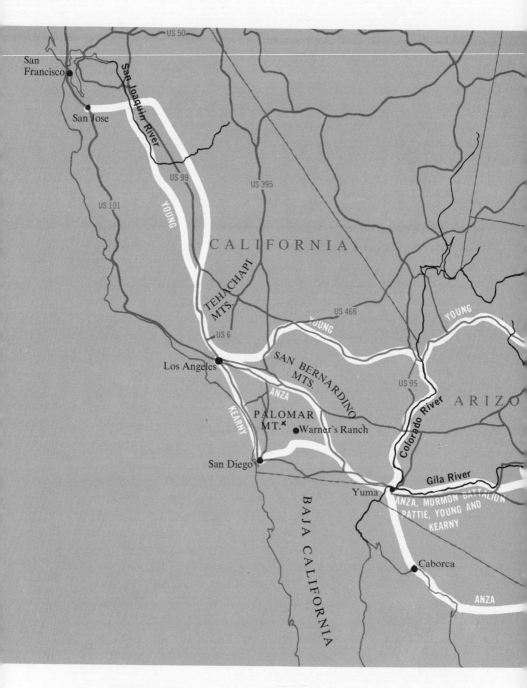

The Gila Trail: routes of Anza, the Patties, Ewing Young, Kearny
with the Army of the West, and the Mormon Battalion. Juan

Bautista de Anza opened the Gila Trail from the Colorado River
to the Pacific and later founded the San Francisco colony for Spain.

Viceroy, who fully recognized the value of the undertaking, he brought in three Franciscan priests, families of Spanish settlers, church paraphernalia, farming tools, horses, cattle, and sheep.

At first the padre's only difficulty was that the Yumas did not take readily to communal endeavor. Although they soon learned to become excellent farmers and stockmen, each preferred to have his own horses, cattle, and little plot of land. With his interest being solely in the welfare of his Indians and the project, Father Garcés let the Yumas have their way, and, as travel over the trail expanded, his mission settlements grew and prospered. Then tension began to rise; the Yumas were honest, but the Spanish settlers, travelers, and soldiers were not. They had no respect for Indian property, and would turn their starving animals into the Yumas' field. By 1781 the tension had become so great that Garcés had to spend all of his time at Mission Concepción, trying to control the Spaniards and pacify the Yumas.

The blowup came in July of that year. Captain Rivera y Moncada, the arrogant military commandant of California, reached the Colorado with forty soldiers, their horses exhausted from too fast a crossing of the desert. While resting there Rivera noticed that the Yumas had excellent horses, and commanded his soldiers to take the best among them. When the owners protested he had them flogged before their women and children. The Yumas were a proud people, and the flogging was enough to erupt the smoldering volcano of their resentment. In one of the most sudden and bloody uprisings in history, they killed every Spanish male in both settlements, including Father Garcés and his three colleagues, destroyed the missions, and took the Spanish women and children prisoners.

The priests were evidently murdered when blood lust was at the boiling point, and probably by irresponsible young warriors. The friars' bodies were the only ones buried, and when Father Garcés's grave was discovered it was covered from end to end with flowers.

With the Yuma uprising and Father Garcés's death, the Gila Trail and virtually the whole of Arizona was abandoned by the Spanish. From then until Mexico won its independence in 1821, the only white settlements remaining in the Gila watershed were at Tubac and Father Kino's old Visita of San Cosme del Tucson, where a small garrison had been posted in 1778. But while the Spaniards were retreating from the Gila, the Americans were advancing toward it.

In 1803 the United States had made the Louisiana Purchase, acquiring from France a vast area between the Mississippi River and the summit of the Rocky Mountains, but the southern boundary of the area was vaguely described. The Spanish Government insisted that its domain extended to the Arkansas River, forbade Americans to trespass, and imprisoned any who were caught south of the river.

In 1821 Mexico won its independence from Spain and opened the border to Americans. Early the following spring William Becknell set out from the little frontier settlement of Franklin, Missouri, taking a small merchandise caravan westward across the prairies to Santa Fe, New Mexico. At the same time William Ashley sent the first American beaver trapping expedition up the Missouri River to the Rocky Mountains.

The westward expansion of the United States owes more to these two expeditions than to any others. Becknell not only established friendly relations and commerce with Mexico, but blazed the Santa Fe Trail, the first permanent link between East and West. The eighty young men Ashley sent to trap beaver—among them Jedediah Smith, Jim Bridger, and Tom Fitzpatrick—were the forerunners of the mountain men, a tough, fearless breed who were to conquer the unknown wilderness and open the way for emigrants to Oregon and California. Furthermore, both expeditions returned with huge profits, and news of fantastic wealth to be found in the Rockies spread throughout the frontier like forest fire. By the spring of 1823 scores of small frontier merchants had entered the Santa Fe trade, and hundreds of hardy beaver trappers were rushing to the mountains by way of the Missouri and the Santa Fe Trail. Among the most famous to go by way of the trail were Ewing Young, Joe Walker, "Old Bill" Williams, and the Carson boys.

The headwaters and tributaries of the Rio Grande and Gila River were teeming with beaver, but the Mexican Government had no intention of letting the valuable pelts be stolen by a neighbor, so passed laws prohibiting Americans from trapping in Mexican territory. The laws made little difference to the mountain men. They set up headquarters near the Indian pueblo of Taos, seventy miles above Santa Fe, and by 1824 had trapped the headwaters of the Rio Grande destitute of beaver.

The pueblo at Taos. From Beyond the Mississippi, *Albert D. Richardson.*

That year the most amazing and controversial of the mountain men, James Ohio Pattie, reached Taos. Much of the controversy, which still exists, arose from his publishing in 1831 *The Personal Narrative of James O. Pattie of Kentucky*. The book was ghost-written from Pattie's recollections by Timothy Flint of Cincinnati, and either James or Timothy had a marvelous flare for fiction. There is, however, no doubt that young Pattie had numerous hairbreadth escapes from the Indians, or that he and his father were the first Americans to discover and follow the Gila Trail.

In Pattie's narrative he tells a fanciful story of having rescued a fair damsel—a relative of the Mexican Governor—from the Comanches, in appreciation for which he was given permission to trap the Gila. He also tells of agreeing to bribe the Governor five percent of his take in exchange for the permission. The latter is doubtlessly true, since Mexican governors of that period were strongly in favor of bribes. But the rake-off would have been for permission to bring the pelts back to Santa Fe for shipment, not for the privilege of trapping. The Mexican Government had no power to enforce its no-trapping laws, but on the Gila it needed none: there the Apaches were the game wardens.

The Apaches were a nation divided into half a dozen separate tribes, the fiercest being the Mimbres of southwestern New Mexico and the Chiricahuas of southeastern Arizona. The Mimbres were the scourge of both the upper Gila and the Rio Grande Valley, having their tribal center at the Council Rock, halfway between the two rivers. This rock was an immense outcropping of rich copper ore, single masses of pure metal often weighing more than a ton. In the late 1700's the chief of the Mimbres had led a Mexican officer to the outcropping and sold it to him for a few trinkets. Peons were brought north, the stockaded little settlement of Santa Rita built, and a mine put into operation.

For a while the mine had been extremely profitable, even though the copper had to be transported more than three hundred miles to Chihuahua on pack mules. Then the Apaches acquired a taste for mule meat, shipments could be made only by heavily guarded pack trains, and the mine became unprofitable. By 1824 it had passed through the hands of numerous owners, and a wagon road had been opened to Chihuahua. Each owner started on a shoestring, and the Apaches let him operate until he had built up a sizable string of mules. Then they swooped down and stole the mules, but were careful not to destroy the wagons, having learned that if they were spared another owner would come in and build up a string of tasty mules.

Soon after James Pattie and his father, Sylvester, reached Taos, they heard rumors of the plentiful beaver to be had in the untrapped Gila. Sylvester at once organized a party of fourteen mountain men and set off for Santa Fe. In early December, 1824, the party followed the El Paso del Norte Trail south along the Rio Grande to a point south of Socorro, then took the well-marked trail westward to the Santa Rita copper mine. There they hired two Mexicans to guide them to the headwaters of the Gila.

From Pattie's description of the river and the country, it is evident that the party followed the Gila westward to the present site of Coolidge Dam in Arizona. He tells of the river plunging into a deep and narrow canyon where the party had to detour through "rough, frowning peaks, rising in every direction high above the clouds." For nearly two weeks the party was unable to find its way back to the river through this "heartbreaking region." Then, according to the narrative, they turned south, probably up the San Pedro, and soon loaded their horses down with furs. But when they were just ready to break camp and head back for Santa Fe the Apaches caught up with them, stampeded the horses, and left the party stranded. Pattie tells of hiding the bulging fur packs in a cache, and of the trappers' nearly dying of starvation as they made their way back to Santa Rita afoot.

There is little doubt of the starvation, but the cache does not square with the Apache account. According to Mangas Coloradas, who later became chief of the Mimbres Apaches, the Indians were quite intrigued by the white men's cleverness at trapping beaver, and watched them furtively from the brush. But the white men were not at all intrigued by the Indians, and took pot shots at any they saw. That was all right with the Apaches. The trappers were doing a better job of catching beaver than they could, and besides, they were doing all the squaw work: scraping, stretching, and drying the pelts. Keeping concealed but dogging the trappers' heels, the Apaches let them go until they started to pack for home, then made their strike, killed half of them and ran the others off with nothing but their rifles. The story checks out, for the Patties reached Santa Rita with only five of their party, and when the Mimbres gathered again at their Council Rock they were decked out in beaver pelts. A giant warrior among them was wearing Sylvester Pattie's red undershirt, from which he was given his name of Mangas Coloradas—Red Sleeves.

Though the course of events is too shrouded in fiction to be clearly followed, Sylvester Pattie took over the copper mine, while his son, James Ohio, rounded up another band of mountain men and made a second try at trapping the Gila. He got about as far as on the first expedition before the Apaches again cleaned him out and ran him back empty handed. In 1826 he tried again, and this time claimed to have trapped the Gila to the Colorado. There the Mohaves turned him back, but not until he had wantonly killed their chief for demanding a horse in exchange for beaver pelts taken by the party. Pattie wrote that he returned over the Old Spanish Trail, though the route was then unknown to white men and his description is so vague as to be doubtful. Then he said he was robbed of his furs in Santa Fe by Governor Armijo for lack of a Mexican trapping license.

By the time young Pattie returned, Sylvester had given up at the copper mine and turned it over to Robert McKnight of Franklin, Missouri—one of the earliest traders, who had since become a Mexican citizen. With both the Patties dead broke in the fall of 1827, they joined a trapping party, and led it the entire length of the Gila to the Colorado. This time the Yumas drove them down river, where their dugout canoe was swamped by the tidal bore from the Gulf of California. In an attempt to reach San Diego, the little party of eight started westward across the deserts. They were on the point of death from thirst when discovered by Indian neophytes, who carried them bodily to Mission Santa Catalina. But both Church and Government officials were suspicious of the Americans. As soon as the trappers had recovered they were arrested, and in April, 1828, transferred under heavy guard to a jail in San Diego, making them the first Americans to reach the Pacific coast by way of the Gila Trail. There Sylvester died as a result of his hardships, and—if his story is to be believed—James Ohio went on to explore the entire West.

McKnight's taking over the Santa Rita mine is connected with the Gila Trail in only one way. In 1826 seventeen-year-old Kit Carson had run away from his home in Franklin, Missouri, found a job with a Santa Fe Trail caravan, and gone to Taos to join his elder brothers as a mountain man. When he reached Taos his brothers had gone to the northwest on trapping expeditions, and because of his size and age no expedition leader would take him along. But Kit had known McKnight in Franklin. He made his way to Santa Rita and got a job driving ore wagons to Chihuahua. With the knack that was to make him famous, he won the friendship of the giant warrior, Mangas Coloradas, learned the Apache language, and learned the country surrounding the headwaters of the Gila River as none but the Apaches ever knew it.

In the spring of 1829 Ewing Young made a trapping expedition down the Gila, had the same experiences as the Patties on their first venture, and was lucky to get back to Taos with his life. That fall he determined to go back with a party strong enough to stand off an Apache attack, so made up a band of forty of the toughest mountain men to be found in Taos, taking Carson along as camp boy and interpreter. All went well until they had made the detour through the mountains that had given Pattie so much trouble. Then the Apaches attacked, and in standing them off Kit proved himself to be the best shot in the outfit, cut the first notch in his rifle stock, and graduated from camp boy to trapper. Standing off several more Indian attacks, Young's band trapped the Gila as far as present Phoenix, worked back along the Salt River to the Verde, and trapped that stream to its source, near Flagstaff.

The catch had been far beyond Young's expectation, the fur packs were as heavy as the pack mules could carry, and there was no sense in trapping back along the Gila and its tributaries. Furthermore, Apache territory could be avoided by following the headwaters of the Little Colorado to the Zuñi villages, then the San Jose and Rio Grande to Taos. Beyond that, Ewing Young had heard rumors of there being an untold number of beavers along the rivers of California. All he knew of California was that it lay to the westward, but he decided to go there. He split his party, sending twenty-two back to Taos with the furs, and starting for California with his eighteen best men, Kit Carson among them.

The route pioneered by Young was roughly that now followed by Highway 66 between Flagstaff and Los Angeles. Only with such a leader could the little party have crossed the hundred and fifty miles of waterless wasteland to the Colorado, and an equal distance across the California desert to the San Bernardino Mountains. Before starting he had three deer killed, their hides smeared with tallow, and made into huge water bags. The meat was stripped to shreds and dried into jerky. Even with such preparations, half the horses and mules were lost, and the men were reduced nearly to skeletons before reaching Mission San Gabriel early in the winter of 1830.

Ewing Young immediately sensed antagonism to Americans at San Gabriel, so gave his exhausted men and animals only one day's rest before pushing on to the north. He bypassed Mission San Fernando, crossed the Tehachapi Mountains to the San Joaquin Valley, trapped the streams northward, and reached the tip of San Francisco Bay with bulging packs of beaver pelts. There he had a stroke of good fortune. Indians had stolen a herd of horses from Mission San Jose and run them away to the Sierra Nevada Mountains. As a gesture of friendship, Ewing Young sent Carson with ten men to trail the thieves and bring back the horses. In appreciation, the Fathers at San Jose invited Young to the mission, and, without asking to see his trapping license or passport, traded beaver pelts for well-shod horses and mules, packsaddles, equipment, and enough supplies to see the party to Santa Fe.

In the early fall of 1830 Young reached the little pueblo of Los Angeles on his return journey. There the Government officials demanded to see his passport, and set out to arrest the party when they found he had none. The trappers were saved by an incident, not at all unique among mountain men. For some time there had been bad blood between two of the men, James Higgins and James Lawrence. The party had no more than reached Los Angeles when most of the men got drunk. The Mexicans were about to make the arrest when Higgins dismounted from his horse and deliberately shot Lawrence dead. That was enough for the Mexican constabulary. It beat a hasty retreat, glad to get rid of men so tough they would kill each other in cold blood.

Young led his party back across the California desert by the route he had taken on the way west, trapped the Colorado to the Gulf, then the Gila and its tributaries eastward. By the time he reached the headwaters of the Gila his fur packs weighed more than two thousand pounds, and were worth several thousand dollars. Without a Mexican trapping license, and having Pattie's experience with Governor Armijo in mind, Young did not dare take his pelts to Santa Fe. When the trappers were nearing Santa Rita he sent all his men except Carson back to Taos. Then the two went on to the copper mine, hid the fur packs in an abandoned shaft, covered them with rubble, and continued on to Santa Fe.

For a small bribe, Young obtained from the Governor a license to trade with the Apaches along the Gila, after which he and Carson filled their saddlebags with colorful trinkets and went back to visit for a couple of weeks with Mangas Coloradas. When they arrived in the plaza at Santa Fe with their ton of beaver pelts they were given credit for the most successful trading venture ever carried on with the Apaches. Ewing Young might have hoodwinked the Governor, but not the mountain men at Taos. Following his successful expedition the Gila Trail became as well known to them as the Santa Fe Trail was to the Missouri traders.

While in California Young had been tremendously impressed by the amount and quality of livestock on the mission ranches. At Mission San Jose, alone, he found thirteen thousand cattle, fourteen thousand sheep, and thirteen hundred horses and mules, all of far better quality than the stock in the Rio Grande Valley. Furthermore, trade over the Santa Fe Trail was booming, there was great demand for horses and mules in Missouri, and the prices were ten times those in California. When, in 1832, the Gila watershed became overrun with American beaver trappers, Young decided to devote his attention to the horse and mule trade, and Carson joined a trapping expedition going to the northern Rockies. He soon organized his own band, the Carson Men, and for a decade roamed the entire western wilderness, learning to know it as well as a farmer knows his fields.

THE ARMY OF THE WEST

It is difficult for neighbors to live in peace when the boundary line between their properties is not clearly defined and agreed upon. It is even more difficult when the children of one neighbor refuse to recognize any boundary line whatsoever. While the mountain men were running roughshod over northwestern Mexico, a horde of other American frontiersmen was advancing from the Mississippi. They pushed farther and farther westward into Texas, establishing settlements, usurping the rich grazing lands, and completely ignoring Mexican authority. In March, 1836, these invaders declared Texas to be an independent nation, including all its present area and most of eastern New Mexico. Mexico went to war in an effort to drive the Texans out, but within less than two months Sam Houston soundly defeated her army, in the Battle of San Jacinto. She conceded most of the territory, but maintained that the western boundary was the Nueces River rather than the Rio Grande.

Even though Texas established itself as an independent nation, it had been taken from Mexico by American citizens. Mexican resentment toward the United States, already smoldering because of the lawlessness and insolence of the mountain men, turned to bitter hatred. When, in 1845, Texas was annexed to the United States, Mexico insisted that the western boundary be the Nueces River. The United States demanded that it be the Rio Grande, and it was evident that if diplomatic negotiations failed war was inevitable.

From the time of the Louisiana Purchase, the Government of the United States had been divided on the question of expansion. Some

Stephen Watts Kearny.
From American Generals,
John Frost.

senators believed the entire region west of the Missouri River to be worthless, while others thought that in order to insure national security the bounds of the United States must be expanded to the Pacific, even at the expense of war. The most rabid expansionist was the influential Senator from Missouri, Thomas Hart Benton. His son-in-law, John Charles Frémont, was a lieutenant in the Corps of Topographical Engineers—with ambitions to become a great explorer and military hero.

In 1843 Benton had succeeded in pushing through a congressional appropriation for mapping the Oregon Trail, and having Frémont appointed to carry out the project. The mapping was simply a subterfuge. Benton's purpose was to discover the military strength of Great Britain in Oregon, and of Mexico in California. But Frémont had conquest in mind. When he made up his "surveying" party in St. Louis, he chose thirty-nine of the toughest frontiersmen he could find, armed them to the teeth, and sent for Kit Carson to guide him through the mountains. Then he embroiled Colonel Stephen Watts Kearny, commander of the St. Louis Arsenal, by hoodwinking him out of a mounted cannon "for protection against audacious Indian tribes."

Frémont's egoism and willfulness made the whole expedition a farce. The cannon had to be abandoned, and catastrophe was avoided only by Carson's extraordinary ability and John Sutter's generosity. Frémont did, however, discover that the Mexican military strength in California was woefully weak and that there were a few hundred American settlers in the vicinity of San Francisco Bay.

Shortly before Texas was annexed by the United States, Senator Benton pushed through another congressional appropriation, and had Frémont appointed to execute the project. This time the avowed purpose was for exploring and mapping the Continental Divide, but this, of course, was another subterfuge. When Mexico won her independence from Spain she was obliged virtually to mortgage California in order to secure loans. Benton knew that Great Britain and France had battleships along the Pacific coast, doubtlessly standing by to foreclose their past-due mortgages in the event of war between the United States and Mexico. As tension mounted between the two nations, the United States also had stationed a small squadron on the California coast, its commodore instructed to protect American rights and citizens in the event of conflict. Headstrong Senator Benton evidently decided to take matters into his own hands and, by supplying conflict, force the American squadron to take action before either Great Britain or France slipped in to plant its flag on California soil.

In any case, Benton hurried Frémont west with secret instructions, supposedly to stir up a revolt by the American settlers in California. In August, 1845, Frémont arrived at Bent's Fort on the Santa Fe Trail with sixty-two heavily armed frontiersmen and two hundred horses, half of them loaded with ammunition and supplies. He stopped for a day's rest, spread the news that he was on his way to explore and map the Rocky Mountains, and again sent for Kit Carson to act as his guide. There is little doubt that Frémont divulged the actual purpose of his mission to Carson while at Bent's Fort, for when the expedition hurried on it included the entire band of Carson Men.

With the Military Department entirely ignorant of Frémont's junket, Colonel Kearny was assigned to recruit and command the Army of the West. In the event of war, he was to lead it westward over the Santa Fe Trail for the conquest of New Mexico. That accomplished, he was to march by way of the Gila Trail for the conquest of California.

Establishing headquarters at Fort Leavenworth, Kearny recruited

United States troops commanded by Colonel Stephen Watts Kearny conquer New Mexico in 1846. From A Pictorial History of the World's Great Nations, *Charlotte M. Yonge.*

sixteen hundred mounted dragoons from Missouri's frontier, and five hundred infantrymen from the Mormons who had recently been driven out of Illinois. Since his line of march was to be across uninhabited country, he gave particular attention to his supply train. For it, he had great prairie schooners built, like those being used in the Santa Fe trade, but heavier and stronger. To pull them, he had Missouri searched for the largest and strongest mules, and hired two hundred of the best civilian teamsters on the frontier. But the finest mules were reserved for the colonel's pride and joy—his artillery division of twenty-one mounted howitzers.

In May, 1846, war was declared with Mexico, and in early June Kearny started his advance supply trains rolling westward over the Santa Fe Trail. On July 4, he led his cheering Army of the West onto the trail and marched rapidly toward Santa Fe, eager for the glory that would surely accrue to the conqueror of New Mexico and California. By making an extremely fast march, Kearny reached Bent's Fort by the end of the month, but much of his anticipated glory had already been stolen.

Ironically, Frémont had succeeded in stirring up the Bear Flag Rebellion at Sonoma just as Kearny was sending his first supply wagons away from Fort Leavenworth. As the Army of the West moved out on the Santa Fe Trail, the ragtag army of the California Republic, with Frémont in command, set out from Sonoma. Before Kearny reached Bent's Fort, Frémont had driven General Castro's weak Mexican army south of Monterey, and joined forces with Commodore Stockton. The American flag was raised, the Carson Men sworn into the United States Navy as mounted marines, and Stockton and Frémont set about the conquest of California, neither of them knowing that war had been declared.

The intrigues and circumstances leading to the conquest of New Mexico had their greatest effect upon the history of the Santa Fe Trail, so will be recounted in that section of this book.

Kearny, newly promoted to the rank of lieutenant general, marched into Santa Fe on August 18 without firing a shot, and the next day New Mexico was formally surrendered in a rousing celebration at the Plaza. For a month he remained in Santa Fe, being entertained and banqueted. Then, on September 22, he appointed Charles Bent, educated at West Point and partner in Bent's Fort, as Civilian Governor.

With New Mexico conquered and a West Point governor named,

General Kearny was anxious to move on for the conquest of California, but the ease with which Santa Fe had been taken led him to believe that his entire force would not be required. He decided to take only five companies of his best dragoons, the artillery, and a supply train. This force was to be followed by the Mormon infantry as soon as it reached Santa Fe.

Although American traders had been taking caravans as far into Mexico as Chihuahua for nearly a quarter of a century, the Military Department knew absolutely nothing about the geography of the Southwest, so Kearny employed Tom Fitzpatrick, one of the most famous mountain men, as guide. If the Army of the West were bound for Oregon, Kearny could hardly have found a better guide, but Fitzpatrick had never been on the Gila Trail, and knew the route only by what he had heard from other old-time beaver trappers. Otherwise, he would have advised the general against starting out with his artillery and a supply train of ponderous prairie schooners.

Fortunately, two of Kearny's officers, Surgeon John S. Griffin and Topographical Engineer William H. Emory, kept detailed diaries, and Emory made excellent maps of the route followed from Santa Fe to San Diego. The first entry in Dr. Griffin's diary gives a good description of the high spirit that prevailed at the outset:

"Sept. 26, 1846. We left Santa Fe yesterday . . . all hands in great spirits at the prospect of the trip. Left camp early & had a hard days march through a perfectly barren country, one that would not feed a single goose to the acre. All the men are mounted on mules—some of them devilish poor at that. One or two gave out to day. This is a bad prospect for California to have the animals giving out the first day. It is said that there is gold in the sands, and that a man can make a living washing dirt, it is well this can be done for I am damned if any one could make a living ploughing."

That first day was only a foretaste, and left some question as to who had conquered whom. When Kearny had swept victoriously into Santa Fe his dragoons were mounted on the finest horses that could be secured in Missouri, but the Mexicans assured him that horses could never stand the heat of the deserts beyond, and he would have to mount his cavalry on mules. Kearny had taken their word for it, since neither he nor his guide had any idea what lay ahead. Dr. Griffin's journal indicates that the crafty Mexicans did all right for themselves. "The mules purchased by the Qr master are extremely weak, many of them are nearly given out . . . the Mexicans,

Kit Carson. From
Pictorial History of
Mexico and the Mexi-
can War, *John Frost.*

we have all come to the conclusion, are great rascals, and are not burthened with any great amount of the article called conscience."

The greatest difficulty was with the transport mules. Kearny's schooners had been fine for the prairies, but were worse than useless in the desert. With wheels sinking deep into the sand, scant forage at night, and scorching heat by day, even the big Missouri mules soon broke down.

Convinced that mules could not get the wagons through, Kearny sent back to Santa Fe for oxen. None were to be had, and the quartermaster brought back word that the officer in command of the Mormon Infantry Battalion had died. On the night of October 3, the doctor entered in his diary: "The news of Captain Allens death was confirmed poor fellow—he is gone. I wonder how many more of us will go, before we return to the United States for I am damned if I do call this Uncle Sam, whatever Mr. Polk says."

Doubtlessly the doctor's entry reflected the feeling of most of the men as, leaving a trail of dead mules behind, they fought the ponderous prairie schooners southward along the Rio Grande Valley. Averaging only twelve or thirteen miles a day, the Army of the West passed the little Mexican settlement of Socorro on October 5. In midforenoon on the sixth a cloud of dust appeared far down the trail, and out of it came a racing band of horsemen, looking and yelling like Indians. It was Kit Carson and his men, thirty days out of San Diego and on their way to Washington with dispatches for President Polk: California already had been conquered, Stockton was Commander-in-Chief, and had appointed Frémont as Civil and Military Governor.

The meeting was hardly a joyful occasion. That evening Doctor Griffin wrote, "This created considerable sensation in our party, but the general feeling one of disappointment and regret. Most of us hoped when leaving Santa Fe that we might have a little kick up with the good people of California but this totally blasted our hopes, and reduced our expedition to one of mere escort duty the Genl taking the same view of the matter. . . ."

As for the general's feelings, the entry was certainly a rank understatement. Kearny's role had hardly been that of a conquering hero when New Mexico surrendered without a shot being fired, and now it seemed apparent that he had been cheated out of the glory of conquering California. Worse still, Carson probably led him to believe that Frémont—a Topographical Engineer, and the man whom Kearny detested more than any other—had captured California single-handedly, since Kit had extraordinary admiration for Frémont.

Kearny's only comfort was that his orders from the War Department directed him to take command of Upper California and establish a civil government there. Even though he was too late to take possession from the Mexicans, he determined to take it from the interloper, Frémont, with all possible dispatch. But without a guide who knew the way, and at the rate he was traveling, it seemed improbable that he could reach California before spring. In desperation, Kearny ordered Carson to turn his dispatches over to Tom Fitzpatrick, and to guide the Army through to San Diego by the fastest possible route.

Kit refused, saying that he was under orders from Commodore Stockton to deliver his dispatches personally to President Polk. Kearny countered by threatening arrest and court-martial, although as an Army officer he had no right to countermand Stockton's orders, and no authority over Carson, since he had been sworn into the Navy as a member of the mounted marines. Kit still refused, planning to let himself be arrested, then escape and continue on to Washington, knowing that Kearny would be unable to catch him. Fortunately for the general, Carson's friend Lucien Maxwell convinced him that refusing to obey a superior officer's command in time of war was equal to treason. Reluctantly he turned his dispatches over to Tom Fitzpatrick and agreed to act as Kearny's guide, but warned him that with wheeled vehicles the direct Gila Trail could not be followed, and it would be impossible to reach California within four months.

Strangely, Kearny accepted Carson's report that all hostilities had ceased in California, but would not accept his statement that the direct Gila Trail could not be traversed with wheeled vehicles. He at once sent three of his five companies of dragoons back to Santa Fe, but insisted on continuing with his heavy transport wagons and mounted howitzers. From the doctor's diary it is evident that the general was determined to prove Carson wrong. "Oct. 7th. From the way the Genl. marched to day, I should say he was on his way in Earnest. We have come some 23 miles."

What neither the general nor the doctor realized was that those were the easiest twenty-three miles on the entire route to California, for they were on the well-worn Chihuahua Trade Road and through the most fertile valley along the Rio Grande. At the end of the valley, mountains pinched in to wall the river on the east, and rugged hills closed down along the west. There the Chihuahua Road crossed the Rio Grande and continued southward over a burning desert called the Jornada del Muerto—the Journey of Death. To reach the Gila Trail, Carson kept to the west side of the river, probably following the trail over which he had just come.

The doctor's entry of October 9 was less optimistic: "We have not made more than 7 or 8 miles to day. It was with the greatest difficulty that the wagons could be brought up at all. The guide Carson declares that he believes it impossible to get wagons through and I think the Genl. is becoming of the same opinion, five of our team mules utterly caved and the remainder were so near to it, that the difference could scarcely be told, it was one succession of hills and what is called in this country cañons (pronounced canyons). The sides of the hills being nothing but beds of Lava, and when on top of the hills chapparal, prickly pear & sand, so withall the poor mules had a devil of a time, this is the poorest country I have yet seen in New Mexico."

From the description of the land it is very probable that Carson was doing a little convincing before it should become too late for

Kearny to send back his wagons. There was a rough but serviceable cart trail from the Chihuahua Road to the Santa Rita copper mine, and it is quite evident that he was not guiding the Army of the West over it. In any event, the transport mules gave out completely on the tenth, and Kearny found himself stalled. On Carson's promise that he would get him to California in fifty days if he did so, the general reduced his supplies to bare necessities, loaded them on pack mules, and sent his wagons back to Santa Fe, but insisted upon taking along two mounted howitzers. The only reason for it seems to have been that he regarded them as a status symbol.

With the decision made, four days were lost while pack saddles were rushed out from Santa Fe and Carson taught the dragoons how to make up and lash packs. While encamped, the doctor made a significant entry in his diary: "Some Mexicans brought mules into camp to trade. The Genl. finding they had been trading with the Apachees without a license confiscated the whole of them." The excuse was, at best, rather thin, and the effect of the confiscation was to prove nearly disastrous to the Army of the West.

Rid of the ponderous wagons, Carson led the Army eighteen miles down the Rio Grande on the 14th. There he left the river and struck toward the old Indian pass through the Black Range mountains, covered another twenty-five miles on the 15th, then had to encamp while the howitzers were brought up. The pass followed a series of deep, narrow canyons, separated by high rocky ridges. Although the trail was rugged, pack mules could travel at two to three miles an hour, but the howitzers had to be hoisted over rock shoulders and boulders. To drag one of them up the steep ridges required a dozen straining mules, with as many men heaving from behind. To get them down into the next ravine was even more difficult. By the time the summit of Black Range was reached, men and mules were nearing exhaustion, but in his haste Kearny drove on, covering eighteen miles on the 16th.

Once the summit was crossed the mountains became less rugged, the grazing plentiful, and the weather cool. The cavalry and pack train could hold a good pace, but the howitzers had to be fought from ravine to ravine, holding the Army back and breaking down mules by the score. It was late on the 18th before the abandoned Santa Rita copper mine, at the site of the Apache Council Rock, was reached.

For the past two days deserted Apache wickiups had been seen along the trail. To the soldiers these were only objects of curiosity, but to Carson they told a disturbing story. The Apaches had doubtlessly been watching the column since long before it left the Rio Grande, and Mangas Coloradas had sent out runners to gather his warriors—a force capable of annihilating Kearny's two companies of inexperienced dragoons within a single hour. The Apaches would not be at the Council Rock, but hidden nearby, where the Army could easily be ambushed when passing through some narrow canyon.

Carson was not surprised when, soon after camp was pitched near the copper mine, Chief Mangas Coloradas strode in, accompanied by one of his warriors. The fact that he showed no surprise at Kit's being among the soldiers was proof enough that the Army had been constantly watched, and his coming with only one companion indicated that his warriors were concealed close by. Carson introduced Kearny as a son of the Great White Father in Washington, who had been sent to whip the Apaches' despised enemy, the Mexicans. The chief appeared to be little impressed by the bedraggled Army of the West, but was all in favor of whipping the Mexicans. With Carson interpreting, he assured Kearny of his undying friendship, and offered to send his warriors along to join in the fun. That was the last thing Kearny wanted. What he needed was mules, but there Mangas backed away. He would get some of his people together and find out if they had any mules to spare, then they would meet the soldiers the next evening, fifteen miles farther along the trail to the Gila. Gifts were passed out, and the chief with his sole witness left to carry the word back to the tribe.

When, on the evening of the 19th, the advance guard reached the designated rendezvous they found no Indians or water, but plenty of mule tracks and the grass grazed tight to the ground. They moved on a few miles to find water and make camp. Soon after the main body of dragoons and the pack train had come up, the Apaches appeared—the men armed to the teeth with Mexican guns, bows and arrows, and lances; the women arrayed in Spanish finery taken in raids made far to the south. But there were no mules. It was apparent to Carson that the Apaches knew all about the confiscation made from the Mexicans, and were running no risk. If the son of the Great White Father wanted to be friendly they would take his presents and let him pass; if not, they had come prepared to defend themselves.

After passing out presents all around, including the biggest officer's uniform that could be found for Mangas Coloradas, General Kearny made an eloquent speech to the Apaches. He told them that he would protect them from their enemies if they would be good and peaceful children of the Great Father in Washington, but that if they molested the whites or stole from them he would come back and punish them severely. Carson gave the speech a rather free translation, leaving out the threat of punishment, but assuring the Apaches that the soldiers were their friends and wanted only to pass peacefully through their country.

The next morning more presents were distributed to Mangas and his subchiefs, and further attempts made to trade for mules, but only two or three could be secured—poor ones, and at an exorbitant price in supplies. With a train of sore-backed pack mules and nearly-broken-down howitzer mules, Carson led the unimpressive Army of the West down Night Creek gorge and to the rock-walled canyon of the Gila, skirted by centuries-old Indian trails.

Cannons and Canyons on the Gila

The Mogollon Mountains at the headwaters of the Gila are still just as they were when Carson led Kearny's Army westward—one of the wildest and most rugged sections of the United States. The doctor wrote of it: "Oct. 21st. When we left camp this morning we followed down the Gila some five or six miles and finally turned the steepest point of the mountain, in following the course of the river, we were obliged to cross it every half mile or so, the mountain jutting down to the very edge of the stream, making a very picturesque affair of it—but damn bad roads—the fact is we have so much of the grand, & sublime scenery that I am tired of it. After turning the flank of the mountain we ascended it, and found it bad enough even at that. Carson said this was a turnpike road in comparison to the other route. . . . Our march to day some 18 miles by my computation. The Howitzers have not come up yet, and it is now 8 P.M.

"Oct. 22d. We arrived late in camp this evening as usual, having marched 18 or 20 miles—Kept the river bottom for a few miles, but was again headed off by another cañon—we then had a rough country, the Howitzers broke down another set of mules yesterday—these devlish things cost us more in the shape of mules than a Company of Dragoons."

[51]

On the 23rd the Army marched sixteen miles, lost the 24th in waiting for the howitzers to be brought up, and struggled ahead another five or six on the 25th. On the 26th Dr. Griffin wrote: "We left camp early, revallie having been sounded at 4 A.M. . . . this was represented as being a hard day—and it was not belied. It was one succession of mountains so covered with sharp stones that I do not believe our mules touched ground once in five miles. A mule without shoes stood no chance, many could not be driven, and many from exhaustion fell by the wayside, and no effort on the part of the men could get them any farther.

"Oct. 27th. The men were coming in last night till one oclock, and five or six had to lay out in the mountains. . . . Howitzers did not get in."

On the 28th Carson led the dragging Army out of the mountains at a point just east of present Safford, Arizona, and for the first time the doctor saw evidence of the old Hohokam culture. He wrote: "No hills or stone, but deep sand and plenty of dust . . . passed the ruins of several buildings, in some places the cedar posts were standing. The buildings were evidently quite large—and pieces of crockery

Fording the Gila River. From Notes of a Military Reconnaissance, *Lieutenant Colonel W. H. Emory. Courtesy of The New York Public Library, Rare Book Division.*

were scattered about in great profusion—some are plane, some painted black & white, & red & black. Who could have done this—there is no record nor tradition that I have heard of, of the Mexicans having lived in this country, and the present race of Indians evidently never either built so extensively or made the crockery. . . ."

Another note: "No game seen . . . the fact is Carson says he never knew a party on the Gila that did not leave it starving, this I am fearful will be our case before we leave—Marched about 16 or 17 miles." There was reason to worry. With the dragging howitzers costing the Army a third of its marching time and breaking down mules by the score, it had been necessary to abandon all but the most necessary supplies, and rations were running low.

For three days the Army moved at a fair pace over the desert, then reached the gorge of the Gila above the present site of Coolidge Dam, where Pattie had been forced into the mountains. Carson had since discovered an easy passage to the south, but there was no way of getting the howitzers across the canyon, and Kearny would not abandon them. To move them thirty miles downstream required six days, and the only way they could be taken through was by dismantling them and dragging the parts over an Indian trail that wound upward between peaks nearly eight thousand feet high.

On November 6 Griffin wrote, "This has been a most weary day, and the great difficulty of getting anything along with wheels caused the loss of another day—they have not got up yet—and the lord knows when they will arrive—though I have no doubt that Hammond and his party have worked like devils to get the cursed things ahead. . . . Every bush in the country is full of thorns—and every piece of grass so soon as it is broken becomes a thorn at both ends—every rock you turn over has a tarantula or a centipede under it, and Carson says in the summer—the most beautiful specimens of rattle snakes are scattered around in the greatest profusion. The fact is, take the country all together, and I defy any man who has not seen it—or one as utterly worthless—even to imagine any so barren. The cactus is the only thing that does grow, and we saw some of them yesterday—I should say 50 feet high. . . . We are now within some fifty miles of a Mexican post in Sonora—lord if they only knew our condition I do think they might trade our Genl off for La Vega." La Vega was a Mexican general captured by the Americans in May, and the post referred to was Tucson.

So many mules had been lost in getting the howitzers over the high mountains that most of the dragoons were afoot and the supplies almost entirely exhausted when, on November 10, Casa Montezuma was sighted and the Pima Indians came out from their villages to meet the bedraggled Army. It was a lifesaver for the Army of the West, though the good doctor was at first a bit shocked: "Their women are ugly and coarse looking, have merely a petticoat girted around the loins—all the upper part of the person being perfectly naked."

By the next day he was much better impressed, and wrote, "They are an agricultural people their fields are well fenced, and the land well irrigated—they are well mounted on fine horses and mules, their houses mud hovels, thatched. They raise cotton, corn & beans in great abundance . . . I think they live better and have more than the people of New Mexico—they are extremely honest. 12th Nov. The trading commenced this morning most briskly again—for meal and flour, and the supply was fully equal to the demand. We are now trading for cattle—they value them at $10 a head."

Although the Indians were eager to trade food and cattle for beads, bright cloth, and trinkets, they would not part with their good horses and mules. This was a hard blow to Kearny, particularly when Carson told him that he would have a ten-day march to the Colorado River, with scarcely any grazing for the animals. Kearny stopped three days at the Pima villages to let the men rest and let what mules he had left recuperate, then moved on, and after incredible suffering by both men and animals came within sight of the Colorado River on the evening of November 22.

It must be assumed that Carson had told Kearny of the manner in which General Castro's army had run away from any engagement with Frémont's forces in California, for in his diary entry for the 22nd, Doctor Griffin wrote, "In the evening as we approached the river, discovered the trail of a large body of horse—supposed this to be a Mexican force sent out from Sonora to intercept us. As we rode into camp—the Genl sent Carson ahead to find the wereabouts of the enemy, and said 'find them Carson and we will fight them tonight.'

"Our men are nearly naked and barefooted. Their feet are sore and legs weary—They have been marching many of them for the last four or five hundred miles. Our mules are all so that they can scarcely get along with a pack or a man on their backs, only the sick have been allowed to ride lately. This is rather a bad picture for men who have a hard campaign before them, but then our powder is dry, and the guns in good order and if they don't pile an unreasonable number up before us we will be able to give them a good sound thrashing. . . ."

Fortunately, the "Mexican force" turned out to be a small band of Mexican traders, driving a herd of five hundred unbroken horses and mules from California to Sonora. Three or four of the men were captured and brought into camp. The news they brought was probably embarrassing to Carson, but would have been heartening to Kearny if he had sent the two howitzers instead of three fifths of his dragoons back to Santa Fe: the California Mexicans had whipped the Americans, José María Flores was Governor, and the traders did not know where Frémont was.

The next day a Mexican messenger was caught, carrying letters to General Castro who had fled to Sonora when his army was routed by Frémont and Stockton. The letters reported that General Flores had reorganized the Mexican army, and bragged of eighty cavalrymen having soundly whipped 450 American sailors. What the letters failed to say was that the cavalrymen were not Mexicans, but Californios. The Californios were a breed apart: mission-raised descendants of the original Spanish soldiers and Indian women from the most advanced and intelligent California tribes. They had been the herdsmen of the missions, were the finest horsemen in the world, and despised the Mexican rancheros who had virtually enslaved them when the missions were secularized. They would not fight under Castro, but admired Flores and fought like fiends for him.

With news that there was yet time to reap the glory for conquering California, Kearny was anxious to push on immediately, but Carson held him back, warning that there would be absolutely no feed for animals, and almost no water, during the six days required to cross the California desert. In consequence, the general laid over for two days at the Colorado, while the mules grazed and the men gathered hay. The delay cut deeply into the supplies secured from the Pimas, and when the start was made on the 25th the heavy howitzers cut deeply into the sand. Before reaching the California mountains the column was barely crawling, and the men had been on quarter rations for four days. The Army of the West was on the point of collapse when, in mid-afternoon on December 2, it reached Warner's Ranch, the extreme frontier outpost of the Gila Trail in California. There beef and mutton were butchered, the men well fed, and grain provided for the jaded mules.

Warner had been arrested and imprisoned, but on the evening of General Kearny's arrival he was visited by an Englishman named Stokes, who owned a ranch some fifteen miles nearer San Diego, and who had kept out of trouble by remaining neutral. Stokes was well posted, and reported that the Mexicans had retaken Los Angeles, but that Stockton was in control of San Diego, and Frémont was advancing on Los Angeles from the north with some four hundred troops, about a hundred of them Indians. He also mentioned that there were several detached parties of cavalry between Warner's Ranch and San Diego, and that a herd of horses and mules belonging to Flores was in a valley some fifteen miles to the north. Although anxious to maintain his position of neutrality, Stokes consented to carry a letter to Stockton at San Diego.

Stokes was no sooner on his way than Kearny hurried off Carson and Lieutenant Davidson, with twenty-five dragoons, to capture Flores's stock. By noon the next day they were back with a hundred horses and mules, most of them wild, and only a few saddle-broken.

San Pasqual and the End of the Trail

Mounting his men on anything that could be ridden, Kearny pushed on to Stokes's Ranch on the afternoon of December 4. Next morning he moved on again, and at noon met Captain Gillespie with a party of thirty-five marines, sent out by Stockton from San Diego. Soon after the meeting a heavy rain set in and Gillespie encamped, but Kearny drove on for another ten miles, impatient to take command in California. How he went about it is best told by his surgeon:

"A party of the enemy being reported in our vicinity—it was first determined that Capt. Moore should take sixty men and make a night attack but for some reason the Genl altered his mind, and sent Lieut Hammond with three men to reconnoiter. Hammond found the enemy at some 10 miles distant, but was discovered—and as he ran off with his party the Mexicans gave three cheers."

Carson was known to be the most clever scout in the entire West, so it is evident that Kearny lacked confidence in his loyalty. Otherwise he would have sent him to spy out the enemy camp, rather than the bungling Hammond, who knew nothing of the country, the people, or the language. If Carson had been sent he would doubtlessly have brought back an accurate report of the detachment's strength, the condition of its horses, and the fact that it was composed of Californio lancers, not Mexican cavalrymen.

Even though Hammond had been discovered and had brought back no intelligence of the enemy's strength, and though his own force was totally unprepared to give battle, Kearny determined to make an immediate attack. Of it, Griffin wrote: "We were all afoot about 2 A.M. and expected to surprise the party of Mexicans. Though we had been in the rain all night our arms were not reloaded, but boots and saddles was the word, and off we put in search of adventure. In two miles from our camp we met Gillespie with his company, which fell in—in our rear—Major Swords was left back with the baggage, and thirty men. Another party some 10 or 15 men were left back with Gillespies four pounder. This reduced our fighting men to about 85 all told—with these and two howitzers we marched forward. The morning was excessively cold, and we felt it more as the most of us were wet to the skin. After passing over a mountain and travelling as near as I can judge some ten or eleven miles we came in sight of the enemys fires. We marched down the mountain. So soon as we arrived on the plain the shout and charge was commenced from the advance." Another officer says that Kearny himself shouted the command.

With Hammond having been detected it is not surprising that the Californios were prepared for the pre-dawn attack. They met it with a volley of rifle fire that threw Kearny's ill-organized dragoons into confusion, then retreated just enough to lead them into an ambush. Doctor Griffin, for some reason riding with the dragoons, gives us a description of the engagement. "... by this time we were very much disordered—our men, some being mounted on fresh horses, and others on poor and broken down mules, could not come. Capt. Moor however ordered the charge to be continued and it was in the most hurly burly manner—not more than ten or fifteen men being in line and not over forty all together. On they went however—the Enemy continued to retreat for about ½ mile further when they rallied and came at us like devils with their lances. Being mounted on swift horses—and most of our fire arms having been discharged or missed fire from the rain of the night previous, our advance was perfectly at their mercy. . . . We lost one of our Howitzers in this action, the mules in it ran wild and ran off with the piece. . . . In all, 35 men killed and wounded and I should think there was not to exceed fifty men who saw the enemy. We took two prisoners."

Among the seriously wounded were Captain Gillespie, Captain Gibson, and General Kearny, who would have been killed if Lieutenant Emory had not saved him by a lucky pistol shot. Among the killed were Captains Moore and Johnston. There is no doubt that the surgeon was loyal to his general, for he took pains to lay the blame for the debacle on the officers who had been killed: "This was an action where decidedly more courage than conduct was showed. The first charge was a mistake on the part of Capt Johnston, the 2d on the part of Capt Moor. After the Genl was wounded and the men were rallied he was anxious for another charge but was persuaded not to risk it."

With General Kearny unconscious from loss of blood, Captain Turner took command and went into encampment on a rocky hill just outside the little Indian settlement of San Pasqual, while the Californios, under Captain Andrés Pico, brother of former Mexican Governor Pio Pico, took up siege positions on the surrounding hills.

Captain Turner's first action was to send a letter to Commodore Stockton, asking that a strong detachment of mounted reinforcements be sent out from San Diego immediately. To carry the message, he chose three scouts, headed by Alex Godey, one of the Carson Men who had been sworn into Stockton's horse marines. The rest of the day was spent in caring for the wounded, making travois on which they might be moved, and guarding the stock and supplies. After dark the twenty-one dead were secretly buried.

The next morning General Kearny was sufficiently recovered that he could sit a horse. He determined to move on toward San Diego without waiting for reinforcements, since the occupied hill had no forage for the animals. The march was started at sunrise, with the wounded and pack animals at the center of the column. In his *Own Story*, Carson reports, "I had command of about 15 men and was ordered in advance. Marched about seven miles. During the night, the

Californios had received reinforcements. They were now about 150 strong. During the day they would show themselves on every hill ahead of us."

In the afternoon the Army of the West reached a ranch near the present town of Escondido. The place was deserted, except for a few Indian laborers, so the general took over the house, had chickens killed and cooked for the wounded, beef butchered for the rest of the men, and the horses and mules watered and fed. Toward evening the Army moved on, "driving many cattle before us."

In his diary, Lieutenant Emory goes on: "We had scarcely left the house and proceeded more than a mile, when a cloud of cavalry debouched from the hills in our rear, and a portion of them dashed at full speed to occupy a hill by which we must pass, while the remainder threatened our rear. Thirty or forty of them got possession of the hill, and it was necessary to drive them from it."

Unfortunately, this was another ambush. The hill had neither wood, water, nor grass. To capture it Kearny had to abandon the cattle he had seized at the ranch, and once on it he found himself completely surrounded and unable to escape. The night temperature dropped to 23 degrees. With no firewood, the wounded suffered terribly, no food could be cooked for the men, and in the darkness several of the pack mules stampeded off the hill in search of water. The sleepless night was followed by an even more hectic day. On the shadeless hill parched men had to fight thirst-crazed mules and horses to keep them from escaping into the enemy lines. All edible supplies had been consumed, and little could be done to relieve the pain of the wounded.

In the forenoon a mule was butchered, and while its raw meat was being wolfed down by the hungry men a commotion was heard on the plain below. Soon after, Captain Pico sent a messenger with a white flag, saying that the returning scouts had been captured, and that he would exchange prisoners. He would not, however, exchange Godey, the only one who knew Stockton's reply, though Burgess, the man for whom the exchange was made, reported that he understood Stockton had refused to send relief.

With his position on the hill untenable, Kearny decided to march at once, regardless of the consequences, but his officers convinced him that such a move would be disastrous. He then called for volunteers to take another appeal to Stockton. Carson and Lieutenant Beale of the Navy stepped forward, and Beale's Indian-boy servant insisted on going with them.

Captain Pico suspected that another attempt to get messengers through to Stockton would be made as soon as night fell. As dusk settled it was evident that he had learned, probably from Alex Godey, that Carson was in Kearny's camp. He set his lancers circling the foot of the hill in a triple ring, just out of rifle range, and as they rode they called to each other, *"Tenga cuidad! Se escapara el lobo!"* (Take care! the wolf will escape!)

The wolf did escape. As soon as darkness fell, Carson, Beale, and the Indian boy wriggled from the camp like snakes, carrying only rifles, a canteen of water, and a chunk of mule meat. They had nearly reached the inner circle of lancers when Beale brushed a rock, and the canteen clanked against it loudly. Instantly the nearest lancers converged on the sound, one of them stopping his horse within a rifle's length of where the three scouts lay frozen to the hillside. Later, Carson said he could hear Beale's heart beat as they lay there, expecting to be discovered or trampled upon at any moment.

For several minutes the Californio sat listening, then rolled a cigarette, lighted it, and took up his circling again. The canteen could not be risked. Carson had Beale take it off his back and leave it. Next he had boots removed and stuck under their belts, for the hillside was covered with loose stones, and a bare foot could feel a stone, while a booted one might set it rolling.

Time and again a lancer passed within a horse's length of the three messengers as they inched their way down the hill and through the circling cordon at its foot. The first two miles required half the night, and as the men crawled their arms, legs, and bodies picked up cactus spines as a magnet picks up steel filings. When, at last, they were beyond the probability of detection, they discovered that all three had lost their boots—and San Diego was thirty-six miles away, across a rattlesnake- and cactus-infested wilderness.

During the rest of the night the messengers made their way southward together. Near dawn Carson had them separate, each to hide out during daylight, then make his way by a widely divergent route as soon as darkness fell.

In the little hamlet of San Diego a small advance force for Kearny's relief was being organized at nine o'clock on the night of December 9, when a sentry challenged and was answered by an exhausted Indian boy. An hour later Lieutenant Beale was brought in, unable to walk, and delirious from the poisoning of countless cactus spines. At three o'clock in the morning Carson arrived, having taken a much more devious route, his feet swollen twice their normal size from cactus toxin.

Back on the hilltop at San Pasqual conditions were becoming desperate. On the evening of December 10, Kearny had all his baggage burned, and Surgeon Griffin wrote in his diary, "The Genl ordered all things to be in readiness for marching in the morning. We all went to bed firmly convinced that we should be obliged to fight our way to St. Diago."

When, later, his brother officer wrote up his report of the night, he put a better face on it. "We were all reposing quietly, but not sleeping, waiting for the break of day, when we were to go down and give the enemy another defeat. One of the men, in the part of camp assigned to my defence, reported that he heard a man speaking in English. In a few minutes we heard the tramp of a column, followed by the hail of a sentinel. It was a detachment of 100 tars and 80 marines under Lieutenant Gray, sent to meet us by Commodore Stockton, from whom we learned that Lieutenant Beale, Carson, and the Indian, had arrived safely in San Diego. The detachment left San Diego on the night of the 9th, cached themselves during the day of the 10th, and joined us on the night of that day."

There was no need to "give the enemy another defeat." The relief force had arrived at two o'clock in the morning. In the darkness Captain Pico could not use his lancers to advantage, so wisely withdrew. At four o'clock on the afternoon of December 12, the exhausted remnant of the Army of the West reached San Diego, where the wounded general at once contended with Commodore Stockton for the position of Commander-in-Chief in California.

A week later he wrote to his wife, "I have been here a week. . . . Lieut Col Fremont is still in California, & we are daily expecting to hear from him. He went up the Coast to raise Volunteers, from Emigrants from Missouri, to attack the Californians, 700 of whom are now said to be in Arms about 100 miles from here. . . . When I get the Volunteers [the Mormon Battalion] into the Country, I can drive the enemy out of it with ease, tho' at present they have the advantage of us, as they are admirably mounted & the very best riders in the world—hardly one that is not fit for the Circus."

[61]

This time Kearny had misjudged the strength of the enemy as badly as at San Pasqual, for though Flores had gathered a force of seven hundred horsemen at Los Angeles they were not Californios but Mexicans, with few usable arms and no taste for battle. Knowing this, Stockton determined to retake the city without waiting for the arrival of Frémont or the Mormon Battalion. But to assert his claim of being Commander-in-Chief, Kearny insisted upon joining the expedition with his Army of the West. The combined force marched from San Diego on December 29. It was made up of 433 sailors and marines, 60 horse marines with Carson as chief scout, and 57 dragoons—all the able-bodied men left in the Army of the West, and afoot for lack of mounts.

It required ten days for this motley army to march the 125 miles from San Diego to Los Angeles. There it fought two "battles" with Flores's army on January 8 and 9, 1847, in which three Americans were killed (one by accident), and ten wounded (two by accident), then the Mexicans scattered like frightened quail, Flores and his officers making a fast run for Sonora. On the morning of the 10th the conquering army marched into Los Angeles, and Stockton again raised the American flag, after which both Commanders-in-Chief made their reports.

General Kearny to the War Department: "I have the honor to report that, at the request of Commodore R. F. Stockton, United States Navy (who in September last assumed the title of Governor of California), I consented to take command of an expedition to this place. . . . Commodore Stockton accompanied."

Commodore Stockton to the Navy Department: "I have the honor to inform you that it has pleased God to crown our poor efforts to put down the rebellion. . . . Having made the best preparation I could, in the face of a boasting and vigilant enemy, we left San Diego . . . aided by General Kearny with a detachment of sixty men on foot."

Ironically, neither claimant to the rank of Commander-in-Chief reaped the glory of obtaining California's surrender. When Flores made his dash for Sonora he left Captain Andrés Pico of the Californio lancers as Commander-in-Chief, and Pico elected to make the surrender to Frémont, who was approaching Los Angeles from the north.

The Mormon religion was founded by Joseph Smith, who gathered followers rapidly. During the 1830's he tried to establish a Zion for his people, first in Ohio, then in Missouri. But the Mormons, a close-knit, aloof, and industrious people, were feared and resented by other settlers. In 1839 they were expelled from Missouri by order of the Governor, and settled in Illinois. Within five years fifteen thousand had gathered there, built a great temple, fine public buildings, two thousand houses, and established hundreds of well-stocked and highly profitable farms. But in their rapid growth and prosperity lay their weakness. They were hated and persecuted, not primarily because of their religion, but for fear they would take over the political power of the state, and possibly the nation. Joseph Smith was arrested on a trumped-up charge of treason, and murdered by a mob at the Carthage jail. Other Mormons were murdered from ambush, much of their stock killed, crops destroyed, and houses burned.

By early spring of 1846 the situation had become so explosive that the Mormons had no choice but to abandon their homes and pull out, with nowhere to go, and no means except their remaining wagons, horses, and oxen. The migration had to be westward, and Brigham Young, Smith's successor, had to have crops in order to feed his people. He sent out four detachments of young men with oxen, wagons, plows, carpenter's tools, and seeds of all kinds. They were to establish temporary settlements between the Mississippi and Missouri rivers, put in crops, and erect dwellings. As soon as the grass was high enough to sustain stock and the earliest crops were ready to harvest, the remainder of the people would follow.

The seed was barely in the ground when war was declared with Mexico, and resourceful Brigham Young believed he saw a way of transporting his people to California at Government expense. Volunteers were being recruited for the Army of the West, obviously for the conquest of California, and the United States was anxious to establish as many settlers as possible there. If the Mormon men could be enlisted in the Army, and permitted to take their families along, the matter of transporting and provisioning the migration would be solved.

Young immediately wrote to Elder Jesse Little, the most influential

Mormon in the East, setting forth his hopes, and urging Little to make a direct appeal to President Polk. News of Young's proposal evidently reached the Governor of Missouri, for he wrote to the Secretary of War: ". . . I doubt the friendship of the Mormons for any cause but their own; or for any government, and especially ours, either state or National. . . . They are a bad and deluded sect, and they have been harshly treated; but I suppose very correctly; yet they do not believe so, and under the treatment which they have received, if they are not enemies, both of our people and our government then they are better Christians and purer patriots than other denominations, a thing which nobody in the west can believe."

Elder Little gained an interview with the President on June 3, but Polk was as skeptical as the Governor of Missouri. That evening he wrote in his diary: "The Mormons, if taken into service, will constitute not more than ¼ of Col. Kearny's command, and the main object of taking them into service would be to conciliate them, and prevent them from assuming a hostile attitude towards the U.S. after their arrival in California." The next day, after consultation with the Secretary of War, he decided that no Mormons should be enlisted.

The Missourians, who had been the Mormons' most bitter enemies, now unwittingly became their benefactors. Three weeks before Elder Little's interview with the President, the Secretary of War had called upon the Governor of Missouri for a thousand mounted volunteers and an equal number of infantrymen for the Army of the West. The mounted force was raised, but the Missourians had no stomach for marching two thousand miles afoot across prairies, mountains, and deserts, so no infantrymen could be enlisted. In consequence, Kearny was authorized to muster not more than five hundred Mormons into the Army of the West at once, but instructed that they must not comprise more than a quarter of his force. Doubtlessly, he was also instructed that they were not to march with the main body of his force.

On June 19, 1846, Kearny issued orders to Captain James Allen to enlist four or five companies of "young and efficient" Mormon men, "each company to consist of any number between 73 and 109. . . . You will have the Mormons distinctly to understand that I wish to have them as volunteers for twelve months; that they will be marched to California, receiving pay and allowances during the above time, and at its expiration they will be discharged, and allowed to retain, as their private property, the guns and accoutrements furnished to them at this post. Each company will be allowed four women as laundresses, who will travel with the company, receiving rations and other allowances given to the laundresses of our army." The daily rations were set at eighteen ounces of bread and twenty ounces of beef or twelve ounces of bacon.

From the viewpoint of the Mormons, no finer man could have been chosen to organize the Battalion than Captain Allen. By the time he had visited the four temporary settlements where they were raising crops to tide them through the coming year he became thoroughly convinced of their loyalty to the United States, of their honesty, their industry, and the fact that they had been unjustly persecuted. In his sympathy for them he somewhat exceeded the authority given him in Kearny's orders. Men were permitted to enlist who were too old or feeble to make good infantrymen. Families were permitted to take the places of the "four laundresses" authorized for each company. An agreement was made with Brigham Young that the men should wear their own clothing, for which each would receive an allowance of forty-two dollars. Also, the volunteers were to receive their first month's pay at the time of enlistment. As Allen knew they would, the men turned these funds over to the Church, a lifesaver to the almost destitute emigrants.

By July 18, 1846, the Mormon Battalion of five companies had gathered at Council Bluffs, and Brigham Young gave them their instructions from the Church: "Let no man be without his under garment and always wear a coat and vest; keep neat and clean, teach chastity, gentility and civility; swearing must not be admitted, insult no man; have no contentious conversation with the Missourian, Mexican, or any class of people; do not preach, only where people desire to hear, and then be wise men. Impose not your principles on any people . . . never trespass on the rights of others. . . . Should the battalion engage with the enemy and be successful, treat prisoners with the greatest civility, and never take life if it can be avoided."

Henry Standage was unusual among the Mormons who enlisted in the Battalion only because he kept a diary. His entry of July 20 reads: "This morning I arose early to prepare for to join my Co., which was 10 miles distant on the Missouri River. Went to Bro. Ira Eldredge and besought him to permit my mother to make her home with him till I could be free to take care of her. When he agreed to be a son to my mother, I accordingly left her with him promising to recompense him, as soon as I was able and opportunity would offer. About 9 o'clock I took my knapsack and left the camp of Israel leaving my wife and Mother in tears, and reached the Co. at noon. This afternoon I received a blanket of Government, and commenced to draw rations."

At noon on July 21, the Mormon Battalion marched away from the little settlement of Council Bluffs, the men keeping time to "The Girl I Left Behind Me."

The condition of some of the enlisted Mormons, and the poor provision for the 180-mile march to Fort Leavenworth are evident in Standage's diary. "July 22 . . . travelled today 18m. One of our number died this evening. July 23. This morning we buried Bowley in his blanket and resumed our march and traveled 26 miles. July 25. Traveled 18m, weather very warm, some of the brethren sick and obliged to ride in the baggage wagons. Battalion generally in good spirits, flour scarce, and last night had parched corn for supper."

The Battalion reached Fort Leavenworth on August 1, and was held there two weeks while a regiment of Missouri mounted volunteers was being gathered and started off for Santa Fe under Colonel Price. During the stopover Captain Allen contracted pneumonia, and the Battalion moved on under the Mormon Captain Hunt until it reached Council Grove on August 27. There it was overtaken by Lieutenant Smith of the Regular Dragoons, who brought word of Allen's death, and orders to take command of the Battalion until it reached Santa Fe.

Allen had planned to march the Battalion, as Kearny had marched, by way of Bent's Fort. But Lieutenant Smith, although unfamiliar with the route, decided to take the Cimarron Cutoff across the New Mexico desert. Much of the three-hundred-mile trek was waterless, and many of the supply mules and oxen were lost through thirst and starvation. By the time Wagon Mound was reached the men, on half rations for several days, were so exhausted that the Battalion had to be divided; the stronger men making a forced march for Santa Fe, the weaker left to get in as best they could. The wagons, with twelve or fifteen families, were left to bring on the men who were unable to walk. The advance division reached Santa Fe on October 9, the second on the 13th. Altogether 486 Mormon volunteers arrived at Santa Fe, sixty of them by that time invalids or unfit for service.

The Mormon Battalion was as fortunate in its third commander as in its first, and equally fortunate to find Colonel Doniphan, a stanch Missouri friend, in command of the post at Santa Fe. When, on October 3, General Kearny received word of Captain Allen's death, he was already a week's travel on his way to California. He at once sent back Colonel Philip St. George Cooke to take command of the Battalion, and with it to establish a wagon road to California by the shortest possible route.

Cooke had seen enough to know that any movement across the Southwest with wheeled vehicles was going to be extremely difficult and attended by severe hardships. When the exhausted second division of the Battalion arrived in Santa Fe, he immediately recognized the folly of trying to take any but able-bodied men into the wilderness.

Upon finding that a migration of Saints from Mississippi had reached Bent's Fort, on their way to the little settlement of Pueblo, Colorado, Cooke and Doniphan conferred and made a proposal: If the Battalion would leave its invalids, unfit, and families in Santa Fe, Doniphan would supply them and give them escort to Bent's Fort, where they could join the Pueblo party. The following spring, and at Government expense, they could join the main westward migration of the sect. The wisdom of this plan was at once apparent to the leaders of the Battalion, and they agreed to it with only one exception: that five of the officers' wives, who were in robust health and had their own wagons, mules, and provisions be allowed to continue with the Battalion.

As guide for the expedition, Cooke chose Paul Weaver—known on the frontier as Pauline. The Mexicans had originally called him Paulino, but the mountain men dropped the "o." His father had been one of the earliest Tennessee settlers, and his mother a Cherokee Indian beauty. He and Kit Carson had been beaver trappers together, both knew the Gila River and its tributaries thoroughly, and both had driven ore wagons from the Santa Rita copper mine to Chihuahua. From his father Pauline had inherited coolness and judgment, and from his mother the Indian's amazing sharpness of eye and ear, as well as the instinct which enabled him to find water where few white men could. Beyond this, he had the friendship and confidence of both Indians and Mexicans, spoke their languages fluently, and could make and read Apache smoke signals.

A week was lost at Santa Fe while a doctor examined the Battalion, rejected eighty-six men, and consigned them to be sent with twenty-five women and children to Pueblo. Meantime the quartermaster laid in the authorized rations for four hundred men, replacements were secured for the mules and oxen lost in crossing the Cimarron desert, wagons were repaired, the paymaster distributed pay checks for the month of September, and messengers arrived with mail from the Mormon camp at Council Bluffs.

On October 18, Henry Standage wrote in his diary: "Today I wrote a long letter to my wife and mother and sent 8.00 to my wife and 1.00 to the twelve [apostles] at the bluffs.—Br. Lee & Egan taking monies to the families at the bluffs.—The sick and the women start to day for Pueblo." This was about the average division of the pay checks: eight dollars to the family, a dollar tithe to the Church, and a dollar reserved by the volunteer for emergencies.

The Mormon Battalion left Santa Fe on October 19 with twenty wagons, fifteen of them drawn by mules, and the remaining five by oxen. On the 21st Standage entered in his diary: "March'd 24 miles a hard days march and encamp'd at 5 o'clock. The Col has started with only 60 days rations or in other words, if we call a days rations what the law recognizes as such, we have only 54 days rations although the Pilot [Weaver] had frequently told Col Cook that it was too little. We are now on ¾ rations and if reduced so soon what will we be obliged to do ere we reach San Diego; for the Col can not obtain it in the settlements."

The shortage of provisions was no fault of Cooke's. The War Department, knowing only that the straight-line distance from Santa Fe to San Diego was six hundred miles, had authorized a day's rations for each ten miles, and six days' food supply had been consumed before the Battalion left Santa Fe.

The Mormon supply wagons, although much lighter than Kearny's great schooners, dragged like anchors through the loose desert sand, but Cooke devised a system to keep them rolling. The infantry companies, changing positions each hour as the leaders tired, were required to march in front, packing the sand enough to keep the wheels from cutting in too deeply. In this manner, fifteen miles were covered on the 22nd.

Even with the men marching in the lead, thirty-nine miles in two days proved much too fast a pace for heavy wagons over a trail so deep in sand. On the 23rd only ten miles were covered, mules and oxen began to break down, and the older men became exhausted long before a day was ended. For the next week no more than twelve miles a day could be averaged, and it was the end of the month before Socorro was reached.

At this rate of travel there was no possibility that the supplies would last through to San Diego, so on November 1 Cooke put the Battalion on half rations and set a minimum of fifteen miles a day. Furthermore, rumors had been brought in that Kearny's dragoons had been attacked at the copper mine, and the colonel was determined to get there with all possible haste. The rumor was doubtlessly started by Mangas Coloradas gathering his warriors, though an attack had been avoided through Carson's discreet interpreting and friendship with the Apache chief.

Regardless of Cooke's haste, fifty-seven miles were all that could be covered in the next six days, though the Battalion was kept on the trail from dawn till dusk. For November, the weather was extremely warm, forage for the animals was scarce, and oxen that had withstood the long trip across the plains without difficulty began breaking down. The beef from those worn-out animals, tough and scanty though it was, would have been a blessing to the men on half rations if they themselves had not had to replace the oxen they ate. Each time an ox fell out a rope had to be attached to a wagon, and a dozen men set to straining on it.

When, on November 6, the camp was reached where Kearny had stopped to send back his wagons, the older men and mules were reaching the point of complete exhaustion. The diaries for the next few days give a good description of the progress and the condition of the Battalion. On the 7th Standage wrote: "March'd 10 miles down the River over small mountains, had to push much at the wagons, and pull with ropes, taking one wagon at a time and placing as many men around it as we could get; mules giving out very fast." On the same day William Coray wrote: "This day nearly all the mules gave out and the men were nearly worn out pushing on half rations. Every man was willing to take ten days rations on his back if the Col. would leave the wagons. He said if the roads did not get better within several days he would leave them, for he knew if we did not gain ground faster we would perish on the plains of Sonora or Chihuahua."

It is very doubtful that Cooke ever seriously considered abandoning the wagons. General Kearny had assigned him the task of opening a wagon road between Santa Fe and California, and he was no man to give up on an assignment. Moreover, his mules could not possibly have packed the necessary amount of supplies. In fact, Weaver had already told him that half of them, even if driven unburdened, were too weak to withstand the trip to the coast. When the condition of men and mules continued to deteriorate, Cooke made the move that probably saved the Battalion from starvation in the deserts. He culled out his weakest men and mules, and sent them back to Santa Fe with the heaviest wagons, thus increasing the supplies available for the remainder.

On the morning of November 10 Standage entered in his diary: "This morning 50 [others show the figure as 55 and 58] of the Battalion were sent to winter at Santa Fe, or if possible to go to Pueblo ... sending back some tents and other things to lighten the loads. We marched 15 miles today, roads still very bad, having to labor almost incessantly, helping wagons through the sand. This is now the 10th day we have been on ½ rations. Some rumors of our going to take the town of Sonora [probably Janos] in the District of Sonora, in order to get a fresh supply of provisions, as it is thought impossible to cross the Mountains to the Pacific sea with as little as we now have."

On the 13th Cooke left the Rio Grande and struck westward toward the Santa Rita copper mine, driving as hard as he could, for he was still unsure that Kearny's dragoons had not been attacked there. With wagons he was unable to follow the route taken by Carson, but had to circle well to the south, losing time and cutting more deeply into his scant food supplies. To make up for it he kept the men on the trail from daylight till dark. Then the weather turned bitter cold. In crossing the Black Range, only three miles were traveled in an entire day, the wagons having to be lifted and pried through the narrowest gorge still known as Cooke's Pass. Even with the backbreaking labor, the colonel did not dare to increase the rations, and on the 17th Standage's entry read in part, "Water a long ways off. I eat guts today for the first time, though many have eat them before. One of our Pilots shot 2 wild goats here."

To reach water Cooke was obliged to drive his weary and half-starved Battalion eighteen miles the next day. The diary note that night was short, "Very much worn out today. The bretheren are daily growing weaker."

Still Cooke drove on another twenty miles the next day to the present site of Whitewater, twenty-five miles south of the copper mine. Late in the afternoon Pauline Weaver sent up signal smokes, but instead of bringing in Apaches the smoke attracted a few Mexicans who had been trading with the Indians. From them it was learned that there had been no attack on the dragoons, and from Standage's diary entry it is evident that Cooke was quite relieved. "Nov. 20. Laid by all day. Very pleasant. The coppermine road passing up this valley. The Col partly concluding to take this road and travel south to Sonora. The passes west of this not known and our Provisions very low, may not be able to get through at all. The American backbone showing very plain from this place, the largest chain of Mountains I have seen."

Standage was mistaken in thinking that the passes to the west were not known. Pauline Weaver knew the headwaters of the Gila as well as Kit Carson did, and knew it would be impossible to get through with wagons. He advised Cooke to follow the old ore road south to Janos, thirty miles below the present International Boundary, then turn northwestward to Guadalupe Pass, and follow Father Kino's old trail back to the Gila along the San Pedro Valley.

Cooke realized that a wide detour must be made, but was opposed to going so far south, and entered in his own journal, "I have determined to follow the Yanos road until I can turn off—probably two days on this side—as the best road or route to the same point of the Gila which I should strike in any route—"

The Mormons had no way of knowing what the colonel had decided to do. Upon hearing that the officers were urging him to take the ore road to Janos, Elder David Pettigrew surmised, "their reason was that they might procure whiskey, tobacco and women, and seeing their determination and influence with the Colonel, felt distressed in mind and had some evil forbodings." That evening he visited every tent and mess fire, imploring the men to pray that the Mormon Battalion might be led directly to California without passing through the wicked country of Mexico.

Although Cooke had written that he intended to follow the ore road to within two days of Janos, he actually followed it only about two miles, then struck off across the trackless desert toward the southwest. Numerous reasons have been given for this change of plans; one that the old ore road veered to the southeast at this point, and others that he turned away in hope of discovering a direct route westward.

The latter is quite improbable, for Cooke, unlike Frémont, never tried to be a pathfinder through unknown country, but relied on the knowledge of his guides. Cooke, though brusk and a strict disciplinarian, was farsighted and diplomatic in his handling of people. He certainly knew the Elders' fear of going to the Mexican settlements, and of the prayers that had been offered the night before. It is most probable that he changed his course slightly, even at the expense of known hardship, in order to retain the trust and good will of the Mormons.

If so, his decision was wise, for that evening Standage wrote: "November 21. Struck tents quite early and started towards the Settlements of Sonora; travelled about 1½ miles, when Col. said he started to go to San Diego, Upper California and he meant to go the near way, and then ordered the Command to turn west leaving the well beaten road for the trackless desert. Travelled 8 miles towards the American back-bone. The Bretheren truly rejoicing this evening to turn west again, trusting in the Lord to guide our Pilots day by day. Found both wood and water."

The pilot knew nothing of the barren deserts lying to the westward of the ore road, but was familiar with the Chiricahua Mountains in the southeast corner of Arizona—the stronghold of Cochise's warlike tribe of Apaches—and knew that Guadalupe Pass formed a gateway through the southern end of these mountains. Setting his course for the pass, he led the way toward modern Lordsburg and on to the dry lakes near the Arizona-New Mexico line. The Mormons, positively convinced that they were being led by divine guidance, trudged on uncomplainingly for forty waterless hours, straining at ropes to help the worn-out mules pull the heavy wagons.

Before the advance guard reached the dry lakes the Battalion was strung out for ten miles or more, exhausted men and animals littering the desert. There a well was dug, good water found, and cask-laden mules led back to revive the stragglers. With his rations running desperately low, Cooke was obliged to lay over a day while men and animals recuperated. The layover was fortunate, for several mules had completely broken down in crossing the desert, and at the dry lakes Cooke was able to secure ten replacements from Mexicans who had been trading with Cochise's tribe of Apaches.

The Mormon camp at the dry lakes was on the route that would later become the mainline of the Gila Trail, and only thirty-five miles east of Apache Pass, the most important gateway of the trail, but at that time it was unknown to Pauline Weaver. With the fresh mules and the men revived, he led the way seventy-five miles to the south, keeping a few miles east of the present Arizona-New Mexico line.

On November 28, the Battalion reached the vicinity of Guadalupe Pass, near the point where New Mexico, Arizona, and Sonora join. But by mistake the guide led them into the wrong canyon. By doubling teams, the wagons were pulled to the summit without too much difficulty, but there the way appeared to be completely blocked. On the western side the trail pitched down a thousand feet, snaking through a narrow, rock-walled gorge. Any commander less ingenious and resolute than Philip St. George Cooke, or with men less hardy and loyal than the Mormons, would have abandoned his wagons there, but both commander and men were determined to complete the task they had begun. On half-rations, their provisions nearly exhausted, and with no expectation of finding more before reaching the Pima villages in thirty days, they drove on. Two days were lost in moving six miles, while wagons were dismantled, let down over precipices with ropes, and reassembled.

The Mormons, cut now to quarter-rations, had moved on for only one day when it appeared to them that Jehovah had rewarded their faith and loyalty with manna from heaven. They had reached the site of the old Spanish settlement of San Bernardino. This had once been a thriving cattle center, with great ranches spread out through the valleys, but the settlers had all been killed or driven out in Apache raids, and their longhorn herds had reverted to wild beasts. Although the Apaches preferred to eat mules or horses, they had no objection to cow beef, but drew the line at bulls. As a result, the area was overrun with the wildest and fiercest bulls imaginable, some of them so old that they had Spanish brands burned on their hips.

Bull beef was a rare treat to the half-starved Battalion, and Cooke decided to lay over a day, so the men might hunt. They had been in camp only a short while when the Apaches appeared, but either because of their friendship for Pauline Weaver or because the Mormons showed no hostility, the Indians were friendly, honest, and hospitable. They showed the Mormons how to jerk and smoke beef, and brought in good mules to trade for knives or trinkets.

With full stomachs and fresh mules, the Battalion moved on for a week, holding a westerly course below the present International Boundary until passing the site of modern Douglas, then turning slightly northwest to the San Pedro River. The hunting was good all the way, and from Standage's diary it appears probable that the men gorged themselves on bull beef. "December 9. I awoke this morning after a very restless night quite sick, unable to carry my gun &c. Permission given me by Lieut Lytle to put my gun and knapsack in the wagon; eat no breakfast and travelled all day in much pain—Crossed San Pedro River a pleasant stream and camp'd on its banks. Wood scarce principally Hackberry. 27m. today."

The brush which Standage believed to be hackberry was actually mesquite, so thick that the Mormons often had to cut an opening for their wagons, and perfect cover for the wild bulls that infested it. On December 11, the Battalion fought its only battle—against the bulls. Private Keysor described it extremely well in his journal:

"The land on each side of the Pedro river bottom is a dense thicket of bramble bush, mostly muskeet, with which millions of acres are covered. Those in the Mormon battalion who had yaugers [probably Jaeger muskets] were permitted to go a hunting this morning. Shortly after we started, two wounded bulls came jumping into our marching column. One of them knocked down and run over Sergeant Albert Smith, bruising him severely; as soon as they passed the column, they received a volley which brought them to the ground. The sergeant was put into a wagon and the command marched on; soon descending to the river bottom we halted to water our teams, where another couple of bulls raging and foaming with madness, charged upon us. One of them tossed Amos Cox of Company D into the air, and knocked down a span of mules, goring one of them till his entrails hung out, which soon died; Cox's wound was four inches long and three deep.

"While these two bulls were performing thus, others stood a few rods off seemingly unable to determine whether they should charge or await the issue; they chose the latter course; meantime, the two bulls retreated, closely pursued. Then our attention was turned to the bulls that were looking on. Some officers shouted 'shoot them,' others cried, 'let them alone'; amid this confusion the wagons and part of the command moved on. After advancing about half-a-mile another bull came rushing out of the muskeet thicket, and charged upon the hind end of a wagon, lifting it partly around, and knocking down a mule, but his career was short for all the command now had their muskets loaded, and soon greeted our fierce opponent with a shower of bullets. These bulls were very hard to kill; they would run off with half-a-dozen balls in them unless they were shot in the heart."

Following the battle of the bulls, the going became easier. Weaver led the Battalion to the present site of Benson, then turned away from the San Pedro, taking a northwesterly direction toward Tucson. Tucson was the only Mexican stronghold between the Rio Grande and Colorado River. The town consisted of a score or so of adobe houses, an arsenal, and barracks for several hundred soldiers, surrounded by thick adobe walls, impregnable to rifle fire. Garrisons from the surrounding area had been gathered there, together with half a dozen brass cannons and a large store of grain and provisions.

Cooke, unlike most of the commanding officers in the Mexican War, was not obsessed by the urge to win himself glory on the field of battle. His concern was with carrying out his mission of opening the shortest possible wagon road to California, and in getting his men there with the least possible loss of life. As soon as the Battalion had left the San Pedro he sent three scouts ahead to negotiate for a peaceful passage of the expedition. One of the scouts was seized and held prisoner, while the others returned to report that the garrison could probably raise a thousand defenders, and that the Battalion would not be permitted to pass.

Although Colonel Cooke was not inviting battle, he was no man to avoid it if necessary. A halt was made, companies formed in marching order, put through drills, and each man issued twenty-eight rounds of ammunition. With the ranks in close file and ready for a surprise attack, the Battalion marched twenty waterless miles over rough country, made a dry camp, and marched on eighteen miles the next day. There Standage takes up the story:

"December 16. . . . Early this morning the 5 Cos. were paraded and march'd at a quick pace to Touson. The Col determined to pass through. Many of the brethren travelled this 18m. without either food or drink suffering much for want of water, having none last night or yesterday. When we arrived at the Town, we found but a few of the Inhabitants, the Soldiery having fled with their Cannon and also having forced many of the people to leave also. We were kindly treated by the people of Touson, who brought Flour, Meal, Tobacco, Quinces to the camp for sale and many of them giving such things to the Soldiers. We camp't about ½ mile from Town. The Col suffered no private property to be touched, neither was it in the heart of any man to my knowledge so to do. 2000 bushels of wheat belonging to the Spanish [Mexican] Government was found out which we were ordered to feed the Animals but none was taken for food for the Soldiers as the teams were too weak to haul the same. . . . I am led to exclaim that the Lord God of Israel will save his people in as much as He knoweth the cause of our being in the United States Service."

After a day's rest in Tucson the Battalion pushed out on the ninety-mile dry march to the Pima villages on the Gila, and the Mormons had need for their unshakable faith in divine protection, for the feat they accomplished has never been equaled by infantry in the history of the United States. For fifty hours they marched without a drop of water, their worn-out clothing hanging in rags, the soles of their boots filed away by the sharp sand, their feet bleeding, and having to tug at the wagons to help along the exhausted mules. On the third morning Weaver discovered water two miles from the trail, canteens were filled and carried back for miles to revive the men and animals that had fallen out, too weak to gain their feet.

On the fourth day Standage believed the Promised Land had been reached, and wrote in his diary: "21. Struck tents early and travelled till 10 A.M. when we came to a point from which we could see the Ela [Gila] River and on the other side the long looked for country of California. The River running west and Sonora being on the south and California on the north [he was mistaken as to his geography; the boundary of California was then unestablished]. At about 2 P.M. when near the River the Pemose [Pima] Indians some 200 in number came to trade with us bringing meal, corn, beans, dried pumpkins, and water melons which they readily exchanged for old shirts &c. These Indians appear glad to see us, many of them running and taking us by the hand. The weather is very warm like unto April in Illinois. Camp'd on the Ela River."

Strangely, where the biographers of the Kearny expedition reported the Pima women to be boorish and ugly, the Mormons found them to be beautiful and cultured, doubtlessly judging them by their hospitality and gentleness rather than by their physical appearance. When the Pimas discovered that the Mormons were destitute, they supplied them freely from their granaries, fed them generously, and made them welcome while men and animals regained their strength. Ten mules that Kearny had left with them six weeks previously, broken down to the extent that they had been worthless, were turned back to Cooke in good condition for the trail, the Indians refusing any reward for their care.

The Battalion stayed with the Pimas until Christmas Day, then set out on the fifty-mile arid cutoff across the Big Bend of the Gila. Here a scant supply of water was carried for the men, but the mules were obliged to travel dry for another forty-eight hours, and before the river was reached most of them were on the verge of collapse. Worse still, the hundred and forty miles from the Big Bend to the Colorado River would be across a barren desert, deep in sand, and with the only forage being the few willows and rushes that grew along the bank of the river. For the next four days the Battalion crawled along the trail at the rate of barely a mile an hour, men pushing the wagons from behind while others tugged at ropes beside the worn-out and famished mules.

On New Year's Day, 1847, Cooke hit upon a plan to relieve the men and mules of a part of their burden. He had wagon bodies lashed together, mounted on drift logs, loaded with provisions obtained from the Pimas, and floated down the river as rafts. The men were not too confident of the experiment, and Standage wrote in his diary: "This plan will certainly lighten the loads for the mules and enable them to travel faster but I am of the opinion it is very risky."

Standage was right. At this time of year the Gila was at its lowest. Although swift and a hundred and fifty yards wide, it averaged no more than three or four feet deep, and was ribboned with sandbars, many of them submerged. Each barge was loaded with twenty-five hundred pounds of provision, together with corn for the mules. They were to be moored to the bank every afternoon, so that camp might be ready when the Battalion reached it. Instead, nothing was seen of the makeshift boats for several days. As soon as launched, they were swept away by the swift current, but soon piled up on sandbars, and could be dragged off only by lightening the load and piling supplies on the nearest dry bar.

In the meantime the Battalion crept on, men and mules so weakened by hunger that no more than ten miles a day could be covered. For the 6th and 7th Standage's only diary entries were: "Detailed for the Col's Orderly. Travelled 10 miles and was kept up very late. Travelled 10 m. today. quite weak and hungry, I purchased a piece of bread & meat of one of the Col's waiters, a Regular." What he purchased it with is hard to imagine, since no provision had been made for paying the Battalion, and no money had been drawn since leaving Santa Fe.

By the 8th the lightened boats had caught up, and a detail with pack mules was sent back to salvage as much as possible of the abandoned supplies. On the 9th the Colorado was reached, but there was nothing left for trading with the once-friendly Yuma Indians, and without a reasonable exchange they would furnish no supplies to white men.

On the 10th the detail returned with only a few sacks of salvaged flour, and the condition of the Battalion became desperate. While some of the men ferried the remaining provisions and equipment across the Colorado on the makeshift boats, Cooke set others to gathering mesquite beans—food for men and mules in crossing the desert to the California mountains. At the same time he sent a few picked men ahead on the strongest animals; their mission being to find cattle and mules at the nearest California outpost, then drive them back to meet the column on the desert. This foresight was all that saved the Battalion.

For five days the Mormons plodded westward across the desert on quarter rations, following the route originally blazed by Father Garcés and Anza. They dug wells wherever a drop of water could be found, and tugged at the wagons when the worn-out mules died of hunger and exhaustion. Late on the afternoon of January 15 running water was reached on the western edge of the Imperial Valley—now, through irrigation, a lush garden spot, but then a barren wilderness. Soon after, the advance scouts returned, driving ten beeves and forty-two mules.

Ten beeves was a small supply for a starving battalion of 350 men afoot in the desert, but there was no complaint, though on the 18th

Standage wrote: "I suffered much this day for want of water, as did also my brethren. We have suffered much in crossing this desert. . . . We are now without Flour, Bread, Coffee or sugar. Nothing but beef and very small rations of it. I was glad today to go and pick up the Pork Rines that were thrown away by the Col's cook although they were in the sand."

The worst seemed over for the weary Mormon Battalion, but when within some thirty miles of Warner's Ranch, it found a canyon with rock walls so close together that the wagons could not pass through. The reasonable solution would have been to abandon them, for there was already a wagon road from Warner's Ranch to San Diego, but neither men nor commander would consider it. With only a few shovels, a couple of crowbars, wagon tongues, and other rocks for tools, Colonel Cooke and his men attacked the walls. By sundown they had broken them down enough that the wagons could be drawn through without being disassembled. The next day was little better. An eight-mile mountain pass had to be crossed where the boulders were so large and close together that wagons could not pass between. A day of backbreaking labor was required to split them, roll them aside, and get the now useless wagons through.

General Kearny's dragoons had straggled into Warner's Ranch on December 3, worn out and in disorder from their eight-hundred-and-fifty-mile crossing of the mountains and deserts from Santa Fe—encumbered only by the two howitzers. On January 21, the Mormon Battalion marched in, each of the five companies in close order and perfect step; heads high and muskets sharply at shoulder-arms, though most of the feet were bare on the ground—and after eleven hundred and fifty miles afoot, dragging or pushing wagons most of the way. As a mark of pride in his Battalion, Cooke had stopped it on the 20th, and again that morning, for marching drills and manual of arms.

For the Mormon Battalion the struggle had ended. After a day's rest at Warner's Ranch, it marched on to San Diego, and as it neared the town on January 28, Standage wrote in his diary: "Last night we camp'd in sight of a farm house but the Inhabitants had gone. Passed two other houses today. Saw thousands of cattle, horses &c. all wild. Was detailed for one of the advance Guard. March'd with very sore feet; came 15 m. Saw little or no improvements around these Spanish dwellings. It is now Spring though in January—everything seems to rejoice; the grass, the trees, weeds, the birds on the trees, all, all seem to rejoice. Travelled in sight of the Ocean nearly all day."

There was cause for rejoicing, not only by the Mormons—but by the United States Government and General Stephen Kearny. Until the arrival of the Mormons—so distrusted and feared that no more than five hundred had been permitted to enlist—Kearny had only fifty-seven able-bodied dragoons in his once-proud Army of the West. There was no reason to question the loyalty of any man in the Battalion, their march was never equaled in history, and the road they opened became one of the most important gateways to the West. Troublemakers that the Mormons were accused of being, the Battalion was the only expedition to cross the Southwest in perfect harmony with the Indians, and without loss of a single animal by theft or raid. After completing their year's enlistment, many of the Mormon volunteers settled near San Bernardino, later brought their families, and established the most thriving farming community in California.

FORTY-NINERS ON THE GILA TRAIL

Within a year after the Mormon Battalion reached California, James Marshall discovered gold at Sutter's Mill, but news traveled slowly in 1848, and it was not until December that gold-rush fever infected the East. Everyone infected was frantic to be first upon the scene, believing that the "sooners" would find nuggets the size of eggs lying about in profusion, but only the wealthy could afford passage around Cape Horn on a fast clipper ship. Although the Oregon and Santa Fe trails were already well-worn wagon roads, the western prairies could not be crossed in the dead of winter, or the snow-covered summit of the Sierra Nevada until early summer.

Here the Texans had a big advantage, and were quick to capitalize upon it. Except for the extreme eastern portion, the Gulf coast, and three inland settlements—El Paso, San Antonio, and Austin—their state was a trackless, Indian-infested wilderness, but the winters were mild enough for travel. Furthermore, the Federal Government was planning to open a military road between San Antonio and El Paso. Envisaging their town as the gateway to the gold fields, and without even waiting for the military roadway to be surveyed, the San Antonians sent off reams of propaganda to eastern newspapers during the winter of 1848-49: months could be saved by taking ship from New York to Galveston, from where, by way of the San Antonio-El Paso thoroughfare and the Cooke wagon road, the diggings could easily be reached in forty-five days. In addition, prospective Argonauts were assured that they would be protected by Government troops, and that there was abundant grass and water all the way. Thousands of fever-ridden easterners were deluded by the propaganda, organized wagon-train parties, and took ship for Galveston. But it was September before the roadway was opened to El Paso, and no wagon train that took it in 1849 reached California before the end of the year. The following spring, however, it became a heavily traveled route and one of the chief branches of the Gila Trail.

The Texans themselves did not wait for roads to be opened. By early February the gold rush was on in earnest. From East Texas and the Gulf settlements hundreds of men were riding toward San Antonio and Johnson's Station, a Mexican War cavalry post near present Fort Worth. Each led a pack mule or two, and drove a couple of longhorn steers as provisions for the journey. But the Comanche Indians were on the warpath in the spring of 1849, and northwest Texas was their stronghold. It was also known to be a barren and almost waterless wasteland. To avoid the Comanches and the arid Staked Plane, the more conservative Texans made their way to San Antonio, organized pack trains, and traveled to El Paso by the general route that later became the San Antonio-El Paso wagon road. The most reckless, frantic to be first in reaching the gold fields, gathered at Johnson's Station, banded together in trail parties, and set out straight to the westward, along the general route which is now Highway 180—many of them to lose their scalps to the Comanches or their lives to the arid wastes. The daring but less foolhardy chose a compromise route. Among them was Benjamin Butler Harris, a former schoolteacher who wrote of his experiences in one of the very few Texas Argonaut manuscripts to be preserved.

Harris left his home in East Texas on March 25, 1849, and reached Johnson's Station in early April.

He joined a fifty-two man, horse-and-pack-mule expedition being organized by Captain Isaac Duval, of which the men "represented nearly every state and several European countries, Texas, owing to its youth, being scarcely able to contribute a grown-up white man.

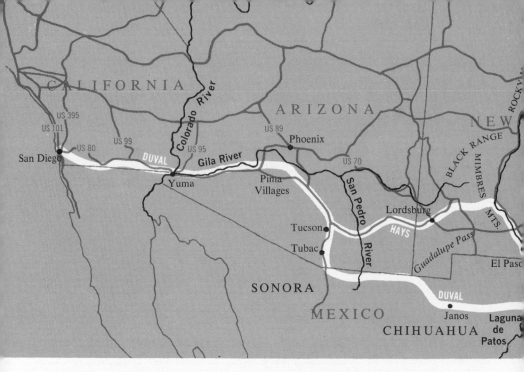

The Gila Trail: routes of the Forty-Niners. Mild winters gave
Texans the advantage in reaching California. Captain Isaac Duval's
gold-rush party blazed a much-followed route between El Paso

About a dozen of our company were discharged Texas Rangers."

The Duval expedition set out from Johnson's Station on April 10,
each man armed with a good musket, leading his pack mule, and
driving his longhorned provisions. Led by a Delaware scout, it followed a well-traveled trail southward nearly to Waco, crossed the
Brazos River, and turned almost straight to the west. This direction
was held for a hundred and fifty miles, across rolling prairies with
plenty of water and abundant grass for the animals, bringing the
party to the Colorado River of Texas at its confluence with the
Concho. The Delaware guide wanted to follow the Concho southwest to its headwaters, but upon learning that he had never before
crossed western Texas, Duval and his men refused to turn aside.
Anxious to reach California by the shortest possible route, they followed the Colorado northwest to Beal's Creek, then turned west
along that stream to Big Spring.

The journey was rather uneventful until the party neared the

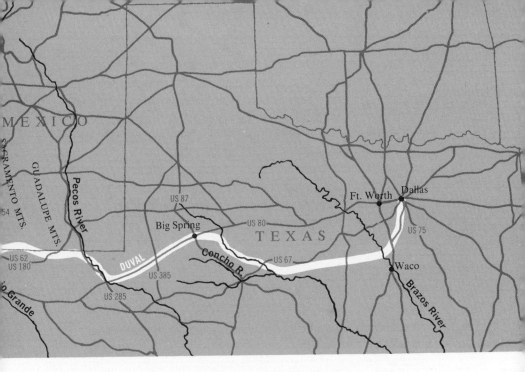

and Tucson. Colonel Jack Hays's cutoff route was later used by the Butterfield Overland Mail.

Colorado, of which Harris wrote: "Game of all kinds, with fresh Indian signs, abounded. One evening about dusk, as the guard for the night was being stationed, a thundering sound of horses was heard, growing louder each moment. We rushed to arms, expecting to receive the onset of thousands of Indians. It seemed to make a circuit, passing half a mile to eastward and died rumbling away in the distance. An intervening ridge screened the cause from view. Whether it was caused by horse, buffalo, or human enemies we did not ascertain nor did we seek to find out. . . . The first drove of wild horses I ever saw saluted us in this section. They came with flowing mane, prancing in regular order, so wild, so free and inspiriting, to within a hundred yards, then by a right face made a complete circle around the train and, following in an exact tangent, disappeared with their leader. Their advance, reconnaissance, and their thundering hooves caused my blood to quicken as in battle."

Upon reaching Big Spring the Duval expedition found itself in a dilemma. Then as now, the spring formed the farthest outpost of running water at the southeast corner of the Staked Plain. Between there and the Pecos River to the west lay a hundred and forty miles of arid tableland, so dry that scarcely a coyote crossed it. To go back and follow the Concho toward the southwest would probably cost a week or more in time. To go on with no assurance of finding water would be dangerous, but it was decided to run the risk. Except for a lone mosquito, the risk, no doubt, would have been fatal.

With animals well watered and canteens filled, the party set off at daylight toward a range of mountains that was barely discernible to the west. At noon a chain of small lakes was sighted far ahead, but when reached the water was too alkaline and brackish to be drunk. In the belief that fresh water would be found nearby, the rest of the day was lost in a fruitless search, and a dry camp made for the night. Forty miles were covered the following day, with a gill of water apiece for the men, but none for the animals. By morning a few of the weaker horses had to be abandoned, and the train plodded on another forty waterless miles, leaving its trail strewn with thirst-famished animals.

At the end of the third day the distant mountains appeared to be little nearer than when first sighted, no living creature had been seen, no buffalo trails crossed, and the plateau stretched away in all directions as flat as a table top. With a hot breeze blowing from the southwest, camp was made, and the men lay down to get what rest they might, too weary, parched, and discouraged to think of eating. Harris had lain for only a short time before he leaped to his feet, shouting with excitement; he had heard a mosquito buzzing about his head. There could be no doubt that water lay at no great distance ahead, and that the brisk breeze had blown the mosquito from it. With the strongest men mounted on the stoutest mules, an advance party set off, carrying anything that would hold water, and riding straight into the breeze. At dawn the mules pricked up their flopping ears and broke into a trot, heading for a range of low sand hills that appeared on the horizon—in all probability the sand hills of Winkler County, west of Odessa. Pools of clear, cool water were found in the hollows between the hills, and a supply hurried back to the prostrate men and animals along the trail.

Men and animals weakened by their three-day ordeal, the forty-mile trek from the sand hills to the Pecos River was devastating. By the time the first thirty miles had been covered nearly half the party were afoot, their animals having given out completely or become too weakened to carry more than their own weight. Every canteen was empty, and the temperature rose to above a hundred degrees, dehydrating men and animals as though they were roasting in an oven. Ahead, the desert appeared to stretch on for thirty miles or more to the foot of the distant mountains, its monotony broken only by an occasional desolate, barren mesa. A few of the men, despairing of hope that they might live to reach water, threw themselves down to die in the scant shade of a bush. Those who staggered on were driven to the verge of insanity, and in their irrational panic plotted to murder Captain Duval for leading them into the desert rather than following the Delaware guide's advice to turn to the southwest.

Below the New Mexico-Texas boundary the Pecos River flows through a winding channel, gouged as with a chisel through the almost level floor of the desert. Its banks treeless, it was, in 1849, invisible from farther than a hundred yards. But at a distance of seven or eight miles the Delaware guide detected signs of nearby water: a buffalo chip here and there, a coyote, and the first bird seen for several days. With hope renewed, those of the party who were still mounted flogged their staggering animals on. An hour later the mules began lifting their flopping ears, standing for a moment like a pointer on set, then driving on at a shuffling amble. Sensing that the mules had smelled water, the horses also quickened their pace. A half mile from the invisible river, the thirst-crazed animals became unmanageable, running until they tumbled down the precipitous bank into twenty feet of water.

Floundering and choking, the weakened men and animals were now in as much danger from too much water as they had been from too little. They had struck the river at a point where it was about a hundred feet wide, the current moving at four miles an hour, and the banks on either side rose in sheer walls, five or six feet high. Fortunately, the animals were sufficiently revived by the water to keep afloat, while the men clung to their tails or saddle leathers until a shelving bank was reached, a half mile downstream. Filling their canteens, they turned back along their trail to revive and bring in the stragglers.

After resting and recuperating for a day, the Duval party followed the Pecos River northward nearly to the point where it crosses the

New Mexico-Texas line, then turned westward, probably along Delaware Creek, to the Sacramento Mountains. There the Argonauts discovered a pass just to the south of Guadalupe Peak, and pioneered the route later followed to El Paso by the Butterfield Stage Line. Along the way they discovered Hueco Tanks, the only reliable source of dry-season water between the Rio Grande and Pecos River. These tanks are natural limestone basins in the Hueco Mountains, catching and holding sufficient pure water in the rainy season to last through the hottest summer. For centuries the tanks had been a gathering place for desert Indians, and the Duval party found the nearby cave walls decorated with crude drawings of birds and animals.

To their surprise, the Texas Argonauts found El Paso (now Juárez) to be a thriving city of eight or ten thousand inhabitants, with a garrison of five hundred soldiers as protection against the Apache Indians. There they learned that the wagon trail blazed by the Mormon Battalion might be intercepted a hundred and fifty miles straight to the west, but that the country lying between was a waterless desert. To avoid the desert they had two choices: They could follow the Rio Grande northward for nearly a hundred miles, intercepting the Cooke wagon road where it left the river. Or they could follow the well-traveled Chihuahua Road southward for some sixty miles, turn westward past the Corralitos silver mines and Janos, reaching the Cooke route at the southeast corner of Arizona.

After restocking with supplies and replacing their lost animals at El Paso, the Duval party decided to take the southern route, it being some fifty miles shorter than that to the north. They followed the Chihuahua caravan road to the vicinity of Laguna de Patos, then turned straight westward, crossing the desert by night to the Santa Maria River. There they found the Mexican silver miners in a state of fear and wild excitement because of recent Apache raids. Several men had been killed, most of the ore-wagon mules run off, and fifty armed men were constantly required to guard the hundred and fifty working in the rich mines. In recent months the Apache raids had become so fierce that ore trains had to be conducted to Corralitos, sixteen miles to the west, by a small army of soldiers under General Zuloaga.

The Duval party moved on to Corralitos, then a thriving smelter

[86]

town, just in time to witness an Apache raid. The Indians swooped down on the town, stampeded the mule herd that was grazing on the outskirts, and drove it away to the hills. The Texans, itching for a fight, joined the Mexican citizens and soldiers in pursuit. A subchief and a couple of warriors were captured, but the Apaches, the most skillful of Indian raiders, escaped without the loss of a single mule. Even so, the Mexicans welcomed the Americanos with open arms. For two or three days they were feasted and entertained lavishly—while General Zuloaga hatched up a scheme for using them to wipe out the enemy.

Janos, the next town on the Texans' line of march, lay a few miles down the Casas Grandes River, in a wide fertile valley. In Father Kino's time it had been the most thriving of the Spanish frontier outposts, with great haciendas and cattle ranches throughout the adjacent hills and valleys, but Apache raids had reduced it to a squalid settlement of *pobres*. The Duval party of fifty-two well-armed Texans had barely set out on the Janos road when it was overtaken by General Zuloaga and his ill-equipped little army. The general was bubbling over with excitement. He had set up an ambush that would wipe out Mangas Coloradas and all his subchiefs at a single blow. All he needed was a little help from the Americanos.

He told the Texans he had arranged for a peace parley in Janos the next day, where the three captured Apaches were supposedly to be exchanged for stolen mules. The Americans and Mexican soldiers who had muskets were to be sneaked into town afoot during the night, so as to be hidden within houses and upon rooftops before the Indians arrived. Then, when the parley was at its height in the plaza, they would open fire, killing every Apache before he could reach his horse and escape.

Although the Texans were still itching for an Indian fight, they had no taste for cold-blooded murder, but agreed that half of their force would take part in the ambush if, upon a signal, they could break from hiding and battle in the open. The general was opposed to any such reckless gallantry, but accepted the inevitable, then was careful to hide the Texans in houses facing on the plaza, while his own men took positions at a safe distance.

Soon after daylight the Indians began drifting into Janos, and by mid-forenoon more than a hundred subchiefs and warriors were gathered in the plaza, a bow or musket concealed under every blanket. But the ambush was ruined by the Texans who were supposed to take no part in it. Over-anxious for a hand in the excitement, they had broken camp too early and traveled too rapidly. Mangas Coloradas had just ridden into the plaza when they came racing up the valley. Before General Zuloaga could spring his trap the Apaches had leaped onto their ponies, streaked out of town, and scattered like leaves in a hurricane.

The people of Janos, living in constant dread of Apache raids, were reluctant to have the Texans move on, and entertained them for two or three days with fandangos, feasting, and *aguardiente*. When, on June 26, the Texans had sobered up enough to continue their march, they themselves were nearly ambushed at a mountain pass by four hundred Apaches. They were saved only by having scouts well out ahead. A square, with the animals in the middle, was quickly formed, and for an hour or so a noisy but ineffectual battle was fought, with no losses on either side. While the Texans poured out a barrage of musket fire the Apaches raced their ponies in a circle around the square; shrieking, yelling, and shooting at random, but keeping well out of range.

The Apaches, like the Mexicans, had no taste for a battle in the open. As soon as Mangas Coloradas became convinced that neither the Texans nor their animals could be stampeded, he raised an arm in the peace signal and called for a parley with Duval. After assuring Duval in excellent Spanish that the Apaches were the undying friends of the Americanos, he explained the reason for having set his ambush: the Texans had upset his carefully laid plans. If they had not arrived in Janos just when they did, he and his warriors were going to have killed the whole population. But he was not angry any longer. The Mexicanos were the enemies of both the Apaches and Americanos. They would join forces and kill all the Mexicanos in Mexico. Then the Americanos could have the land, and the Apaches would take the horses, cattle, and whatever else they could carry off.

Duval managed to avoid the alliance without again arousing Mangas's wrath, but when, after making presents all around for permission to pass, he tried to trade for fresh horses and mules the chief shook his head; the Apaches would need all they had in order to carry on their war against the Mexicanos.

With Apaches trailing along to stampede the pack mules at the first opportunity, or to steal any that strayed or lagged, the Texans made their way to the Cooke wagon road, over Guadalupe Pass, and westward to the deserted settlement of San Bernardino. After resting there for two days they moved on toward Agua Prieta, "encountering along the way a herd of wild cattle variously estimated by us as numbering from five thousand to fifteen thousand head. As we passed, tall ranges of timbered, table-top mountains loomed as a distant wall on the right, from which streams ran Pacificwards and from whose distant summits Indians continually sent up sky-reaching signal smokes, telegraphing our movements."

The smoke signals were disturbing enough to change the route of the Gila Trail. The wagon road Colonel Cooke had blazed led down the San Pedro River valley, through mesquite thickets ideal for an Indian ambush. The country straight on to the west, "was broken, fairly well watered, well adapted to grazing, sparcely timbered, oft-indented with vale and dell. . . ." To get out of Apache territory as quickly as possible, the Texas Argonauts continued westward below the present International Boundary, past San Pedro Palominos, Santa Cruz, and on to Nogales. There they turned down the Santa Cruz Valley on the road pioneered by Father Kino, and found few more white inhabitants than had been there in his time. Tubac was completely lifeless. About six months earlier the Apaches had raided it, and Harris wrote, "the wheat crop in the fields was ripe for the sickle. The bell and costly pictures, the other ornaments, were still in the church. Peaches and other fruits were ripening on the trees. Streets were uninvaded by weeds and the buildings still shone with new whitewash. There was not a human soul to enliven all this silence."

San Xavier del Bac had been deserted by the Mexicans, and the Texans found only a few Papago Indians around the magnificent old cathedral. Not far beyond, they again reached the Cooke wagon road, where it crossed from the San Pedro Valley, and followed it on to Tucson. Some idea of the intensity of the gold rush is shown by the next entry in the Harris memoir: "During our two-day stay there, immigrants to the number of four to five hundred filled the little frontier town, it being the last Mexican town on our route this side of San Diego."

The experiences of the Duval party between Tucson and San Diego were very much the same as those of the countless parties that followed: suffering for the men from thirst and hunger in the deserts, and a devastating loss of animals from starvation and exhaustion. The great contribution of the Duval expedition to the Gila Trail was that its route from El Paso to Tucson was followed by a large portion of the earliest Argonauts to reach California by land.

THE TUCSON CUTOFF

The last significant change in the route of the Gila Trail was made by Colonel Jack Hays. A hero of both the Mexican War and the Texas War of Independence, he was appointed Indian Agent for the Gila District in the spring of 1849. At that time Mangas Coloradas and his Apache warriors were raiding in the Janos area, where they were encountered by the Duval party. But in late summer they moved eastward, devastated the Rio Grande Valley to the south of El Paso, and on September 12 soundly whipped the U.S. cavalry detachment stationed at Fort Hancock. Although the raided area was not in the Gila Indian District, the homeland of the Apaches was, bringing Mangas Coloradas under Hays's jurisdiction. He at once set out for the Rio Grande Valley, hoping to arrange a meeting with Mangas and effect a peace treaty, but the wily chief withdrew into the mountains of Mexico.

Failing in his attempt to negotiate with Mangas Coloradas, Hays decided to go into Arizona, in hope of working out a treaty with Cochise, the great chief of the Chiricahua Apaches. On his way he stopped at El Paso, and found the city crowded with panic-stricken gold-rushers, afraid to move on for fear of the Apaches. Even though Hays was accompanied by only a few soldiers, his reputation as a war hero was so well known as to inspire confidence, and the frightened Argonauts pled with him to lead a caravan through to Tucson. He agreed, and in late September set out with a combined caravan of a hundred pack animals and the first eight wagons to have traveled over the San Antonio-El Paso road.

Enforcing strict military discipline, Hays led the caravan north along the Rio Grande Valley, to intercept the Cooke wagon road where it turned westward from the river. Well mounted and armed scouts were kept far out in front, on either side, and at the rear, to guard against surprise Indian attacks. No night camp was made without posting sentries, and each man was assigned his position and the hours he would stand watch. The caravan forded the Rio Grande about sixty miles above El Paso, crossed the Black Range by way of Cooke's Pass on October 12, and moved westward onto the New Mexico deserts. Then hostile Indian signs began to appear. From the Mimbres Mountains to the north, the Burro Mountains ahead, and the brush-covered desert on either side, smoke signals rose by day and specks of light blinked by night. Hays knew this to be the Apache telegraph, a system no white man had ever been able to decipher, but by which the Indians could send detailed information hundreds of miles within an hour or less.

There could be no doubt that the caravan was being watched constantly, that its strength was accurately known to the Apaches, and its every move reported. To provide the greatest possible defense, Hays doubled his number of scouts and formed the caravan into a compact column. In two days of forced marches he reached the point where Cooke had turned southward to circumvent a region unknown to his guide. Camp was pitched, and at midnight an advance scout rode in to report that no water had been found along the wagon road for a distance of nearly forty miles. Since Hays's position was reasonably defensible and there was grass and water for the animals, already jaded from the forced marches, he decided to lay over for a day and explore to the west. He had a map of Cooke's route, show-ing the long detour, and estimated that at least a hundred miles could be saved if a practical cutoff could be discovered.

Next morning an exploring party was preparing to set out when a chatter of distant gunfire was heard from the west. Hays trained a spyglass in the direction of the sound, and saw a low bank of dust that appeared to be blowing northward across the desert. But as he watched, its forward movement stopped, and its bulk slowly ex-panded. Such a dust bank could be raised only by a rapidly moving column of several hundred riders, and it had turned to come straight on toward the camp. At the colonel's first command, the cry of *Apache!* was shouted throughout the camp, and only his calmness kept the frightened Argonauts from panicking completely. As the dust cloud swelled and swept nearer, he had the animals brought in and tied at the center of the camp, wagons tipped over to form breastworks, ammunition issued, muskets reloaded, and canteens filled in the event of a long siege.

The letdown was tremendous. The expected Apaches proved to be a ragtag army of a thousand Mexican volunteers, under the command of General José María Elías, and its compaign had terminated in the customary manner. When Apache raids in Chihuahua became unbearable, the Mexican Government offered large bonuses for volunteers, opened the jails and prisons to fill the ranks, and organized an army to annihilate the enemy. As soon as it took the field, the Apaches retreated to their mountain strongholds, where the Mexicans had no stomach to follow. Instead, they usually managed to surround an isolated family band in the brush, killed a few old men and women, captured a few children, and returned triumphantly with their trophies of war. Secure in their strongholds, the Apaches waited for the army to disband, then continued their raiding. The Chiricahua Mountains were some seventy miles to the southwest of Colonel Hays's camp, but General Elías had taken care to stay well to the east of them. In a skirmish with a family band he had lost six men, but taken five Apache scalps and four child prisoners. With his mission completed, he was on his way back to Chihuahua with his trophies.

Hays had no interest in the gruesome scalps, but great interest in the child prisoners. He believed that by returning them to the tribe he might be able to establish friendly relations with Cochise, and effect a peace treaty to protect travelers on the Gila Trail. Also, he was anxious to discover information about the country lying straight to the west; whether it was crossable with wagons, and whether or not water could be found at reasonable intervals.

After much negotiation and, no doubt, an appropriate present, General Elías agreed to give up one of his prisoners, a ten-year-old boy, but he knew nothing of the country lying to the west. The territory bounded by the Gila River on the north, the San Pedro on the west, and the New Mexico-Arizona boundary on the east was considered to be Chiricahua stronghold, and it was a brave Mexican indeed who dared invade it. The general was not one of them, but said he had a sergeant in his ranks who had once hunted there and knew of a pass across the mountains. The sergeant knew little more than his general, except that there was a stream on the east side of the Chiricahua Mountains, and that a well-worn trail crossed their northern end.

In hope of a meeting with Cochise, and since there was no water within forty miles along the Cooke route, Hays decided to attempt the cutoff. Next morning he moved the caravan westward across the unexplored desert to the present site of Lordsburg. There he turned southwest, along the line that is now Highway 80, until reaching the New Mexico-Arizona boundary, where he again set his course as straight as possible to the west. Good grass and water were found at the foot of the Chiricahua Mountains, and after circling their northern rampart, a low pass—since known as Apache Pass—was discovered. The crossing was made with little difficulty, and an excellent spring of clear water was found at the top of the pass. Although this was the center of the Chiricahua stronghold, no Indians were seen, and no meeting had with Cochise, but smoke and fire signals made it clear that the caravan was being watched. And animals straying from night camps were seldom found, indicating that the Indians were escorting the invaders from hiding.

Beyond the pass, long-used Indian trails led westward across Sulphur Springs Valley, and to the San Pedro River about ten miles north of the point where Cooke had left it in turning west to Tucson. Except for the last thirty or forty miles, the passage was not difficult, and a hundred and twenty miles of travel had been saved. Although the cutoff pioneered by Hays was to become the main line of the Gila Trail, and the route of the Butterfield Stage Line, no other party is known to have used it until 1851. This was, no doubt, due to the travel of 1850 being entirely westward, so that maps of the cutoff failed to reach the East until the following year.

Of the more than eight thousand American Argonauts who passed over the Gila Trail in 1849, most of those who came by way of El Paso followed the route through Nogales pioneered by the Duval party. Those who came by way of Santa Fe followed the Cooke road to Guadalupe Pass, then continued along the Duval route to Tucson. When the Hays caravan reached the Cooke road at the San Pedro Valley, they found that it had not been traveled since the Mormon Battalion marched over it in 1846.

During the gold-rush years, sixty thousand people, and more than double that number of beef cattle and sheep, entered California by way of the Gila Trail. In 1856 the first California overland mail service was inaugurated when James Birch established the San Antonio-San Diego Mail Stage Line. For nearly a year it was a stage line in name only, since it consisted of a rider leading a pack mule. In 1857, light wagons were put over part of the route, though few, if any, passengers were carried, and no schedule was maintained. But the following year the firm advertised proudly:

OVERLAND TO TEXAS!

THE SAN ANTONIO AND SAN DIEGO MAIL LINE

Which has been in successful operation since July 1856, are ticketing PASSENGERS through to San Antonio, Texas, and also to all intermediate Stations. Passengers and Express Matter forwarded in NEW COACHES, drawn by six mules over the entire length of our Line, excepting from San Diego to Fort Yuma, a distance of 180 miles, which we cross on mule back. Passengers GUARANTEED in their tickets to ride in Coaches, excepting the 180 miles, as above stated.

Although the Californians were glad to have any overland mail and passenger service, they were far from satisfied. Railroads had long since been pushed westward to the Mississippi Valley, and ever since California had been granted statehood in 1850, its people had been insistent that the Federal Government construct a transcontinental railway connecting with one of the Mississippi Valley lines. Although the transcontinental railway would not be completed for nearly two decades, the insistence of the Californians resulted in the establishment of the first dependable mail and passenger service between the Mississippi Valley and the Pacific coast—the Butterfield Overland Mail Stage Line.

BUTTERFIELD OVERLAND MAIL

The Great Oxbow Route

When, at the close of the Mexican War, the Treaty of Guadalupe Hidalgo was negotiated, the Gila River was established as the southern boundary of Arizona, and that of western New Mexico was set at 32° North Latitude. This left almost the entire Cooke wagon road between the Rio Grande and Colorado rivers in Mexican territory. With the discovery of gold in California and the tremendous traffic it caused to move over the Cooke road, the United States Government found itself in an embarrassing position, since it could not protect its citizens from Indian attacks while in a foreign country. Furthermore, the demand of the Californians for a transcontinental railroad was becoming too insistent to be entirely ignored, and to avoid crossing high mountains a route south of the Gila appeared to be the most feasible. To relieve the situation, the Gadsden Purchase was made in 1853, establishing the present International Boundary.

Tension over slavery had split the Senate before California was admitted to the Union as a "free" state. With one of the chief purposes of the Gadsden Purchase acknowledged to be the acquisition of a railroad route to California, the tension flared into anger. Antislavery partisans demanded that the Government build a transcontinental railroad along the Oregon Trail, crossing the Rocky Mountains at South Pass. Proslavery adherents insisted just as vehemently that the Government consider no transcontinental railroad route except one lying through the South, across Texas, and to California along the Gila Trail. Since the Senate was equally divided between proslavery and antislavery forces, an unbreakable deadlock resulted.

In 1856, a presidential-election year, California was a doubtful state. It was also a fabulously wealthy state, far removed from the national capital, and disturbing rumors had been drifting back; some that there was a movement afoot for outright secession and forming a separate nation. There was no possibility of breaking the transcontinental railway deadlock, but in December, 1855, California's Senator Weller took advantage of the rumors to secure a temporary alternative. He introduced a bill authorizing the construction of two bridged and fortified wagon roads to California; one from Independence, Missouri, to San Francisco by way of South Pass, Salt Lake City, and the Humboldt River; the other from El Paso to Los Angeles over the Gila Trail route.

California was too great a prize to be risked by either faction. Its lower half was largely populated by southerners who had migrated over the Gila Trail, and the proslavery Senators believed that the state could be won to their cause if joined to Texas by means of rapid communication. The antislavery forces were content to compromise on two roads, so long as one of them joined the North with Upper California, for it was there that nearly all the gold had been discovered. A bill was speedily passed "for improvement of overland transportation"; appropriating $300,000 for the Independence-San

Francisco road by way of South Pass, and $200,000 for the El Paso-Los Angeles road by way of the Gila Trail. The bill required that streams be bridged, wells dug, cavalry posts established, and freight depots constructed along each route.

The next problem to face Congress was rapid transportation, as both factions were anxious to keep in the closest possible communication with their constituents in the Golden State. Road construction was barely under way before bills were presented for the establishment of fast semiweekly mail-and-passenger service to California. Again a deadlock resulted, as each faction insisted that only one Federally-subsidized means of rapid transportation be provided, and that over the route of its choice.

After a year's wrangling, an ingenious bill was presented. It provided that the Post Office Department be authorized to call for bids "for carrying the entire letter mail from such point on the Mississippi River as the contractor may select, to San Francisco," each trip to be made in twenty-five days or less. The contract was to extend for six years at an annual Government subsidy not to exceed $300,000 for semimonthly, $450,000 for weekly, or $600,000 for semiweekly mail service, the frequency to be determined by the Postmaster General.

With the bill clearly stipulating that the western terminus of the mail line be San Francisco, northern Senators permitted the attachment of a rider authorizing the Postmaster General, not the Congress, to determine the route to be followed. This was a great victory for the South, since Aaron V. Brown, an ardent proslavery partisan from Tennessee, was Postmaster General, and sole power to determine the route freed him from any necessity of accepting the bid most advantageous to the Government. Brown immediately advertised for bids, making it clear that each bidder must designate his Mississippi Valley terminus and the route he proposed to follow to San Francisco.

Few bids were expected, since a vast amount of capital would be required to undertake such a venture. But the reward would be tremendous if the Postmaster General could be induced to grant a contract for service over the shortest route, and at the maximum subsidy authorized by the legislation. Nine or ten hastily formed companies entered bids, most of them designating the route through South Pass.

With Aaron Brown's proslavery convictions well known, it was generally expected that the rich "plum" would be picked by a southern contractor. Nevertheless, a New York firm was finally awarded the coveted contract, but not without a great deal of influence and compromise. The organizer and moving spirit of the group was John Butterfield, a close personal friend of President Buchanan. Those who had joined him to form Butterfield and Company were all partners in one or another of the four largest express companies in the United States: Adams, American, National, and Wells Fargo.

Possibly to avoid winter snow in the Rockies, but more probably because of his friendship with President Buchanan, John Butterfield designated a route which, though far more expensive to equip and somewhat longer than the northern road, would offend neither North nor South. He specified St. Louis as eastern terminus, and proposed a route by way of the Santa Fe Trail to New Mexico, thence to California along the 35th parallel, now the route of the Atchison, Topeka, & Santa Fe Railway.

Although the proposed route lay largely through the Southwest, it bypassed Texas, and therefore the "solid South," so Aaron Brown refused to accept it. He suggested to John Butterfield that his firm might be given the contract if Memphis were made the eastern terminus of the line, and the route were southwest through Arkansas to the Red River, across the entire state of Texas to El Paso, and on to California by the road along the Gila Trail.

There had been several reasons for Butterfield's choice of St. Louis as his eastern terminal and the Santa Fe Trail as a part of his proposed route. The first of these was that St. Louis had direct rail connections with all the large cities of the East, whereas Memphis had none. The second was that the Missouri Pacific Railroad was then building a line westward across Missouri, and had already reached Tipton, a hundred and sixty miles west of St. Louis. It had been Butterfield's plan to transport mail over the railroad, starting his coaches from the various railheads as the line was extended westward. This would not only reduce his firm's operating expense, but materially add to its passenger business, since western Missouri and eastern Kansas were already well-populated.

The route Aaron Brown had designated was eight hundred miles longer, and there would be no local passenger business, for the only town of any size on the fourteen-hundred-mile roadless stretch from Memphis to El Paso was Little Rock, Arkansas. It would not only be tremendously expensive to equip such a roundabout route through

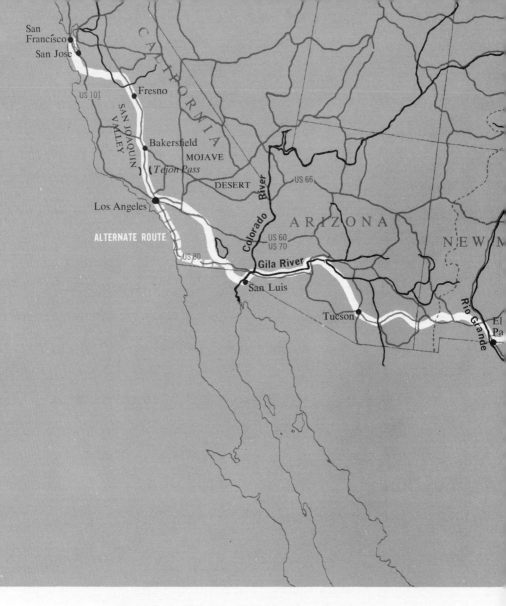

The Gila Trail: route of the Butterfield Overland Mail. Because of slavery issues, the Butterfield route ignited a bitter political conflict. Butterfield's original proposal was carefully drawn to offend

an uninhabited wilderness, but extremely doubtful that coaches could travel the distance in twenty-five days and nights. Brown, however, was adamant in his demands.

It is difficult to deal with a zealot holding dictatorial powers,

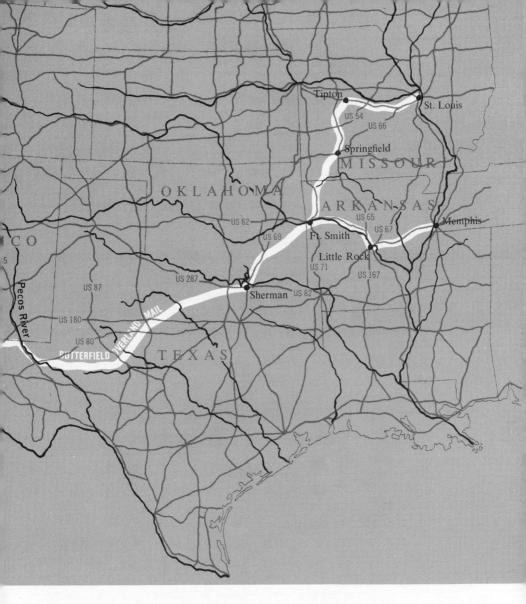

*neither North nor South, but the plan finally approved reflected the
bias of the Postmaster General, a southerner.*

but John Butterfield was as clever at negotiation and compromise as
at operating stagecoach lines, and he had two advantages: Brown
was determined that Memphis, his home town, should be eastern
terminal of the line, but the law provided that the contractor have

free choice. Secondly, Missouri, though admitted to the Union as a slave state, might swing to the northern cause if St. Louis and Springfield were excluded from the transcontinental mail line.

After carefully considering the political aspects and studying several possible routes, Butterfield negotiated a compromise for semi-weekly mail service at an annual subsidy of $600,000. It provided for two routes as far as Fort Smith, Arkansas: one from Memphis by way of Little Rock, the other from St. Louis by way of Tipton and Springfield. From Fort Smith the route would follow the Marcy-Simpson Trail to El Paso, the newly improved Gila Trail road to Los Angeles, and continue to San Francisco by way of the San Joaquin Valley. The compromise bid was accepted, and the contract signed on September 16, 1857, with a provision that service be inaugurated within one year from that date.

When news of the Butterfield contract was released, showing its $600,000-a-year subsidy and 2975-mile route from St. Louis to San Francisco, the newspapers of the North sent up a howl of protest. The *Chicago Tribune* and other papers called it, "one of the greatest swindles ever perpetrated upon the country by the slave-holders." The *Sacramento Union* blasted it as "a foul wrong, a Panama route by land." New York editors referred to the route as the "horseshoe" or "ox-bow," declaring that it lay over impassable savage-infested deserts, avoided every population center, and would prove too expensive to operate, even with its scandalous subsidy.

John Butterfield and his partners paid no attention to the newspaper blasts. The course of the route and its length were regrettable, but unavoidable under the circumstances. Though the line would be expensive to stock and equip, it would be snowless during months when a northern route might be completely closed to travel. As to their ability to operate within the subsidy, the partners had their own opinion. Their greatest concern was in being prepared to operate within a year, as specified in the contract, and so well prepared that there would be no danger of defaulting on the twenty-five-day time limit for mail deliveries.

The contract was no sooner signed than fifty-six-year-old John Butterfield set out on a rapid but thorough survey of the route, taking with him a staff composed of the most capable construction and operating superintendents of the four great express companies. Nor did Butterfield depend upon these men alone. He had long since sent representatives to hunt out and employ guides, scouts, and frontiersmen who were friendly with the various Indian tribes, and who knew every spring, water hole, stream ford, or mountain pass on the entire route. No more expert group of men could have been assembled for planning, laying out, and constructing a stagecoach line through a wilderness than that which John Butterfield led out of Fort Smith.

Between Fort Smith and El Paso lay a thousand miles of wilderness, arid plains, deserts, and mountains, inhabited only by bands of roving Indians. The Marcy-Simpson Trail was a trail in name only, being no more than an indefinite route between rivers, springs, and water holes. Its general course was southwest across Indian Territory, now Oklahoma, to the present city of Sherman, Texas. From there it continued in a more westerly direction across the Texas prairies to Big Spring, then followed the route taken by the Duval party—to water at the Odessa dunes, on to the Pecos at Horsehead Crossing, up the treeless river to Delaware Creek, and westward along the New Mexico-Texas line to El Paso.

The Government had somewhat improved the road over the Gila

Traveling in a coach of the Butterfield Stage. From "The California Overland Express," William Tallack, in Leisure Hour.

Trail from El Paso to Los Angeles, following the Apache Pass cutoff. Fort Yuma, with a Government-operated ferry, had been built on the Colorado River at the mouth of the Gila, but Tucson remained the only settlement between the Rio Grande and California. Wells had been dug at widely spaced intervals across the deserts, the roadway slightly graded over the worst hills, and a few small military posts scattered along the route for control of the Apaches. Beyond Los Angeles, a very passable road had been opened across the Tehachapi Mountains to the San Joaquin Valley, and across the Coast Range to San Francisco Bay.

There were still great stretches along the way where neither a drop of water nor blade of grass were to be found, but within a year the route must be converted into a thoroughfare over which coaches could roll day and night with comparative safety and comfort for passengers. The entire distance must be divided into relays, each short enough that it could be traveled at a rapid pace under any weather conditions and without danger of exhausting mules or horses.

At the end of each relay, living quarters, stables, and corrals must be constructed, two or three experienced frontiersmen employed as guards and hostlers, and a plentiful supply of hay, grain, food, firewood, and water provided. Accurate but definitely attainable time schedules must be worked out, and at the end of each day's travel a way station established with sleeping and feeding accommodations for passengers and drivers. These stations must be staffed with half a dozen well-trained and experienced keepers, equipped with blacksmith and harness shops, stocked with relay horses and mules, and supplied with enough feed, fuel, and provision to meet any emergency. Streams must be bridged, ferryboats built for crossing the larger rivers, creek banks cut down to provide fording places, boulders removed from the roadway, wells dug, passes through the mountains cleared, and the road graded enough to make it safely passable over the roughest hills and deepest gulches.

When John Butterfield had completed his survey he separated the route into two major divisions, one east of El Paso and the other west, and placed each under the management of a general superintendent. Both major divisions were broken into nine minor sections, each with a road boss or superintendent, who was held responsible for maintaining friendly relations with the Indians, as well as hiring suitable employees and constructing his own section of the line. After the division was built, provisioned, and stocked, he would make his headquarters at one of the way stations, supervise the relay posts on either side, and be held strictly accountable for the maintenance of time schedules and the safety of passengers and mail.

While Butterfield directed the construction his partners were equally busy at either end of the line, gathering building materials and starting them away from river landings and seaports in great freight caravans. They sought out the toughest and fastest horses and mules available, had hundreds of sets of harness made, and ordered the necessary vehicles—freight wagons for hauling the thousand tons of hay, grain, and provisions that would be required each month, tank wagons for supplying water to relay posts and way stations in arid regions, and luxurious Concord coaches for California, the El Paso area, and the eastern end of the line. For travel over most of the route, celerity wagons were bought. These were rugged low-wheeled vehicles, with canvas tops and side curtains, and having seats for six or eight passengers.

Within a year from the time the contract was signed, more than a million dollars had been poured into the enterprise, and John Butterfield had driven his men relentlessly, but Butterfield and Company was prepared to carry the California mail on schedule. More than two hundred way stations and relay posts had been erected along the 2975-mile route. There were two hundred and fifty Concord coaches, and double that number of other vehicles ready to roll. Over eighteen hundred of the best obtainable horses and mules stood in the corrals and stables. Nearly three thousand tons of hay, grain, and provisions were stored in stacks and warehouses. Wells had been dug or water stored in tanks at every relay post in the arid regions. Over twelve hundred highly skilled superintendents, road bosses, drivers, guards, conductors, keepers, blacksmiths, harness-makers, hostlers, and clerks manned the line.

Most of the men John Butterfield had chosen for his line were rough, tough frontiersmen, with the courage of wildcats and the endurance of lobo wolves, for no other men could have withstood the hardships and performed the tasks he demanded of them. On his last inspection trip over the route, he gathered his men at various way stations and gave them their final instructions: Above all else, passengers and mail must be protected and schedules maintained, but this could be accomplished only by keeping on friendly terms with the Indians.

Although drivers and conductors would be armed, they would use their weapons only when the lives of passengers or safety of the mail were definitely endangered. To avoid the possibility of attacks by highwaymen, no shipments of gold or silver would be transported under any circumstances. In the event of mules or horses being stolen by the Indians, it was the responsibility of the division superintendent to secure their return by peaceful means. Failing in this, a report was to be made to the nearest U.S. military post, but no other action taken.

Keepers of way stations and relay posts would be held accountable not only for the safety of passengers and mail, but for the condition and protection of company property and animals in their care. But in case of Indian attack, they were to shoot to kill only if passengers' or their own lives were endangered. Teams of well-shod horses or mules were to be kept ready for the road at all times, and harnessed immediately when, from two miles away, the conductor of an incoming stage sounded a trumpet call. Ten minutes was the maximum time allowed for a relay stop, unless passengers were to be fed, and keepers would be discharged if their unreadiness caused delays. In the event the driver of an incoming stage was incapacitated for any reason, the keeper was to take his place.

In order that coaches might roll swiftly and safely through the darkest night, drivers must know every twist and turn of the road. To make this possible, each driver would have his own route, a section approximately sixty miles long, over which, except in dire emergencies, he would do all the driving in both directions. He would be housed and fed at the way station or relay post at each end of his route, but regardless of rest he must take any incoming coach out within ten minutes of its arrival. He would not treat horses or mules with brutality, but would not spare them at the expense of running behind schedule, and he would not spare his own life in order to protect passengers and mail.

No coach would roll without a conductor seated beside the driver, and his route would be from one way station to another, a distance of approximately a hundred and twenty miles. He would have absolute charge of passengers, mail, and express, guard them with his life if necessary, and be relieved of his responsibility only when he had received a detailed receipt from the next conductor. If, when he reached the end of his route, the conductor for the next section was not there and entirely capable of assuming responsibility, he would continue on without sleep or rest. The passenger fare between San Francisco and St. Louis or Memphis would be $200; for shorter distances, fifteen cents per mile. At each meeting, John Butterfield's last words to his men were, "Remember, boys, nothing on God's earth must stop the United States mail!"

The Wheels Begin to Roll

At one minute after midnight on September 16, 1858, exactly one year from the day on which the contract had been signed, the first Butterfield Overland Mail stage rolled away from the post office in San Francisco. It carried a sizable load of mail and six passengers, few if any of whom rode through to the Missouri end of the line.

At daylight the next morning a Butterfield spring wagon dashed away from the St. Louis post office, carrying the postmaster and "two diminutive bags" of mail, since he had included only letters that were marked, "Per overland mail." At the depot the bags were turned over to John Butterfield himself, and the Missouri Pacific flyer for Tipton pulled away as soon as he had swung aboard. With him went William L. Ormsby, special correspondent of the *New York Herald*, the only through passenger on the first westbound trip.

The wood-burning engines of the mid-1850's were none too dependable, the fireman had trouble keeping up a head of steam, and although the distance was only a hundred and sixty miles it was 6:15 in the evening before the flyer reached Tipton. There John Butterfield, Jr. waited with a Concord coach and six fast horses. Within nine minutes his father, the mail, and the lone passenger had been transferred to the Concord. The engineer blew a blast on his whistle, the townsfolk screamed in excitement, and young Butterfield whipped away toward Springfield.

Fresh teams were waiting at each relay post, and a fresh driver at each way station. At 1:50 on the morning of September 19, the people of Fort Smith, Arkansas, leaped from their beds and raced to the Butterfield station. The first Overland Mail stage had just dashed in from Memphis, a full day ahead of schedule. The fact that it carried no passengers and only one small bag of mail made no difference to the townsfolk. They whooped and shouted in celebration of Fort Smith's first scheduled communication with the outside world. Fifteen minutes later, their shouting rose to a frenzy. The sound of racing hoofs was heard from the north, and the Tipton stage swept in with the St. Louis mail, the president of the line, and his weary passenger.

John Butterfield rode only to Fort Smith, where the mail bags and William Ormsby were quickly loaded onto a celerity wagon. The conductor climbed to the high seat, and the driver whipped away across Indian Territory, over "two hundred miles of the worst road God ever built." At some of the streams, a fording could be found in the darkness only by having the conductor walk ahead with a lantern. With the coach a day ahead of schedule, few of the relay posts had teams ready. Stops had to be made while the keeper lassoed mules or horses that had been turned out to graze. Those that were caught were often so wild they could hardly be harnessed, and a fight of a half hour might be required to get them hitched to the wagon. Time and again a celerity wagon was tipped over by runaways, and one pair of mules kicked the top off before being brought under control.

Across the prairies and deserts of western Texas, the road was barely discernible in daylight. On the first westward trip the weather was stormy, the moon and stars hidden behind a thick layer of clouds. Although the drivers knew the route better than any other men in the country, they were helpless in black darkness, having no landmarks to guide them and mules unaccustomed to the trail. Even with the mail a day ahead of schedule on leaving Fort Smith, it was two days late in reaching El Paso. From there on, the road had been sufficiently improved and traveled to be followable in darkness, the weather cleared, and the drivers poured the bullwhip onto the backs of their mules. Bouncing, swaying, and skidding, the low-wheeled celerity wagon careened across the deserts, through deep gulches, dry washes, and over rocky hills and mountain passes, while William Ormsby clung to the seat for dear life, or tried to catch a cat nap when too exhausted to sit up.

By the time Tucson was reached, one of the lost days had been made up, and the entire population of eight hundred—two thirds of them Mexican, and most of the others the white scum of the frontier —turned out to cheer the first westbound stage from Missouri. For the Forty-Niners, the four hundred arid miles from Tucson past the Pima villages, along the barren bank of the Gila River to the Colorado, and across the burning California desert to Warner's Ranch, had been devastating to both men and animals. Now, with way stations and relay posts reasonably close together and well stocked with feed, water, and provisions, this section of the route was one of the less difficult. The load was light, and the drivers kept their bullwhips cracking while Ormsby caught up on a little of his lost sleep. Whether planned or not, a race was on between the eastbound and westbound stages, and the westerners had no intention of losing it.

When Warner's Ranch was reached, the second of the two lost days had been made up, but there was no slacking of the pace. William Ormsby and the mail sacks were quickly transferred to a Concord coach that stood waiting behind six high-spirited horses, and the driver whipped away as soon as the hostler jumped back from the lead team's bridles. On through the Laguna Mountains, the Santa Anas, and down to the Los Angeles plain, the great coach rolled and pitched. There an extra span of horses was added, the hard climb made across the San Gabriel Mountains, and to Tejon Pass at the summit of Tehachapi Range. Down the tortuous, precipitous grapevine to the San Joaquin Valley the horses flew to keep ahead of the swaying coach, while billows of smoke rose from grinding brake blocks.

On the level floor of the valley the road was firm and good, and the drivers took full advantage of it, keeping the coach rolling at a smart trot past the cheering crowds at Bakersfield and Fresno. A few miles south of Merced the stage road turned westward toward the Coast Range, and darkness had settled before Pacheco Pass was reached at the summit. From the pass the road pitched downward to the Santa Clara Valley, twisting and writhing like a tortured snake. Here the driver used the whip instead of the brakes, and when Ormsby shouted for him to take it a little easier, he called back nonchalantly, "It's best to keep the wheels rolling, or they'll slide."

A light or two blinked in San Jose, but only the way-station keeper and his hostler were awake to change teams, then speed the racing coach back onto El Camino Real, the old Padres' Trail to Mission San Francisco de Asís. In the first gray light of October 10, the hills of San Francisco came into sight. As the sun rose over the bay the driver whipped his tiring horses to a brisk gallop, scattering early risers as he skidded the rocking coach around the last corner, pulled up at the Butterfield office on the plaza, and delivered the first overland mail just twenty-three days and twenty-three hours from the time it had left St. Louis. Actually, the elapsed time was twenty-four days and one hour, due to the two-hour difference between Central and Pacific coast time.

On the eastbound run the drivers encountered about the same difficulties as those on the westbound, but there was no possibility of making a final sprint through the rolling hills of Arkansas and Missouri. The San Francisco mail and passengers reached Tipton at 9:05 on the morning of October 9, were transferred to a special train on the Missouri Pacific Railroad, and reached St. Louis at 4:45 in the afternoon—being twenty-four days, fourteen and three-quarter hours of actual elapsed time on the way.

At both ends of the line there was a great celebration to mark the inauguration of a rapid, regularly scheduled overland mail. The *San Francisco Bulletin* exulted: "To-day for the first time, we experienced an inward consciousness that our State is practically independent of the steamship monopoly." Colonel J. B. Crockett, chairman of the celebration committee, went even further. "In my opinion," he told his cheering audience, "one of the greatest blessings that could befall California would be to discontinue entirely and at once all communication by steamer between San Francisco and New York." William Ormsby was a little less enthusiastic about the superiority of stagecoach to steamer travel, but he was more diplomatic than most newspaper correspondents. When asked to comment on his enjoyment of the journey, he simply remarked, "Had I not just come out over the route, I would be perfectly willing to go back." A later passenger expressed it more bluntly. "I know what Hell is like. I've had twenty-four days of it."

John Butterfield had met the eastbound stage at Fort Smith, and from Tipton he telegraphed news of the mail's arrival to his friend President Buchanan. The President replied, "I congratulate you upon the result. It is a glorious triumph for civilization and the Union. Settlements will soon follow the course of the road, and the East and West will be bound together by a chain of living Americans which can never be broken." A chain which would never be broken had been forged to bind California to the Union, but settlements along the course of that long-abandoned road are still few and far apart.

In spite of its unreasonably long route through desolate and almost completely uninhabited country, and in spite of the punishment inflicted upon passengers riding night and day over barely passable roads, Butterfield and Company prospered. Its success was due entirely to the rules laid down by John Butterfield before the first run was made, and to his insistence thereafter that they be adhered to without deviation. No more than three or four runs were required to convince not only Californians, but the East and Europe that schedules would be maintained, and that the Butterfield Overland service was far more rapid and dependable than that of ships sailing around Cape Horn. Within a month Butterfield stages were carrying ninety percent of the California mail, newspapers from every part of the East, and so many express packages that extra wagons had to be put on.

Back in New York, William Ormsby was popularizing the line with humorous stories in the *Herald*, telling of his experiences on the first westbound trip. *Harper's Weekly* praised the service, and commented that, "California is no longer a colony of the East." In London, *The Times* described the Butterfield Overland service as: "a matter of greatest importance to Europe, inasmuch as it will open up a vast country to European immigration, will be the precursor of the railroads, and will greatly facilitate intercourse with British Columbia." Evidently, the London writer knew nothing about the unreasonably circuitous route, its remoteness from British Columbia, or the arid, desolate region through which it passed.

Passenger travel over the Butterfield line was small for the first several months, largely due to fear of Apache attacks. The fear was well founded, for the Americans had given the Apaches, particularly Mangas Coloradas's Mimbres, every reason to take reprisals.

The Apaches and Lieutenant Bascom

As in all migrations, many who started for California in the gold rush never got there. Some stopped where they found a fertile valley, built a log cabin, and settled to till the soil. Others, having gone broke and lost most of their animals by exhaustion, squatted in the homeland of the Mimbres to make a living for their families by hunting.

For a couple of years Mangas Coloradas drove them out by what he considered peaceful means—stealing their remaining stock, frightening them by shrieking mock attacks, destroying their crops, and burning their haystacks.

In 1851 he found himself faced with a new and strange problem. Gold was discovered at Piños Altos, not far from the tribal Council Rock. Within a few weeks a hundred and forty American miners were digging feverishly into the hillsides. They would not leave when he had a few of their tents burned and their mules stolen, they had no crops to be destroyed, and they would not frighten at mock attack. With the careful thought that eventually won him the reputation of being the greatest strategist among all the American Indians, Mangas Coloradas worked out his problem. Gold had brought the Americans rushing into the Mimbres's homeland, so a greater amount, if it could be had with less labor, should take them away, and he knew where it was to be found, deep in the Sierra Madre Mountains of Mexico.

The Apaches had no use for gold, and held it of little value, so Mangas went alone to direct his unwelcome guests to the rich veins in Mexico, but they suspected him of trying to lead them into an ambush. He had no sooner entered their camp than he was surrounded by a score of men, bound to a tree, and bullwhipped until his back was stripped to ribbons. When their arms tired, the miners released him, hooting and jeering as he staggered out of camp. That night a few of the miners managed to escape with their lives, and in the months that followed a few of the settlers who had remained in the Mimbres homeland were able to escape. The rest were killed, but not until they had been given a taste of the American brand of torture.

Such was the condition in the Mimbres's homeland when John Butterfield set out to build his stage line. Fortunately, only about a hundred miles of the route, that between the Rio Grande River and Cow Springs, lay in Mimbres territory. From there to Tucson the cutoff lay through the heart of the Chiricahua Apaches' homeland, and though they often stole horses or mules from emigrants on the trail, they were at relative peace with the Americans, for neither they nor Cochise, their great chief, had suffered brutality at American hands.

Still, Apache Pass was the most vulnerable spot along the 2975 miles of the Butterfield route. For this reason, John Butterfield had a solid stone way station built in the narrow canyon leading up to the pass, though nearly all the other buildings along the line were adobe. As keeper of the station he chose a man named Wallace, a frontiersman who spoke the Apache tongue and had an unusual knack for winning the friendship of Indians. The early success of the Butterfield venture was, in a large measure, due to Wallace's gaining Cochise's confidence and friendship before the construction of the line was begun.

Cochise had married Mangas Coloradas's beautiful daughter and had more influence with him than any other. To please his friend Wallace, he had extracted a promise from Mangas that the Mimbres would not molest the stage line. In appreciation, Wallace did whatever he could to please Cochise. Among the Apaches, as with practically all other Indians, the women did the heavy work, while the men hunted, loafed, and performed the religious ceremonies. While the Apache Pass station was being built, Wallace made a deal with Cochise to furnish the stone. It was dragged or rolled in from the mountain by the women, and Wallace paid a fair price for it in goods that the Apaches prized highly: bright gingham and calico, tobacco, sugar, cooking utensils, blankets, saddles, sparkling ornaments, and almost anything except firearms and ammunition.

When the station was completed Wallace made a deal for the women to bring in firewood, and though they brought more than could be used, he continued to pay a good price for it in the coveted goods of civilization. As a result, Cochise pitched his headquarters camp a short distance from the station, and often came with his subchiefs and relatives to visit with his friend. On numerous occasions, when some outlaw band of young bucks, such as Geronimo's, made off with a few Butterfield horses or mules, Cochise sent his warriors to punish the thieves and bring back the stolen stock.

As soon as it became evident that the Butterfield stages were safe from Apache attack, the passenger business boomed. And in spite of the punishment attendant upon twenty-three to twenty-five days of jolting night and day over rough roads, it continued to boom for two years. Then Lieutenant George N. Bascom, a shavetail just out of West Point, stepped into the peaceful picture.

Johnny Ward, a degenerate Irishman, was a squatter on Sonoita River, not far from the foot of the canyon leading up to Apache Pass.

He had a small herd of cattle which the Chiricahuas had never raided, and a little shack where he lived with his Mexican mistress and her small son. The woman had been captured by the Coyotero Apaches, and a warrior of the tribe was the boy's father. One day in October, 1860, when Ward was away from the place, a band of Coyotero raiders, probably including the child's father, swooped down on the little shack, stole a few cattle, and carried the boy away. When Ward returned and discovered his loss, he raced a horse twelve miles to Fort Buchanan to report the raid to Colonel Morrison, and demanded that a detachment be sent to punish the thieves and bring back the missing boy and cattle. Lieutenant Bascom, with a detachment of sixty dragoons, was the man sent out.

This was Lieutenant Bascom's first assignment, and he was determined to win himself a reputation in a hurry. He did. Although he knew practically nothing of the country, and had no experience in dealing with Indians, he had heard of Cochise's friendship with Wallace, and that the chief was quite likely to be found at or near the Butterfield station. Heading for Apache Pass at a smart trot, Bascom led his troops into the station yard and demanded that Wallace send for Cochise immediately. Before a messenger could be started away Cochise came in accompanied by one of his "lesser" wives, three warriors, and two subchiefs.

The Indians had no sooner reached the station than Bascom demanded arrogantly that Cochise return the stolen boy and cattle immediately, threatening him with military punishment of his tribe if he failed to do so. For a moment the chief was nonplused, then decided that the military threat must be a joke, for it was well known that the entire U.S. military force in the Southwest would be unable to cope with the Chiricahua warriors in battle. Smiling, Cochise told Bascom that he had heard nothing about the raid, and that it had not been carried out by any of his people, but that he would do his best to find out where the boy and cattle were and, if possible, have them returned.

Bascom flew into a rage, sure that this breechclouted Indian was not only lying but ridiculing him. Regardless of Wallace's protest, Bascom ordered his dragoons to seize the entire party, disarm it, imprison it in a tent, and keep it closely guarded until Cochise had the missing boy and cattle returned.

He might better have tried to imprison a whirlwind. The Indians had no sooner been flung into the tent than Cochise whipped a hidden knife from under his breechclout, slit the canvas as he shouted an insult at Bascom, and burst through the ring of startled dragoons. Ducking and dodging, he raced across the station yard and up the little hill where the Fort Bowie graveyard is now located. At Lieutenant Bascom's frenzied command, the dragoons poured a volley of lead after him, but under the excitement their aim was poor. One ball hit Cochise in the shoulder, knocking him off balance for an instant, but he bounded on over the hill and disappeared among the boulders and brush of the mountainside.

The confused dragoons had barely reached the boulders where Cochise disappeared before a signal smoke rose from the Chiricahua camp, near the spring at the top of Apache Pass. Keeper Wallace needed no one to tell him the Apache telegraph was clicking, and that the tribe was being gathered for war. Within minutes muskets began to bark along the mountainside. The fire increased steadily until a rain of lead was raking the station yard. Several dragoons were hit, and Bascom was beside himself with rage. He could launch no attack, for there was nothing to attack. His dragoons could only dive behind corrals, outbuildings, and the stone station house, firing blindly into the mountainside and trying to hold off an inevitable massacre. But Cochise had no desire for a massacre. His interest was only in keeping the "boy soldier" and his men bottled up until he could get his wife and people back unharmed, and he went about it in true Apache fashion: an exchange of prisoners. He knew where two Americans, Jordan and Lyons, were prospecting in the mountains nearby, and sent a few warriors to bring them in.

Even the stubborn and egotistical Bascom realized that his situation was hopeless if the Apaches decided to storm the station. As soon as darkness fell he sent a volunteer to sneak across the mountains and try to reach Fort Buchanan for reinforcements. With Jordan and Lyons already in camp, Cochise let the messenger get through. If the soldiers wanted to make a war out of it he was willing, but he sent an unmistakable message to Wallace. Late that night the stage from California struggled into the station yard. One horse had been left dead on the road, the driver's leg had been shattered by a bullet, and one of the passengers had been shot in the chest. The whole party might easily have been wiped out, since the coach had been obliged to stop while the dead horse was being cut loose, but then there would have been no message. Wallace must understand that the stages rolled only by Cochise's permission, and that they would roll no more unless the prisoners were safely returned and the soldiers called off.

Since there had been no attack during the night and it was not resumed at daylight, Lieutenant Bascom's egotism again got the better of him. He released Cochise's wife with instructions to tell the chief that the hostages would be removed to Fort Buchanan and held there until the missing boy and cattle were returned. A few minutes after she had disappeared among the boulders on the mountainside, Cochise came out onto a little hill where he had last been seen, just out of musket range from the station. He was carrying a white flag, and with him were four warriors, holding Jordan and Lyons. In a booming voice that echoed across the canyon, he shouted that he was ready to exchange prisoners, and that if more were needed he would be glad to get them.

Disregarding Wallace's warning that he would start a war, Bascom shouted back that unless Jordan and Lyons were released instantly he would have the hostages killed. To an Apache, this was simply horse trading, and Cochise was a well-experienced trader. It might help the deal if Jordan and Lyons did the bargaining, since it would save the need for an interpreter. At a nod from their chief, the warriors began to twist the prisoners' arms. Jordan and Lyon screamed in pain, pleading with Bascom to let the hostages go.

Now Bascom's sergeant, an old campaigner in Apacheland, added his pleas to those of Wallace and the prisoners, but the young shavetail ignored them, shouting back his threats to kill the hostages. In desperation, Wallace ran toward the hill, convinced that he could talk reason to his friend Cochise if not to Bascom. To the chief, this placed Wallace squarely on the side of the soldiers. Cochise let him come on, then had him seized, and shouted that he now had three prisoners for exchange. When Bascom refused, Wallace was given the same treatment as Jordan and Lyons, and pleaded as loudly for the young lieutenant to release his captives. Instead, Bascom lost his head completely, and ran toward the hill brandishing his sword. He was met by a hail of lead that ripped through his uniform and sent him into a hasty retreat, still shouting his threats.

Whether at a signal from Cochise or from uncontrollable anger, a subchief spurred his horse from cover, swung a rawhide lasso around Wallace's neck, and dragged him to death across the rock-strewn hill. Then the Apaches vanished among the brush and boulders of the mountainside—and the smoke signals continued to rise.

When, next day, Lieutenant Bascom was reinforced and made a cautious retreat, he found the bodies of Wallace, Jordan, and Lyon hanging from the limbs of an oak tree, together with those of two teamsters from a captured freight wagon. In retaliation Bascom hanged his prisoners, and for many months no wheel rolled through Apache Pass.

But the Butterfield Overland Stage Line would have been short-lived even without the assistance of Lieutenant Bascom. Two months after his fiasco South Carolina seceded from the Union, to be followed by six other states, including Texas. The North could not risk having its overland communication line with California run through Confederate territory, where it might be cut at any moment. Congress passed a bill requiring that the service be transferred to the northern route, and Butterfield and Company sold out to Wells Fargo. But during its short period of operation the line was a tremendous success. Schedules were always maintained within the twenty-five-day limit, no stage was ever held up by highwaymen, and the profit from the mail contract amounted to $100,000, together with more than that amount from passenger fares.

THE BATTLE OF APACHE PASS

Lieutenant Bascom's abortive bid for glory touched off a powder keg that had been smoldering ever since James Ohio Pattie first made his way along the Gila Trail. In the next eleven years Bascom's blunder cost the United States hundreds of lives and millions of dollars in property loss and military expense, for Cochise resolved to exterminate every American in the territory between the Rio Grande and Colorado River. What is more, he came very close to keeping his resolution.

Soon after the outbreak of the Civil War, the North was obliged to abandon most of the forts on the western frontier. But before the official orders had been received, more than half of the officers and men of the Arizona and New Mexico forts had left to join the forces of the Confederacy. They were soon followed by those called back for service with the Union regiments.

From the day of the Bascom fiasco, the Apache tribes had combined for war against the Americans, with Cochise as commander-in-chief and Mangas Coloradas the incomparable strategist. The stage line buildings were plundered and destroyed. Mining camps, settlements, and ranches were struck by lightning-like dawn attacks, the inhabitants killed—often after the most gruesome torture—buildings burned, crops destroyed, and stock driven away. Every trail in an area nearly four hundred miles square was watched by Apache scouts. Day and night fires blinked or smoke columns rose from mountaintops, flashing messages over the Apache telegraph, a communication system then unequaled by any other military organization in the world. No military detachment left a fort without Mangas Coloradas's knowledge, and one seldom returned without at least a few empty saddles.

Cochise kept small bands of cavalry scattered throughout the entire region of Apacheland, far better mounted than the U.S. forces. At a signal from a distant mountain, two or three bands would converge on a moving column of soldiers, but the Coloradas strategy permitted no unnecessary risk of Apache lives. It was senseless to meet an enemy in open encounter, or to reveal hiding places by the report of a gun. Reaching a vulnerable spot on the trail well in advance of the soldiers, the Apache warriors left their horses and muskets far back in the brush, then hid along both sides of the trail for a mile or more. As the column passed, it was always the last man who fell from his saddle with an arrow through his heart. A commander often lost as many as a dozen men before realizing that he was under attack.

Although the Apaches had the best military communication system in the world, they had no way of knowing that the Civil War had been declared. When the soldiers left the territory it was only reasonable for the Apaches to believe they had driven their enemies away. With the soldiers gone the Apaches concentrated their attention upon the few remaining settlers, or any emigrants unwise enough to invade their territory. By the end of 1861 they were satisfied that they had completely beaten the Americans. Then, in the spring of 1862, the telegraph brought disturbing news: a mighty army was marching eastward along the Gila Trail. To Mangas Coloradas this could mean only one thing: the Americans had raised reinforcements, and were coming back in an effort to steal the Apache homeland. Signal smokes rose from every mountain peak, and the warriors were called in to make raids on Mexico for an additional supply of arms and ammunition.

At the outbreak of the Civil War, California had raised a great many volunteers for the Union, put them in training under Regular Army officers, and equipped them with recently developed firearms —breech-loading carbines and shell-firing field pieces. In April, 1862, General James H. Carleton led the first California column eastward to join the Union forces. It consisted of two regiments of infantry, a battalion of cavalry, and a battery of artillery—twenty-five hundred men in all. From the time the column left the Colorado, its every move was watched from hiding by Apache scouts, and every detail of the march transmitted to Mangas Coloradas and Cochise by the Apache telegraph.

To any other Indian chiefs, the California column would have been appalling, for although the Apache homeland spread over more than 120,000 square miles, the combined tribes could put no more than seven hundred warriors in the field. And in spite of intensive raids on Mexico, scarcely half of them could be equipped with muskets and an adequate supply of ammunition. Furthermore, no such force as Carleton's could be whittled down, as the dragoon detachments had been, by bowmen hidden along the trail. To save the homeland, the Americans must not only be turned back but annihilated, and to do it would require an ambush of gigantic size, as well as taking full advantage of the region's aridness. After much thought and studying of the California column's movements, Mangas Coloradas prepared his ambush, then sent bands to fill every well east of Tucson, and to obliterate all signs leading to its location.

In early June General Carleton led his forces eastward from Tucson, into a desert as seemingly uninhabited as though it had been on the moon, and as hot as though it had been on the equator. His maps showed the location of wells that had been dug at reasonable intervals all along the old stage line, but none could be discovered. Attempts to dig new ones, by soldiers unfamiliar with the secrets of the desert, resulted only in dry holes. Men and animals famished for water and dehydrating rapidly under the hot June sun, the California column staggered on from one widely spaced spring or water hole to another. With scant grazing and forced marches, the mules and horses began to give out from exhaustion, and at each watering place a stop of several days had to be made to revive them. Since no

Apache had been seen on the entire march, both Carleton and his officers became careless. The column was no longer kept in close formation, but allowed to string out for twenty miles or more, one unit well in advance to scout for water.

Only one officer under General Carleton's command knew anything of the Arizona deserts. He was Captain John Cremony, who had been a member of the Bartlett party on its survey of the International Boundary. Cremony was sufficiently familiar with the region to know that the most devastating march would be forty waterless miles between Sulphur Springs and Apache Pass, over barren alkali flats, but he was not at that time sufficiently familiar with the Apaches to interpret the disappearance of wells and Indians from the desert.

At Sulphur Springs the customary stop was made to recruit men and animals. Then, soon after midnight, the advance guard, under the command of Captain Thomas Roberts, moved rapidly out across the alkali flats. It consisted of three companies of infantry, a troop of cavalry under Cremony, and two howitzers—a total of about three hundred men. Because of the stifling alkali dust raised by the horses' feet, Captain Roberts kept the cavalry well behind the infantry, and set a fast pace in order to reach the springs at Apache Pass before the noonday heat should make marching intolerable.

Any officer leading a detachment through Indian country, regardless of the tribe, should have known enough to keep scouts far out in front and to either side, but Captain Roberts was so intent upon reaching water for his famished men and animals that he took no precautions. As though he were marching them up Market Street in San Francisco, he led his infantry into the canyon leading up to Apache Pass, followed by the two howitzers and Cremony's cavalry troop. Roberts and the front rank of infantry were nearing the summit before the last cavalryman rode into the narrow canyon. Then a bloodcurdling Apache war whoop turned the scene into a pandemonium. Frightened horses reared and pitched, unseating many a weary cavalryman caught lolling in his saddle. In utter panic, infantrymen knocked each other down and dropped their carbines as they dived for shelter, trying to escape the rain of lead and arrows that poured from boulders high on the mountains at either side.

With no visible enemy to attack, and his troops panicked into wild confusion, Captain Roberts's position was completely defenseless.

He could only shout for his bugler to sound retreat, and follow his men as they raced back out of the canyon in ignominious rout.

The Apaches made no attempt to trap or follow the soldiers. To do so would only expose them to unnecessary casualties. Thirst in the desert would kill their enemies as surely as lead and arrows in the canyon. The warriors slipped from behind boulders only long enough to gather the carbines that had been dropped, and to strip the few soldiers who had been killed.

Although Captain Roberts had found himself defenseless while in the canyon, he realized that he was in a more desperate situation after retreating. If he camped where he was, the Apaches could massacre the entire detachment as soon as darkness fell. If, with his men and animals already nearly exhausted, he tried to retreat forty miles to Sulphur Springs, the greater part of his command would die of thirst in the desert. Regardless of losses, the canyon must be forced before nightfall, and the springs reached at the summit of the pass.

Rallying his troops, Roberts again sallied into the canyon; the two howitzers in front, the infantry in open formation, so as to furnish the least possible target, and the cavalry at the back to guard against an attack from the rear. With the Apaches raining down a withering fire from the heights, and infantrymen falling like trees before a tornado, Roberts drove on until he reached the abandoned stone Butterfield station, six hundred yards short of the springs at the summit of the pass. There he found himself stalled. On high cliffs bordering the roadway Mangas Coloradas had set up a seemingly impassable fortification. Great boulders had been balanced on the edge of the cliffs, ready to be rolled down by the hundreds on anything passing below. There, also, Mangas had stationed bands of his stoutest bowmen, safe from musket or cannon balls from below, but in position to pour a hail of arrows down onto the roadway.

Except for the expense California had gone to in equipping its troops, and modern inventions of which Mangas Coloradas had never dreamed, his fortifications would have been as impregnable as he believed them to be, and the whole California column would have died of thirst.

Captain Roberts's two howitzers, unlike most of the cannons used in the Civil War, were shell-firing, and the muzzles could be elevated to any desired angle. After two or three disastrous sallies from the station, he had the howitzers wheeled into position, elevated the muzzles, and lobbed a volley of shells onto the cliff tops. Three or four shells would probably have done the trick, for as each exploded it sent a barrage of rock splinters flying in all directions, and the concussions rolled down the boulders balanced on the cliff edges. With the warriors on the cliff tops killed by flying shrapnel, the famished soldiers ran for the springs, but the victory was far from won, for the Apaches still had the detachment safely bottled up in the canyon. Cochise held the eastern exit with a strong band of cavalry, and another waited in a side canyon at the west, ready for Mangas Coloradas to take command in the event another retreat were attempted. If not, the soldiers would be picked off one by one from hiding.

Lack of communications proved as valuable to the Californians as good communications had been to the Apaches. Captain Cremony, in his rear guard position, had no way of knowing that Roberts had forced his way through to water, but it suddenly occurred to him that if the slow-moving supply train and artillery should get too far from Sulphur Springs before being warned of the ambush, they would be unable to return without tremendous losses from thirst. He immediately started a dozen riders back to caution General Carleton. The news of their departure was flashed to Mangas Coloradas the moment the messengers raced out of the canyon.

After a breech was made in his fortifications and water reached by the soldiers, Mangas could not risk having reinforcements come up before the advance detachment had been annihilated, and he could only believe that the messengers had been sent to hurry along the main body of the column. Racing to his hidden cavalry, he leaped onto a horse, shouted for fifty warriors to follow him, and streaked away in pursuit of the messengers.

It was hardly a race, for the Apache horses were the best of thousands taken in raids, well rested and fed, while those of the soldiers were nearly exhausted from a day of travel and thirst. Soon the Apaches were within musket range, and there they stayed, taking pot shots now and again as the desperate soldiers flogged and spurred their faltering mounts. That of nineteen-year-old John Teal was the first to give out. As it lagged behind, John turned sharply off the road, hoping the Apaches would pass him by. But there was no hurry now, and Mangas Coloradas had no intention of letting a single American get away. He could easily catch the others after this one was taken care of.

Teal was no sooner off the road than his horse collapsed and fell, but the boy held onto his carbine, flattened himself, and fired at the oncoming Indians before they were in range. That was exactly what Mangas wanted, for he had no knowledge of breech-loading arms, and a man with an empty muzzle-loader was safe to deal with. The moment Teal's carbine barked, the giant chief raced his pony in for the kill, but he had covered little more than half the distance when the boy slipped another cartridge into the breech and fired again. From close range, the bullet ripped through Mangas Coloradas's chest and knocked him to the ground.

The Battle of Apache Pass was ended by that single shot, and it doubtlessly saved the lives of the entire California column. Teal was forgotten as the warriors crowded around their unconscious chief, panic-stricken and lost without his leadership. Although in his late sixties or early seventies, the giant Apache had the constitution of a grizzly bear, and his heart was beating in a steady rhythm. A few braves were sent to take the horses and news of the tragedy back to Cochise, while the rest fashioned a litter and set out to reach the nearest doctor—at Janos, more than a hundred and twenty miles away. All through the night and the next day they ran, shifting off in squads of four, and carrying the litter with its nearly three-hundred-pound load on their shoulders. At Janos they assured their chief the best possible care, and in a truly Apache manner. The spokesman's instructions to the doctor were short and to the point, "You make well! He no die, everybody live. He die, everybody in Janos die."

Great general and field commander that Cochise was, he had no heart for the battle without Mangas Coloradas. When morning came the Apaches had slipped away into their mountain fastnesses, and Apache Pass was as safe as Captain Roberts had believed it to be when he first blundered into the ambush. When news of the Battle of Apache Pass reached Washington, the War Department ordered Carleton to remain in Arizona, using his forces to control the Apaches, and annihilate them if necessary to the safety of the Gila Trail.

The doctor at Janos saved Mangas Coloradas's life, but it was many months before the aging chief was strong enough to take the warpath again, and during those months he thought long and deeply about the future of his people. In his wisdom he realized that civilization was rolling inward toward their homeland from every direction, and that the white man's power to invent and make new and amazing weapons was a threat that the Apaches could never match with cunning, courage, and stamina. If his people were to survive, peace must be made with the white men, and if it could be made at the cost of one worn-out life that cost would be small.

Mangas Coloradas had been out of the doctor's care for little more than a month when he walked alone into a soldiers' camp, saying that he had come to make a lasting peace. They gave him a peace that lasted forever, then lopped off his magnificent head and shipped it to the Smithsonian Institution. It was found to be somewhat larger than that of Daniel Webster, and the brain was of the same weight. In retaliation for the murder, Cochise continued at war against the white men for nine more years, and during those years many hundreds of lives were lost on both sides, but the backbone of Apache dominance in the Southwest was broken with the death of Mangas Coloradas.

Now the Southern Pacific Railway follows the route of the Old Gila Trail through Apacheland. Across burning deserts where the famished oxen of the Forty-Niners crept at seven miles a day, automobiles of tourists now whiz at seventy miles an hour, but the spirit of the old Hohokam people still pervades the land, and the Pimas irrigate their fertile fields along the river.

3

El Camino Real

THE FABLED LAND

California well might be called the fabled land, since its name and the discovery of the portion now lying within the United States were due to the Spanish propensity for accepting fiction as fact. In 1510 the Spanish author Ordóñez de Montalvo invented California, an island lying east of the Indies and inhabited by a race of Amazons. He let his imagination run wild, and wrote: "Their island was the strongest in all the world, with its steep cliffs and rocky shores. Their arms were of gold, and so was the harness of the wild beasts they tamed to ride: for in the whole island there was no metal but gold." The tale so caught the fancy of the Spaniards that when, in 1533, a mountainous peninsula lying to the west of the Mexican mainland was discovered, it was named California. Settlements and missions were hastily established on the lower end of the peninsula and expeditions sent into the mountains to locate the gold, but the colonies failed when no rich deposits were discovered.

The second fable was of the Strait of Anián. From the time of Columbus's second voyage, a notion had persisted in Europe that the Pacific could be reached by a watercourse through the North American continent. To the French and British this imaginary watercourse became known as the Northwest Passage, and to the Spanish as the Strait of Anián. It was believed that whichever nation first discovered such a passage would be made wealthy through trade with India and the Orient.

Magellan, on his world-circling voyage of 1521, had discovered the Philippine Islands, and New Spain opened a highly profitable trade with them in 1542, sending out a great seven-hundred-ton galleon from Navidad, a little Pacific port straight west from Mexico City. But the Spanish Crown was extremely anxious for a direct trade route between Spain and the Philippines. In 1542, Juan Cabrillo, an expert sailor and explorer, was sent northward along the Pacific coast of Lower California with only a small frigate and an open boat to discover the Strait of Anián. Mapping the shore line carefully as he fought his way against the prevailing winds, he discovered San Diego Bay, and continued charting the coast for another four hundred miles. He was nearing Monterey Bay when a terrific storm came up from the southeast, and for two days the unseaworthy little ships were driven like cockleshells before the gale. Then, far to the eastward, Cabrillo sighted a high point of wooded land, and was successful in bringing both ships into a snug harbor behind it. Because of the tall trees that covered it, he named the headland Point Pinos. It has since been named Point Reyes, and the harbor Drake's Bay, a few miles north of San Francisco's Golden Gate.

When the storm subsided, Cabrillo explored the coast northward to the present California-Oregon boundary, where he was driven back by fog, shortage of supplies, and bad weather. He returned along the coast, but after rounding Point Reyes, sailed far enough offshore that he failed to discover either San Francisco or Monterey bays. Port was made on San Miguel Island, opposite Santa Barbara, and there Cabrillo died of an injury in January, 1543.

After Cabrillo's failure to discover the Strait of Anián, the Spanish abandoned the search temporarily, but each spring a great galleon sailed from Navidad or Acapulco to the Philippines with hides, tallow, and Mexican gold, returning in the fall with spices, silks, and other goods from the Orient. On the return voyage, the galleons followed the Black Current of Japan eastward until making a landfall some two hundred miles north of San Francisco Bay, then sailed down the coast to their home port, two thousand miles to the southeast. In the belief that they had gained unquestionable control of the Pacific, the Spanish made no further explorations northward, but concentrated their attention on establishing settlements and ports in South America. Their belief was shattered by one of the greatest English seamen of all time.

In 1577 Sir Francis Drake was sent to make, "a voyage into the South Sea, and therehence about the whole Globe of the Earth." The expedition, however, had four undisclosed purposes: to do all the injury possible to Spanish settlements and shipping in South America, establish a foothold for England in the New World, discover the Northwest Passage, and chart a trade route to the Orient. Drake rounded Cape Horn and sailed up the Pacific coast of South America, boarding and plundering a score of Spanish merchant vessels, and sacking every important settlement.

The *Golden Hind* loaded to the gunwales with Spanish treasure, Drake set off in search of the Northwest Passage, and reached the California-Oregon boundary in June, 1579. But since his ship had become unseaworthy and there was no indication of a Northwest Passage, he turned back to carry out the third purpose of his voyage —the establishment of a foothold for England in the New World. Although positive proof is lacking, it is believed by most scholars that the harbor he chose was the one in which Cabrillo had found refuge from the storm, and which has since been known as Drake's Bay. After more than a month of repairing ship and exploring inland, he claimed the entire region for England, then failed to discover San Francisco Bay by sailing straight away to the west.

Seven years later another British privateer nearly duplicated Drake's feat, but was more ruthless in his destruction of Spanish settlements, and plundered one of the great galleons. The Spaniards became more convinced than ever that the Strait of Anián existed, and that the privateers had sailed through it in returning to England. To stop British raids in the Pacific, Spain resolved to discover and fortify the strait. In the spring of 1602 it sent out from Acapulco an expedition under Sebastián Vizcaíno to explore the coast as far north as the Strait of Anián and select sites for presidios and missions.

Vizcaíno was an ambitious man, and far more adept at writing convincing fiction than at commanding an exploration. He made no new discoveries, but lost forty-two of his men from scurvy before reaching the California-Oregon boundary. There he turned back, writing in his journal that he had sighted "Cape Blanco and the trend of the coast line onwards towards Japan and Great China which are but a short run away."

From Monterey Bay Vizcaíno wrote to the King of Spain: "This port is sheltered from all winds, while on the immediate coast there are pines from which masts of any desired size can be obtained, as well as a great variety of game. . . . It is thickly settled with people whom I found to be of gentle disposition, peaceable and docile, and who can be brought readily within the fold of the holy gospel and into subjection to the crown of Your Majesty. They manifested great friendship for us . . . are well acquainted with silver and gold, and said that these were found in the interior."

King Philip III was so impressed by the letter that he issued orders for Monterey to be established immediately as an impregnable fortress and refitting port for the Philippine galleons. The orders were never carried out, and for 167 years no further attempt was made to explore or establish settlements in Upper California. Numerous endeavors, however, were made to found mission settlements in Lower California, but until 1697 none was successful. By that time Father Kino's mission empire in Pimería Alta was nearing the height of its prosperity. Through his urging, and with stock and supplies which he furnished, fifteen widely scattered Jesuit missions were established on the southern half of the peninsula. Until Kino's death in 1711 these missions prospered, but without his driving influence the movement soon stagnated.

FATHER JUNÍPERO SERRA

The eventual settlement of Upper California was brought about by a religious upheaval, fear of invasion by the Russians, and the indomitable determination of a semi-crippled Franciscan priest, Father Junípero Serra.

Father Serra, with a score of other young Franciscan missionaries, arrived at Veracruz in 1749. While walking from that seaport to Mexico City he was bitten on the left foot by a scorpion, and the poison spread throughout his leg. For the rest of his life he was lame and tormented by painful running sores, but never allowed his infirmity to interfere with his priesthood. Although of a different order and generation, he was an ardent admirer of Father Kino, had studied his methods thoroughly, and shared his conviction that heathens could be civilized and converted to Christianity only when taught that it resulted in a more abundant and enjoyable life. Furthermore, Kino and Serra were almost identical in the driving force of their personalities, the amazing variety of their talents, their determination to push missions ever farther into the wilderness, and their ability to win the cooperation and affection of Indians.

In the Sierra Gorda Mountains, north of Mexico City, lived the fierce Pame tribe of Indians. For a century and a half they had baffled every attempt to establish missions or control them by military strength. They raided ranches and settlements throughout the surrounding area, murdering, plundering, and burning, then escaped to their mountain strongholds which were inaccessible to Spanish cavalry. In a last desperate effort to bring the Pames under subjection, it was decided in 1749 to again attempt the establishment of Franciscan missions in the Sierra Gorda Mountains, and to man them with the young priests newly arrived from Spain. In January, 1750, ten of them were sent out, with Father Serra appointed Prefect of Missions, and his friend, Father Palou, as Vice Prefect.

Limping at the head of his little task force, Father Serra led it into the Sierra Gordas, taking with him a few cattle, and burros loaded with axes, spades, hoes, seed, and the necessary religious articles for conducting Masses. Within ten years five thriving missions had been established, each surrounded by gardens, orchards, grain fields, and great herds of horses, sheep, and cattle. The granaries were filled to capacity, and the Pames had become one of the most civilized tribes in Mexico. Not only in Mexico but Spain, Father Serra became famous as the Conqueror of the Sierra Gordas.

In 1767 the Jesuit Order fell into disfavor with King Charles III of Spain, and he decreed its expulsion from his domains. To carry out the decree and replace Jesuits with Franciscans, he sent José de Galvez to New Spain as Visitor-General, and Captain Gaspar de Portolá as Governor of California. At the time of Galvez's arrival, numerous of the Kino missions in Pimería Alta had been destroyed, and the Indians were in open revolt. On Lower California the situation was nearly as bad, and there Spain had an ever greater worry. In 1741 the Russians had discovered Alaska, and each year had been extending their fur-trapping expeditions farther southward along the Pacific coast. How far the Russians had come was unknown, but it was feared that they might invade Lower California at any time, and it was imperative that the missions on the Peninsula be revived and strengthened as quickly as possible. As the two most forceful prefects among the Franciscans, Galvez assigned Father Serra to Lower California, and Father Garcés to Pimería Alta.

Father Serra gathered the sixteen priests allotted to him, and led them afoot over five hundred miles of mountains to the little Pacific port of San Blas, two hundred miles north of Navidad. There they met Governor Portolá, but the two small ships which were to transport them, the *San Carlos* and *San Antonio*, were only partially built. Portolá obtained passage to the Peninsula in December, 1767, expelled the Jesuit priests, and placed military guards at the missions to keep them from being plundered by the Indians. The two ships were completed and sailed up the Gulf of California in the early spring of 1768, delivering the Franciscan priests at ports nearest their respective missions. In April, Father Serra reached Loreto, the headquarters mission, to find it in deplorable condition, gardens and orchards uncared for, stock untended, and most of the Indians still naked and entirely uncivilized. He left Father Palou in charge, and set off afoot at once to inspect and organize the other fourteen missions, strung out more than five hundred miles along the Peninsula.

Serra had barely begun his long journey when General Galvez received an urgent message from King Charles of Spain, instructing him to parry by appropriate measures an attack which the Russians were rumored to be contemplating. Galvez believed this could best be done by building fortifications at Monterey and establishing missions where troops could be housed at other strategic points along the coast of Upper California. He at once sailed to the Peninsula and dispatched a vessel up the Gulf to find and summon Governor Portolá and Father Serra to La Paz. Serra was discovered at one of the northern missions, nearly four hundred miles from La Paz, and sent word that he would visit the general when making his circuit at the end of the Peninsula. Galvez rushed a message back immediately: "The King has need of you. Come at once. We are going to found new missions. I beg of you, Most Reverend Father, hurry!" The promise of new missions was enough. Father Serra set off for La Paz with all haste.

In the 166 years since Spanish explorations had been carried out along the coast of Upper California, much of the information gathered by Cabrillo had become lost in the cluttered archives of New Spain. It is evident that when Galvez, Portolá, and Serra gathered to lay plans for settling Upper California they had only Vizcaíno's journal and the exaggerated reports he had written to impress King Philip III.

Father Serra insisted that missions could not successfully be founded without livestock, but experience had taught the Spaniards that cattle could not be transported any great distance on small ships without heavy losses. It was therefore decided that such livestock and provisions as could be spared from the Peninsula missions would be taken overland to San Diego Bay through territory never traversed by any white man. Building materials, church equipment, farming tools, seed, and supplies and provisions for at least a year would be transported by sea in the *San Carlos*, the *San Antonio*, and the *San Jose*, then being built in San Blas.

In January, 1769, the *San Carlos* sailed for San Diego under Captain Vila, taking building materials, farming tools, seed, saplings for planting orchards and vineyards, the French doctor Pierre Prat, and twenty-five soldiers under Lieutenant Pedro Fages. A month later the *San Antonio* followed under command of Juan Perez, taking two priests, twenty-five soldiers, and a cargo of provisions and supplies. At the end of April the *San Jose* sailed with a similar personnel and cargo.

Meanwhile Governor Portolá had been organizing the overland expedition, and Father Serra continuing his circuit of the missions. As he went he had hundreds of cattle, sheep, horses, and mules, together with tons of dried meat and other provisons sent to Mission Santa Maria, five hundred miles north of La Paz. But there was insufficient pasturage there for so much livestock, so Portolá moved his headquarters to Velicatá, fifty miles north. When, in mid-May, Father Serra had completed his circuit and reached Velicatá, his leg was swollen to double its normal size and covered with festering abscesses. Portolá tried to persuade him against attempting to go with the expedition unless carried in a litter, but the only concession the Prefect would make to his infirmity was to ride a mule instead of walking.

At dawn on Trinity Sunday—May 21, 1769—Father Serra said Mass at the newly founded Mission Velicatá and placed Father Palou in charge of the Peninsula Prefecture. Then he had himself lifted onto a mule and, with Governor Portolá, led the expedition out into the mountains, in the general direction of San Diego. Behind them followed one hundred and seventy heavily loaded pack mules, one hundred milch cows, and a rabble of donkeys, sheep, and goats. Driving, herding, and guarding them were muleteers, cooks, common laborers, twenty-five mounted soldiers, and thirty neophyte Indian bowmen. Captain Rivera led another caravan of four hundred head of livestock, twenty-five soldiers, and forty-two neophytes armed with bows and arrows.

The route pioneered northward from Velicatá that Trinity Sunday morning was destined to become known as El Camino Real— The Royal Highway—and is unique in that it was the only important route blazed through the old West which followed neither a stream nor an ancient Indian trail. The few scattered tribes living on the Peninsula were isolated from each other, and there were no trails connecting their settlements. Furthermore, any Spanish exploration of Upper California had been made by sea, and the location of harbors recorded in terms of latitude and longitude. Portolá's only means of finding a direct route overland was by use of an astrolabe, a navigation instrument now replaced by the more accurate sextant.

Far out in front of the expedition rode Sergeant Ortega and a navigator, seeking passes through the high mountains and camp sites with abundant grass, wood, and water. When a passable way was discovered it was marked by messages left on stones, and sappers followed the markings to hack openings through thickets and pry boulders from the trail. The course was northwest across the mountains for 165 miles, reaching the Pacific near present Ensenada, then following the shore line on to San Diego Bay. The march required forty days, eight of them lost in turning back from impassable mountains, but in spite of his infirmity and the ruggedness of the trail Father Serra gained strength on the journey.

The wisdom of sending part of the expedition overland became apparent when the caravan reached San Diego Bay. The original plan had been that this port would be used simply as a point of rendezvous. The ships were to put in there, and wait no more than twenty days for the overland division. Then, with or without it, they were to proceed to Monterey Bay, where supplies would be put ashore for founding the first settlement in Upper California. When, on July 1, 1769, the Governor and Prefect rode within sight of the bay they were amazed to see the *San Carlos* and *San Antonio* riding at anchor, but they were little more than ghost ships. Scurvy had run rampant on the sea voyage. Only two of those who had sailed on the *San Carlos* were still living, and all but a few from the *San Antonio* were desperately ill, being cared for in a makeshift camp that Dr. Prat had set up on the beach.

Portolá at once had the camp moved to higher ground, now known as "Old Town" San Diego. A crude shelter and stockade were built, but deaths from scurvy continued so rapidly that within a week two thirds of the men who had come by sea were in their graves. The only apparent hope of saving the expedition was to send the *San Antonio* back while there were still enough seamen left to sail her. Captain Perez set out on July 9, with instructions to inform General Galvez of the tragedy, then return as rapidly as possible with new crews and provisions that would be desperately needed before another spring.

The *San Jose* had been wrecked on the coast of Lower California but in hope that it had missed San Diego Bay and sailed on to Monterey, Portolá at once readied an expedition for an overland march. On July 14 he set out for the north, taking two priests, a navigator, forty-nine mounted soldiers, fifteen neophyte Indian bowmen, and a hundred mules laden with provisions. At San Diego he left only eight soldiers; two to guard the *San Carlos*, and six to protect the stockade from Indian attack. On the 16th a great cross was set up on a hill above the stockade, Father Serra said Mass under a canopy of branches, and Mission San Diego was founded. It consisted of a little mud-walled chapel, two large tents, and several small ones.

GASPAR DE PORTOLÁ

With Sergeant Ortega and the navigator exploring ahead, Portolá blazed the route from San Diego to San Luis Obispo which became El Camino Real. There he turned northwest to the Pacific, a costly mistake that could have been avoided if Vizcaíno had reported the hundred miles of shore southward from Monterey Harbor as being extremely rugged, with high mountains rising abruptly from the sea. For three weeks Portolá fought his way through and over the Santa Lucia Mountains, keeping as near the coast as possible in order not to pass Monterey Bay. On September 26 he was forced to turn eastward across the summit of the range and into the broad, fertile Salinas Valley, now called the salad bowl of the world. He followed the river downstream and reached Monterey Bay on the last day of

*Monterey Bay as it looked early in the nineteenth century.
From* California: A History of Upper and Lower California,
*Alexander Forbes. Courtesy of The New York Public
Library, Rare Book Division.*

September. The bay, shaped like a football, is twenty-five miles from
end to end. Its southern tip lies behind a high hill that juts out into
the Pacific, its western side is open to the sea, and its eastern shore
is an arc of flatlands, bordered by rolling sand dunes. Near the center
of the arc the dunes give way to marshes through which the Salinas
River flows into the open bay.

This was the harbor that Vizcaíno had described as being at latitude thirty-seven, "sheltered from all winds, while on the immediate
coast there are pines from which masts of any desired size can be
obtained. . . . And it is thickly settled with people whom I found to
be of gentle disposition."

It is little wonder that Portolá was unable to recognize the open
roadstead with its flat treeless eastern shore as the snug harbor Vizcaíno had described. And as for the Indians, what few they had seen
were naked, skulking thieves. Still, observations taken with the astrolabe showed them to be at latitude 36° 42'. Presuming the protected
anchorage to be on the south side of the headland, Portolá crossed

the high hill to the present site of Carmel, and became further confused. There was no protected harbor there, nor could the shallow creek be the great Carmel River which Vizcaíno showed as flowing into the Pacific just to the south of Monterey Bay.

In the belief that he had missed the bay by turning eastward to the Salinas Valley, Portolá spent three days in fruitless climbing through the Santa Lucia Mountains along the coast south of Carmel. Then, after a consultation with his officers, he determined to continue the search northward, to at least another degree of latitude. Surely Monterey Bay must be somewhere near at hand, the *San Jose* waiting there with provisions that were urgently needed. All the vegetables and vinegar had been used from the mule packs, and some of the men were showing symptoms of scurvy.

Ironically, it required ten heartbreaking days for Portolá to circle the east shore of the bay for which he was hunting. By the time he reached the present site of Santa Cruz, his only food supply was a few sacks of flour and meal, and sixteen of his men were so ill with scurvy that they had to be carried on litters. Each day more men were stricken, and a week was lost in marching twenty-five miles farther up the rugged coast. Then a steady, cold rain set in, and a seemingly worse malady struck the expedition. Every man, including Portolá, was brought down with a violent attack of diarrhea.

Unable to travel, the discouraged explorers made camp, most of them believing death to be near, and the last rites of the Church were administered to those who were not expected to live through the night. But for those afflicted with scurvy, the purging proved a blessing. By morning the swelling in their legs and gums had been considerably reduced, and they were able to take a little nourishment. Two days later, improved but still weakened from their ordeal, the Spaniards pushed onward, hoping that beyond each hill they would find Monterey Bay and the waiting *San Jose*. Unable to travel more than three or four miles a day, they passed Half Moon Bay, and on October 30 reached Point San Pedro, now within twelve miles of San Francisco's city limits. There the way was blocked by the Montara Mountains which extend into the Pacific, ending in high, impassable cliffs.

Camp was again made, and Portolá sent Ortega and the navigator to find a way across the mountains. They were soon back in great excitement. From the summit of the Montaras they had seen a high headland reaching far out into the sea, and recognized it as the one Vizcaíno had named Point Reyes.

With most of his men still weak from their illness, Portolá decided to remain in camp while Ortega and a band of sappers opened a trail across the mountains to the northward. The next day a few of the soldiers who had regained their strength asked permission to go hunting deer, as there had been no meat in camp for more than a week. They climbed the high hills to the east, and returned after nightfall, as excited as Ortega had been. From the top of the hills they had seen a great body of water, extending so far inland that its southern end was beyond view. Along its shores were flatlands covered with trees, and from the number of rising smoke columns it was certain that many Indians lived there.

The following day Ortega and his sappers returned from their exploration northward with even more exciting information. They had met friendly Indians, and understood from their signs that a ship lay at anchor in a harbor two days' travel farther to the north, but had been stopped from reaching it by an estuary that connected the Pacific with a great inland bay. Doubtlessly the ship was a Russian fur-trading vessel at Drake's Bay, but the ill and half-starved Spaniards were positive that it must be the *San Jose*, and that it lay at the mouth of another estuary connecting the inland bay with the Pacific. Portolá decided to cross the Peninsula, circle the end of the bay, and march up its eastern shore to the location of the *San Jose*.

On November 5, 1769, 227 years after Cabrillo sailed past the entrance of San Francisco Bay without discovering it, Portolá and his lost expedition reached its shores, marching down San Francisquito Creek near the present site of Stanford University.

As most of his men were still too weak to travel far, Governor Portolá pitched camp, sending Ortega to circle the end of the bay and discovered a route to the harbor where it was supposed that the *San Jose* rode at anchor. Led by friendly Indians, Ortega made his way northward along the east shore to San Pablo Bay, followed around to Carquinez Strait at the mouth of the Sacramento River, and returned discouraged. He had found no way of crossing the water, seen no ship, and was convinced that he had misunderstood the Indians when believing they were trying to tell him of one.

Portolá failed to realize that he had made history by discovering

San Francisco Bay, and was sorely disappointed at having passed
Monterey Harbor without finding it. He returned by the way he
had come, and reached Monterey Bay at the end of November. Several days were spent in searching for the port that was sheltered from
all winds, and finally he decided that it must have been filled in by
sand dunes during the century and a half since Vizcaíno had been
there. With supplies run out and no hope of finding the *San Jose*,
there seemed little doubt that the entire party would die of starvation
before reaching San Diego. Portolá had a large cross set up, and
carved on it, "Dig; at the foot you will find a writing." There he
buried a bottle containing the names of those in the expedition,
where they had been, and why they were forced back.

The men were obliged to live on mule meat until they reached the
coast at the Santa Barbara Channel, where they found the Indians
generous and well supplied with food. From there on the danger was
past. On January 24, 1770, Governor Portolá arrived in San Diego
"with the command in good health and without the loss of a man."

During the Governor's absence Father Serra had little success in

*San Francisco Bay as it looked in the early nineteenth century.
From* California: A History of Upper and Lower California,
*Alexander Forbes. Courtesy of The New York Public
Library, Rare Book Division.*

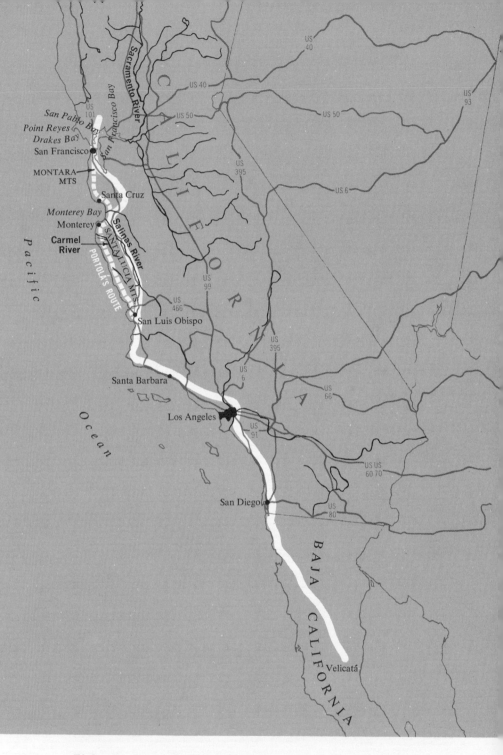

El Camino Real. The King's Highway connected Spanish missions from San Diego to San Francisco and unified the Spanish in California.

his attempt to establish a mission and convert the heathen at San Diego. Upon the arrival of the overland caravans from Velicatá the Indians had taken fright and gone into hiding, mistaking mounted men for invincible demons from the spirit world. Their fear was short-lived, however, and they soon learned that a large number of the Spaniards were ill and incapable of defense.

When Portolá rode away with most of the able-bodied soldiers, the Indians began sneaking into the camp to run off stock and steal anything they could lay their hands on. At first they could be frightened away by the sound of shots fired above their heads, but when they found themselves unharmed by the roaring guns they became bolder. In mid-August they made a raid in force while the soldiers were attending Mass. Storming the stockade, they rushed the hospital tents, stripped the beds of linen, and tore the clothing from the helpless patients.

Before the soldiers could run from the chapel the Indians had arranged themselves in battle line outside the stockade, and were pouring in a barrage of arrows. Behind them their women shrieked and howled, waiting to rush in and complete the plunder when all the white men had been killed. The battle raged for half an hour before the Indians realized that the soldiers' armor was turning aside their arrows, and that there was death in the roar of the guns. Suddenly they broke and ran, dragging their wounded and dead with them. Fortunately, only one of the patients had been killed, though several were wounded, and Father Serra barely escaped serious injury. A few days later some of the Indians returned, bringing their wounded to be cared for by Dr. Prat, and assuring Father Serra of their friendship, but at the same time stealing anything left unguarded.

At best, the relationship between the Spaniards and Indians remained no better than an armed truce for several months, the Indians watching for any opportunity to annihilate the invaders, and the Spaniards trying desperately to cover up their weakness and the number of their losses. Before the scurvy could be brought under control, both Dr. Prat and Father Serra had been stricken, and nineteen more men had died, each being buried at night to keep the Indians from knowing of the loss.

In the Sierra Gordas, Father Serra had won the confidence of the Pame Indians by interesting them in planting crops and constructing mission buildings. Because of scurvy he was unable to do so at San Diego, and the natives remained suspicious and aloof, venturing into the stockade only on pretext of coming to see their wounded, then making off with whatever they could steal. Serra never allowed them to be punished for their thievery, but treated them with kindness, and as the wounded were healed he began to win their reluctant confidence.

When Portolá returned from his expedition, he and Serra each believed his efforts to have resulted in failure, but each recognized the importance of the other's accomplishment. Although the Prefect had made no converts, he was winning the goodwill of the Indians, and had proved beyond doubt that Spanish settlements could be established in Upper California with little military protection. As for Portolá's expedition, Father Serra fully realized its importance. From the description, he was sure the Governor had discovered one of the finest landlocked harbors on earth, and did not believe he had failed to find Monterey Bay. "You went to Rome and did not find St. Peter's," the priest told him. "For it is indeed Monterey, thank God, where you have planted the cross." Captain Vila agreed, pointing out that Vizcaíno had been extravagant in all his descriptions, and had doubtlessly exaggerated the advantages of the harbor in an effort to gain glory for himself.

The Governor was sufficiently convinced that he would have returned to the north at once if either the *San Antonio* or *San Jose* had arrived. But without a fresh supply of provisions such a journey was impossible, and without building materials it would be useless. There could be little doubt that the *San Jose* had been lost at sea, and the *San Antonio* was long overdue. If it, too, had been lost the situation of the entire expedition would soon become desperate, since supplies and meat on the hoof were running low and there had been no opportunity to plant crops.

After making a thorough inventory of all available food, Portolá estimated that on short rations it would last no more than two and a half months, and forty days of that time would be required for a return to Velicatá. Since the time could be extended only by reducing the number of men, he started Captain Rivera and a force of twenty-four for the Peninsula on February 9. They were to gather whatever beef cattle and provisions were available at the nearest missions and return as rapidly as possible. If, by March 15, the *San*

Antonio had not arrived, the rest of the expedition would start its march, meeting Rivera somewhere along the trail.

Father Serra realized the soundness of the Governor's judgment, but was reluctant to turn back, fearing that failure of the expedition would result in abandonment of the undertaking and blast his dream of founding a new mission system. His faith in the protection of the saints was unshakable, and he was convinced that they were more inclined to perform miracles upon their name days than at any other time. He agreed to Portolá's plan, but pleaded with him to postpone the departure until after March 19, as that would be St. Joseph's Day, and he was certain the saint would send them deliverance. Deeply religious himself, Portolá agreed to extend the time, but not beyond March 20.

The 19th came and dragged to its close with no sign of the *San Antonio*, so preparations were made for starting the march to Velicatá on the following day. Then, just at sunset, a sail was sighted by the lookout, from high on Point Loma. The men ran to the beach in wild excitement, but their jubilation was short-lived. The sail was far out on the horizon, and held steadily northward until it disappeared from sight. There was little doubt that it was the *San Antonio*, and even less doubt that it was bound for Monterey Bay, its captain believing the entire expedition to have long since moved there. To wait for the ship to reach Monterey and return would be disastrous, since it might require several weeks, and Rivera could not be expected back with food from Velicatá before May.

There is much disagreement among historians as to why the retreat to Velicatá was not begun the following day. But the cause may well be disclosed in a recently discovered letter which Father Serra wrote at that time to Father Palou, evidently intended for transmittal by the returning caravan. In part, it reads, "Only one thing is talked of: that is to abandon all. But though the hope of seeing help come must vanish, I shall hold on to the end. So long as there is grass in the fields, Father Crespi and I will not go away."

It is quite possible that Father Serra's decision moved Portolá to postpone the retreat, and who can say that the devout friar's prayers were not answered. In any event, rescue came through a chain of unusual circumstances. The *San Antonio* encountered strong headwinds soon after passing San Diego Bay, slowing her progress enough that Captain Perez had to put in at the Santa Barbara Channel for a supply of fresh water. There he learned from the Indians that Portolá had returned to the south two months earlier.

Perez found himself in a dilemma. With no one at Monterey Bay, it seemed pointless to take provisions there when they might be desperately needed at San Diego, but his orders from General Galvez were to sail straight to Monterey. At first he considered disobeying, but fearful of the consequences, set sail for the north. Here destiny lent a hand. As Perez left the Santa Barbara Channel he lost his anchor, making it impossible to moor his ship, and leaving him no choice but to make for San Diego Harbor and tie up alongside the *San Carlos*. On March 24, 1770, the *San Antonio* sailed into port and, whether or not in answer to Father Serra's prayers, the California settlement project was saved from abandonment.

Preparations were made at once for carrying out the original objectives of the expedition. In mid-April Portolá again marched northward over the trail he had originally blazed, and the *San Antonio* with Serra aboard sailed for Monterey Bay.

Because of strong headwinds, the overland party arrived first, and this time Portolá, allowing for Vizcaíno's exaggerations, was able to

San Carlos Mission at Monterey early in the nineteenth century. From California: A History of Upper and Lower California, *Alexander Forbes. Courtesy of The New York Public Library, Rare Book Division.*

recognize the harbor. After exploring the shore, he chose a site for the presidio and mission where the city of Monterey now stands. A week later the *San Antonio* arrived, and on June 3, 1770, the mission and presidio San Carlos Borroméo de Monterey were founded. Bells and an altar were brought from the ship, and Father Serra celebrated the founding Mass under the same great live oak tree where, 167 years before, an altar had been set up and Mass celebrated by Carmelite friars who accompanied Vizcaíno.

THE APOSTOLIC FLAME

Among dispatches brought by the *San Antonio* was one from General Galvez, instructing Governor Portolá to turn the command in Upper California over to Lieutenant Fages and return to Mexico City as soon as a presidio had been established at Monterey. Trees were felled on the nearby hillside, logs dragged down to the shore, and set deep in the ground to form a solid stockade. Within it was built a thick-walled log and adobe barrack, a small chapel, a hut for the priests, and a storehouse. Cannon were mounted facing the sea as defense against invading ships, and on the landward side smaller pieces for protection in the event of Indian attacks. By July 9, the work was well advanced, the supplies were safely stored, and Governor Portolá had sailed away, leaving the establishment of other California missions to Father Serra. The moment Portolá sailed Fages set himself up as a despot, treated his men and any Indians who came near the presidio with brutality, and blocked the founding of other missions by refusing the necessary provisions and materials.

Although Vizcaíno had written that the Monterey area was thickly populated by friendly and intelligent Indians, the reverse proved to be the case. There were but few natives, and they were among the most primitive discovered along the coast; naked, and living mostly on shellfish, insects, roots, and reptiles. After months of effort, Father Serra was able to make friends among them and baptize some twenty children, but with Fages's opposition he could make no further progress. It became apparent that the mission project would fail entirely unless intervention were obtained from Mexico City, and unless the mission at Monterey were removed from Fages and the presidio, but the separation could not be made without authority. By a devoted Indian neophyte, Father Serra sent messages nearly a thousand miles back to La Paz, reporting Fages's interference, and pleading to the Mother Church for thirty more priests, together with authority to found six additional missions and relocate the one at Monterey.

The supply ship promised for October, 1770, did not arrive until late the following May, bringing only a small cargo of provisions and ten priests instead of thirty. But among the dispatches was an order to Fages from the Viceroy, instructing him to cooperate in the immediate establishment of six missions: two between San Diego and the Santa Barbara Channel, two between the Channel and Monterey, and two at San Francisco Bay. There was also a dispatch authorizing the separation of the Monterey mission from the presidio, and word that Captain Rivera had been sent overland to San Diego with a large herd of livestock for establishing the new missions.

With direct orders from the Viceroy, Fages was obliged to make a pretense of cooperation in the founding of new missions, but insisted upon laying all the plans. He announced that upon the *San Antonio*'s return to Mexico, he would sail to San Diego, set up headquarters there, and send for the Prefect when he was ready to start founding missions.

Fages sailed on July 7, taking with him about half the garrison and six priests. The following day Father Serra set off for the Salinas Valley with two of the newly arrived priests, a few Indian neophytes from the Peninsula, twelve cattle, two hogs, eight mules, and a hen with her chickens. He pioneered the route that is now El Camino Real some sixty miles southward along the valley, and discovered a clear stream flowing from the Santa Lucia Mountains. Naming the stream the San Antonio, he followed it to a broad meadow sheltered by surrounding mountains, set up an altar beneath a great live oak, hung a bell from one of the branches, celebrated Mass, and founded Mission San Antonio. After laying out plans for gardens, orchards, vineyards, and the first temporary chapel, he hurried back to Monterey, leaving the construction in the hands of the neophytes and young priests.

Anxious to relocate the Monterey mission before leaving for San Diego, Father Serra set out immediately to discover the best possible site. The one he chose was on a knoll where the town of Carmel now stands. It commanded a beautiful view of the sea, there was abundant timber for building, and the valley, protected by high hills, was ideal for stock raising and irrigated farming. With Fages out of the way,

the Prefect had no difficulty in gaining the wholehearted cooperation of the soldiers who had been left at Monterey, and they pitched
into the building with vigor. By the end of August construction at
Carmel was well advanced, and Serra was anxiously awaiting a sum-
mons from Fages, but none arrived, and none would.

The commandant had no sooner reached San Diego than he won
the hatred of Captain Rivera and his men by his tyrannical behavior.
A week later nine soldiers deserted, taking with them fifty mules and
a herd of cattle. No doubt hindered by the ill will of Rivera and the
remaining troops, Fages was unable to run down the deserters, and
was obliged to send one of the priests to bring them back. He then
decided to found the missions demanded by the Viceroy, but without
the Prefect. In spite of pleading and protests, he ordered two of the
young priests to set off for the location chosen by Portolá as the site
of Mission San Gabriel. On August 5 they started out on their 125-
mile march northward along the trail Portolá had blazed, leading a
few pack mules, and driving a small herd of cattle. Ten days later
they arrived at their destination, now on the outskirts of Los Angeles,
and hundreds of highly intelligent Indians soon gathered from the
surrounding hills. Their confidence was quickly won by the priests,
and they proved to be gentle, tractable, and adept in the use of tools.
Ground was cleared, trees felled, a barracks and chapel built, and the
founding Mass for Mission San Gabriel Arcángel was celebrated on
September 9, 1771.

In the meantime Fages was having more trouble than he could
handle at San Diego. His men continued to desert, and he barely
escaped being killed when trying to recapture them. Convinced that
San Diego presented too good an opportunity for desertions, he
decided to move back to Monterey, founding missions along the way.
At the end of October he arrived at San Gabriel, leading a caravan
of two hundred pack mules, and all the livestock intended for the
six missions specified by the Viceroy.

The harmony at San Gabriel was quickly disrupted. To Fages, as
to many Spanish officers, all Indians were savages, the men to be
subjected to slavery, and the women to be used as the soldiers pleased
for their own pleasure. In order to keep his men from deserting, he
permitted them to make sport of the Indian women at San Gabriel,
and of their behavior one of the priests wrote: "Every morning they
would go out in groups of six, on horseback, and spread far over the

countryside. Accustomed to lassoing cows and mules, they would chase the native women and catch them in a running noose, and they would strike down their husbands with gunfire when these attempted to defend their own. . . ."

Frightened by the wanton killings, the Indians made no concerted resistance until the wife of their chief was raped and he was killed while trying to defend her. They then attacked the mission in force, but their primitive bows and spears were no match for the Spanish guns, and they were quickly driven away. As a reminder of Spanish might, Fages had the chief's head chopped off and mounted on a pole outside the stockade gate. He then marched away, leaving eighteen soldiers to put down any further hostility. On the pretext that he had insufficient soldiers to control the fierce savages along the Santa Barbara coast, Fages made no attempt to found missions, but continued on to Monterey, arriving there in mid-November. The milch cows were kept at the presidio to supply milk for the soldiers, and the rest of the stock moved to Carmel, to be pastured and cared for by the priests. In making his report to the Viceroy, Fages blamed his failure to found missions upon Father Serra, claiming that the Prefect had urged the priests not to obey his orders, and that their disobedience was entirely responsible for desertions by the soldiers. The report, although intended to kill the mission movement, eventually resulted in its salvation.

Even though the mission was now separated from the Monterey presidio by three miles, controversies arose as soon as Fages returned, largely because Father Serra insisted upon founding missions. The commandant blocked every effort by refusing to release supplies, recalled the soldiers who had been helping to build the Carmel mission, and began having its cattle butchered to provide an abundant meat supply for the presidio. By spring the herds for stocking new missions were badly depleted, provisions in the warehouses nearly exhausted, and the supply ships expected from Mexico failed to arrive. They reached Monterey Bay in late May, but the winds were too strong for anchoring in the open roadstead and they were obliged to turn back.

There were few localities on this continent richer in food resources than the Monterey area. The land was fertile, the bay teeming with fish, and the surrounding mountains with deer. It is difficult to believe that famine could strike in the midst of such abundance, but due to

Spanish military ideology famine struck Monterey when the supply ships were obliged to turn back. From the earliest settlement of New Spain, Indians had been enslaved to perform all menial tasks, and the military had become an indolent class, its only duty being to keep the Indians under subjection. Largely for this reason, all Spanish expansion in the New World was accompanied by the founding of missions. It was not only the duty of the priests to convert the heathen, but to exploit their labor and furnish subsistence for the military.

The Indians in the Monterey area took readily to the care of animals, but had no interest in agriculture, and would work in the gardens only under the most patient persuasion, so the first crops at Carmel and San Antonio were negligible. What little was raised had to be distributed among those who had been induced to work, so that others might see the advantages of labor and be more easily attracted to the mission way of life. Under these circumstances the priests were hard pressed to provide their own meager subsistence, and could contribute nothing to the support of the military. Still, by the spring of 1772 considerable progress had been made. Many Indians had come to live at the missions. Orchards and vineyards had been set out, small fields put under cultivation, a hundred or more children baptized, and adults were being instructed in the Christian faith.

When, in August, a messenger arrived at Monterey with news that the supply ships had discharged their cargoes at San Diego, the food situation had become desperate. Except for a few cows hidden at San Antonio, the mission herds had been entirely consumed by the soldiers, the gardens stripped of everything edible, and most of the Indians had drifted back to their old way of living.

Fages at once set out for San Diego, taking the soldiers and every available mule to bring back supplies. Father Serra followed with three priests, but went by way of Mission San Antonio, where they had been able to save nine cows and a little hoard of food. Guided by a convert from the mission the priests continued southward nearly to the headwaters of the Salinas River, then crossed the mountains to San Luis Obispo by way of Cuesta Pass. With very little variation, El Camino Real now follows their footsteps. On September 1, 1772, a location was selected, a rude shelter built, and Mass sung for the founding of Mission San Luis Obispo. Destined to become one of the most prosperous of the California missions, its beginning was far from impressive, consisting of a cross, two priests, nine cows, fifty-five pounds of meal, thirteen quarts of wheat, a box of chocolate, and a box of brown sugar. These last were the priests' only hope of survival, for the Indians would trade large quantities of fish and game for small amounts of sugar or chocolate.

Upon reaching San Diego Father Serra found among the dispatches brought by the supply ships one addressed to him from Father Verger, head of the Franciscan Order in Mexico City. It censured him severely for teaching his priests and the soldiers disobedience to Commandant Fages, causing desertions, and hindering the founding of new missions. Also among the dispatches was news that General Galvez had returned to Spain, and that Don Antonio Bucareli had been appointed Viceroy. It was only too evident that Fages had blamed his failures entirely upon the Prefect, and that his reports had been believed by the new Viceroy. Under such circumstances, the mission project would surely fail unless the true situation in Upper California were made known to the highest Church officials and the Viceroy. Fortunately, the *San Carlos* was still at San Diego, preparing to set sail for San Blas within a few days, and Father Serra determined to sail on it.

In a fury of rage, Fages forbade the Prefect to leave the country, and forbade the captain of the *San Carlos* to let him come aboard. Both refused to obey the orders, and on October 20, 1772, Father Serra sailed on the greatest mission of his life. On the five-hundred-mile journey afoot from San Blas to Mexico City, he nearly died of a malignant fever from the infection in his leg, and did not reach the capital until February, 1773. He found Viceroy Bucareli on the verge of abandoning the settlement of Upper California, and that he had already written the Prime Minister, "Everything, alas, augurs the ruin of this colony which will have cost so much in arduous labor and in money."

The Junta of New Spain, a governing body on the order of a senate, was equally discouraged, and had written the Viceroy, "The royal funds are being wasted, since our inability to navigate in this part of the Pacific puts Monterey out of reach. Has Russia ever succeeded, we ask, in making a landing there? And we who have done so, what a price we have paid! The *San Jose* is at the bottom of the sea, with its cargo; . . . dissension prevails between the military authority and the friars; as for the soldiers, all of them will soon have deserted. While we are waiting for the King to order the abandonment of the venture . . . let us confine our efforts to dispatching the indispensable minimum of aid, by way of Loreto, to the soldiers and the missionaries who are still in those regions."

Even Father Verger was in agreement that Upper California could not be settled, and wrote, "The farce staged by Galvez has lasted long enough."

Some have called it a miracle that in the face of all this opposition Father Serra was able to convince the Viceroy, the Junta, and his own superiors in the Church that the settlement of Upper California must not be abandoned. From the sixth to the thirteenth of February he pleaded his case before Viceroy Bucareli, won not only his confidence but affection, and told him, "If you remove the obstacles which I point out to you, and grant the assistance for which I beg, we shall make of these pagan tribes a great Christian people, and of their land the most beautiful of all colonies of the King."

The obstacles were, of course, the interference in mission affairs by the military, and the lack of a dependable source of supplies and provisions until such time as the missions could become self-supporting.

To supply Upper California by sea from San Blas had proved entirely too expensive and undependable, due to strong headwinds and the inability to control scurvy. To supply it from Loreto was impossible, since the barren peninsula had already been stripped of all the animals and provisions that could be spared. But Father Garcés had so revived the old Kino missions in Pimería Alta that there was an abundance of livestock and grain. Furthermore, in 1771 he had explored a land route from the mouth of the Gila River to the mountains east of San Gabriel. Father Serra urged that every effort be made to supply the California missions by that route, and that a distinct separation be made between supplies sent for military use and those sent for the missions.

Viceroy Bucareli granted the requests with only a few minor exceptions, and agreed that the Church should have title to upwards of one hundred thousand acres of land surrounding each mission. In June he issued a *reglamento* to become effective January 1, 1774, restricting the military, and giving the Church complete authority over the missions, their property, supplies, livestock, and all baptized Indians, excepting only those proved guilty of capital crimes.

There can be no doubt that Junípero Serra alone saved Upper California from abandonment by the Spanish, for of his visit Bucareli wrote: "He was half-dying when I saw him arrive here. The apostolic flame that burned in him made an extraordinary impression on me; it was his views and his desires which inspired my decisions."

ON THE KING'S HIGHWAY

Upon issuing the *reglamento* Viceroy Bucareli sent dispatches to Captain Bautista de Anza, commandant of the garrison at Tubac, instructing him to attempt the opening of a land route and supplying the California missions from Pimería Alta. In January, 1774, Anza set out by way of Caborca, the most prosperous of the old Kino missions, with Father Garcés, thirty-four soldiers and muleteers, sixty-five cattle, and a pack train of one hundred and forty horses and mules. Their suffering was great, and many of the horses and mules were lost in crossing the deserts, but late in April the Anza expedition arrived at Monterey with most of the cattle and provisions, and without having lost a man.

Father Serra had remained in Mexico until the *reglamento* became effective, and arrived at Monterey just after Anza had left on his return journey to Sonora. He found Fages completely transformed by the "stern orders" he had received from Viceroy Bucareli, cordial in his welcome, and wholehearted in his cooperation. During the nearly two years the Prefect had been away his priests had done what they could to keep the struggling missions in operation, but little had been accomplished, and few Indians baptized. Upon Father Serra's return a new start was made, and with the backing of Viceroy Bucareli and the cooperation of Commandant Fages it prospered.

With livestock brought by Anza small herds were founded at each mission, and with the supplies hundreds of Indians were drawn to the missions by feeding and clothing them there. Through infinite patience they were taught the Spanish language, instructed in the Christian faith, and induced to cultivate the land. Within a year the herds had nearly doubled, irrigation systems had been put into operation, orchards and vineyards replanted, several hundred acres of fertile land brought under cultivation, and more than a thousand converts baptized. To find the Indians and bring them in, the priests journeyed far into the surrounding mountains and valleys. From Carmel Mission they crossed the rolling hills to the east of Monterey Bay, discovered the rich Santa Clara Valley, and followed it northward to San Francisco Bay, and the paths they wore in the sod became El Camino Real.

Greatly encouraged by the progress, Bucareli determined that, regardless of cost, California should be held against any possible penetration by the English or Russians. He issued instructions that two missions and a presidio be established immediately at San Francisco Bay, and that additional soldiers and livestock be sent from Pimería Alta, together with whatever colonists could be recruited there. Captain Anza was placed in command of the venture, and authorized to offer colonists mules for transportation, complete outfits of clothing and farming implements, and daily rations of food for a period of five years.

As was to be expected, the colonists were largely the riffraff of the Mexican frontier, but their privations of the past had prepared them well for the hardships of the trail and life in a new and unsettled land. In late September, 1775, Anza left Mission San Miguel, near the present site of Nogales, Arizona, with five hundred and thirty horses, one hundred and sixty-five mules, three hundred and fifty cattle, and two hundred and forty colonists, among them twenty-nine women and one hundred and ten children. On this expedition he blazed the route which was followed by the Forty-Niners coming over the Gila Trail, and which is now closely paralleled by Highway 99 between El Centro and Los Angeles. On January 4, 1776, the caravan reached Mission San Gabriel, having lost scores of animals in the deserts, but with one more colonist than had left San Miguel, for on Christmas Day the wife of one of the soldiers had given birth to a son, the first white child born in California.

Twelve soldiers and their wives were left at San Gabriel to establish the first Spanish colony, then Anza moved on to set up others at San Luis Obispo and San Antonio, reaching Monterey on March 10. Ten days later he set out for the north, and pioneered the fifty miles of El Camino Real that now connect San Francisco and San Jose through an unbroken chain of wealthy suburbs. A site for the presidio was chosen near the present San Francisco end of the Golden

Gate Bridge. Knowing Father Serra's preference for having missions separated from the forts, Anza chose a location five miles inland for Mission San Francisco de Asís. Near the southern tip of the bay a site was chosen for Mission Santa Clara, and a few miles farther down the valley a location selected for the settlement of San Jose. The San Francisco presidio was completed and occupied in September, 1776, and Mission San Francisco de Asís was founded in October. The following January, Mission Santa Clara was established, and San Jose settled soon after.

Upon the arrival of the second Anza expedition and the occupation of San Francisco Bay, the crisis for the California missions was passed, though the great work of Father Serra and his priests was barely begun. The only remaining portrait of Junípero Serra is one painted at the time of his persuading Bucareli not to abandon the settlement of Upper California, and which now hangs in the Dispensary of the Church of San Fernando in Mexico City. He was then sixty years of age, and although Bucareli described him as half-dying, he wrote, "The apostolic flame that burned in him made an extraordinary impression on me." But the portrait shows Serra to be no more than forty, with fat cheeks, an unwrinkled brow, large and expressionless eyes, and a saccharine-sweet mouth. The hand appears as soft and smooth as a woman's, and the entire attitude is one of gentleness and mild composure.

There can be no doubt that the artist painted a portrait of what he believed a Franciscan Prefect should look like, and that Bucareli described Serra accurately. A vast amount of his correspondence and material written about him by his contemporaries has been preserved, and it all shows him to have been a veritable storm center. His one burning ambition was to convert the Indians of California to Christendom, and he let nothing stand in his way. There was almost never a time when he was not embroiled in a battle: with a viceroy, governor, commandant, the heads of the Franciscan Order at Mexico City, some of his own priests, and anyone who hindered the expansion of his mission system. He drove himself to the very limit of his physical ability, and drove his priests as relentlessly. Like most forceful men of destiny, he was almost equally loved and hated. Time and again his enemies succeeded in having his authority curtailed, but each time his friends had it restored, and under his driving force the California missions grew and prospered.

For eight years after the founding of Mission San Francisco de Asís, Father Serra journeyed back and forth between the missions, scattered for six hundred miles along the California coast. A few of his journeys between Monterey and San Diego were made by sea, but the others were over the trail known as El Camino Real—afoot when he was able to hobble on his infected leg, and on muleback when he could no longer walk. At each mission he confirmed the converts who had learned the catechism since his last visit, inspected herds, crops, granaries, and the living quarters of the neophytes; planned the expansion of farm lands, and supervised the building of churches and other structures.

His disappointments and frustrations were many, but each year the number of converts increased, the Indians became more skilled and adapted to the ways of civilization, the herds multiplied, thousands of additional acres were put under cultivation, and the walls of the great churches and cathedrals rose higher. But the Prefect was never content. From the beginning he had envisaged a continuous line of missions along the King's Highway, stretching from San Diego to San Francisco Bay, with no two of them more than a day's journey apart.

His vision was far beyond the ability of any man, particularly of one who was crippled and already well past the age of sixty, for as soon as the California missions became self-supporting assistance from Mexico was cut off, and expansion had to be made entirely from the resources of the existing missions. More beloved by his thousands of Indian converts and the priests under his jurisdiction than any other Prefect, save Kino, Father Serra died on August 28, 1784. But by that time he had built the foundation of the California mission system so solidly, and imbued his fellow priests so thoroughly with his own zeal that his dream was soon to be realized.

At the end of the century, sixteen years after Father Serra's death, eighteen great missions stood between San Diego and San Francisco bays, each of them a thriving community inhabited by hundreds of contented and industrious Indian neophytes. Joining them together, no one of them more than a two days' journey from another, was El Camino Real—The King's Highway. Although still a rough trail, it was the longest and most heavily traveled trade route on the continent. Over it passed long trains of pack mules, carrying on the commerce between the missions, priests on their rounds of conversion and supervision, soldiers moving between the presidios at San Francisco, Monterey, Santa Barbara, and San Diego; travelers between the little settlements of Yerba Buena (San Francisco), San Jose, and the newly founded pueblo of Los Angeles; and rancheros on their way to the seaports to trade hides and tallow for merchandise brought by Yankee skippers.

By the time Mexico won its independence from Spain, the number of California missions had been increased to twenty-one, and El Camino Real had jumped the Golden Gate, extending to San Rafael and Sonoma. Today it is the main thoroughfare of the most populous state in the Union, and its course still follows the paths worn deep by the sandals of Junípero Serra and his devoted priests and Indian neophytes.

4

The Old Spanish Trail

THE GREAT SLAVE TRAIL

The name, The Old Spanish Trail, is inclined to conjure before our minds the concept of an ancient thoroughfare, blazed by the earliest Spanish priests, and worn deep by the trampling horses of Spanish conquistadores. Nothing could be farther from the truth. Spanish rule in North America had been ended by the Mexican Revolution long before the first white man ever traveled the length of the trail, and a considerable portion of it was blazed by a young man from Binghamton, New York.

Like all trails of the old West, the Old Spanish Trail followed the route of the least resistance, and was never a single, well-worn thoroughfare, but a multiplicity of trails that converged and separated, like cow paths leading to a pasture gate. Much of it was originally blazed by wild animals, and most of it had been used by the Indians for centuries before Leif Ericson landed on this continent.

In 1598 Juan de Oñate founded San Gabriel, the first Spanish settlement north of the present International Boundary. It was located at the confluence of the Chama River and the Rio Grande, about thirty miles north of Santa Fe. But long before that Taos Pueblo, some forty miles farther up the Rio Grande, was a well-established trading center. There the Ute Indians of western Colorado and Utah came to trade with the Pueblo people and tribes from the Great Plains.

San Gabriel failed as a settlement, and Oñate was recalled to Mexico City, but at the urging of the Church the Viceroy appointed Pedro de Peralta as Governor of New Mexico, and directed that his first duty be the founding of a new settlement in a more favorable location. Santa Fe was founded in 1610, and though destined to become the commercial center of the Southwest, its economic growth was slow, due to a lack of nearby fertile lands or mineral deposits. But the Church burgeoned. By 1630 twenty-five missions had been established throughout the Pueblo Indian territory of northwestern New Mexico and northeastern Arizona. Sixty thousand Indians from ninety pueblos were claimed as converts, and fifty priests were teaching Christianity, reading, writing, and the simpler arts and skills of civilization.

The Spanish mission system flourished for half a century. Then, because of a weakness within itself, was wiped out by the Pueblo uprising of 1680. As early as the 1490's the *encomienda* system had been established in the West Indies. The *encomiendas* were estates or areas granted by the Spanish crown, and the *encomiendero* was obligated to "Christianize and civilize" the heathen within his domain. To discharge the obligation by friendly persuasion, particularly with the language barrier, was next to impossible, so the natives were herded into conversion and placed under virtual bondage to the priests.

When the conquistadores invaded the mainland and conquered the Aztecs, they found them to be in possession of slaves captured from weaker and less civilized tribes. The Spaniards, already familiar with the *encomienda* system, were quick to adopt outright slavery. Expeditions were sent far to the north to capture strong young Indian men, who were chained together by leg irons, and driven back to work in the mines or on the ranches. But these Indians, mature when captured, proved to be poor slaves. They were too fierce and rebellious for use on the ranches, and if put to work in the mines they soon sickened and died. On the other hand, Indian children raised in captivity grew up to be docile, made excellent house servants, and could endure work in the mines.

By the end of the sixteenth century the Indian slave trade had become one of the most profitable activities in Spanish America, but the demand was entirely for young women and children. An intelligent, well-formed, and tractable girl of eight years would bring as much as four hundred dollars in the Mexico City market, and a strong, healthy boy of the same age would bring two hundred or more. This was largely responsible for the route followed by the Old Spanish Trail.

In New Mexico the Church itself took no direct part in the slave trade, but employed the *encomienda* system by teaching the Indians fear of damnation, then using that fear to exploit them for exorbitant contributions of labor and an unreasonable share of their scanty crops. It did, however, take an indirect part in the slave trade by introducing to the Indians the two objects of Spanish civilization which they most coveted—horses and firearms. Moreover, it gathered the Indians from a wide area into mission centers where they could easily be reached by Spanish traders, and through exploitation kept them so destitute that they had little or nothing to trade for the coveted horses and arms except slaves captured from other tribes.

The most enterprising Indian slavers were the Utes. Their homeland extended from the eastern ramparts of the Colorado Rockies to the western side of the Wasatch Range in Utah. Beyond lay the Great American Desert of Nevada, the homeland of the Paiute Indians, known to the earliest pioneers as Diggers, and the most undeveloped of any humans discovered on this continent. For the most part they built no shelters, but lived in burrows like wild animals, and fed upon lizards, rodents, insects, and roots. With little or no tribal organization, and no weapons except clubs or primitive bows and arrows, these Indians were no match for the intelligent and warlike Utes. But their children, if captured at an early age, grew to be exactly the type of slaves the Spaniards liked for servants and herdsmen: docile, tractable, easily taught the simpler skills, and not prone, as most other Indians were, to run away.

Here was a rich source of trade material for the Utes. In spring, when the Diggers were weakened by a winter of semi-starvation, the Utes would swoop down on the little bands, kill the men and older boys, and capture the young women and children. With their plunder they crossed the Wasatch Mountains in central Utah. There they turned almost directly southeast, forded the Green and Colorado rivers at the only accessible points along their awesome canyons, cut across the southwest corner of Colorado, to the Spanish settlements on the Rio Grande.

There are no available records to indicate when the earliest slave trading began between the Utes and Spaniards, but it must have been in full swing by the middle of the seventeenth century. One reason for this belief is that the earliest French explorers in the Northwest found Indians in Montana mounted on Spanish horses soon after 1700. It is most probable that the ancestors of these horses had been acquired by theft or trade from the Utes, whose only source of supply was from the Spanish traders in the vicinity of Santa Fe, and whose only trade goods in any quantity were Paiute slaves.

In any event, the trade was cut off sharply in 1680. By that time the exploitation of the Church had become unbearable to the Pueblo Indians. Under the leadership of the medicine man, Popé, they revolted, destroyed the missions, killed four hundred Spaniards—about one quarter of the New Mexico population—and drove the rest south to El Paso.

It was 1692 before the reconquest of New Mexico was attempted, and six years of bloody fighting were required before Spanish rule was again established. But the complete domination of the Church was broken. In time the Pueblo Indians along the Rio Grande, and the Zuñis, were brought back into the fold, but the Navajos and Comanches remained enemies. The Hopis were peaceful if left alone, but would tolerate no Spaniards, priests or otherwise, in their northeastern Arizona territory. Although the Utes resisted reconversion, they were more than willing to trade Paiute slaves for horses, mules, and firearms, so the slave trade was reopened in 1694. As for the Apaches, they had been everyone's enemy from the beginning, and remained so.

FATHER ESCALANTE

The history of the Old Spanish Trail begins on July 29, 1776, twenty-five days after the Declaration of Independence was adopted at Philadelphia. Seven years earlier, Father Serra had founded the first California mission at San Diego. By 1773 five California missions had been established, but the Spanish found it impracticable to supply these outposts by sea. The cost was too great, too many men were lost by scurvy, and cattle and horses could not survive the long sea voyage on small sailing ships. If the missions were to prosper they must be stocked and supplied by an overland route. In 1774 Anza, with the help of Father Garcés, had pioneered a route from Sonora to Monterey, but the crossing of the Arizona and California deserts had proved costly in the loss of animals.

By the time Anza's second expedition was being planned—the one resulting in the founding of San Francisco—Sante Fe had become a thriving city, largely due to trade with the friendly Utes. The missions were again flourishing, a wagon road had been opened to Mexico City by way of El Paso and Chihuahua, and a brisk commerce was being carried on by caravans. Fray Silvestre Velez de Escalante, priest at the Zuñi mission on the New Mexico-Arizona border, conceived the idea of supplying the California missions from Santa Fe.

Father Escalante knew only too well the aridness of the land straight westward from Santa Fe, and the hostility of the Hopis, Navajos, and Apaches. But he knew the friendliness of the Utes, and that the country a hundred miles north of Santa Fe was far less arid. Having some knowledge of astronomy and navigation, he also knew that Monterey was at the same latitude as the present Colorado-New Mexico line. From this combined knowledge, he reasoned that a northern route to California would provide ample grazing for animals, thus avoiding losses such as Anza had suffered on the desert route from Sonora, and that it would also circumvent the homelands of the hostile tribes. After giving the matter much thought he wrote to the Governor, and to his ecclesiastical superior, proposing that an expedition of twenty well armed and mounted men be sent from Santa Fe to explore such a route. He proposed that the trail blazers travel northwest to the latitude of Monterey, thence westward in as straight a line as possible. He also offered to, "accompany them in order to aid them in matters spiritual and keep a diary with the greatest exactitude."

The proposal was accepted, though somewhat halfheartedly, and a makeshift expedition was organized. Instead of the twenty men Escalante had recommended, the party was made up of six men—probably Spanish soldiers—under the command of Don Bernardo Miera y Pacheco, a retired frontier militia captain of considerable ability. Instead of Escalante's being appointed spiritual adviser, that honor was given to a visiting missionary, Father Francisco Dominguez, who was designated as titular head of the expedition.

Fortunately, Father Escalante was sent along to, "keep a diary with the greatest exactitude." He was the driving force of the undertaking and, though it failed of its purpose, it was of inestimable value, for Escalante's journal is one of the richest sources of early American history. It not only details every step of a five months' journey through the wilderness, but gives the first accurate description of the vast territory lying between the Rocky and Wasatch mountains, together with a vivid account of its people and their mode of life.

The little party, now generally referred to as the Escalante expedition, set out from Santa Fe on July 29, 1776. Riding saddle horses and driving a few beef cattle along with the pack mules, the explorers followed a well-worn trail northward to Mission Santa Clara, at the confluence of the Chama River and the Rio Grande. Next day they moved on to Abiquiú, about twenty-five miles up the Chama, and the farthest outpost of Spanish civilization to the northwest.

Abiquiú, permanently established in 1754, was then very much as it is now; a picturesque little adobe village, clinging to a hillside above the Chama Valley. The explorers stopped for a day to celebrate Solemn Mass and pray for divine protection and guidance on their journey. On August 1, they set off into the wilderness, continuing up the valley for about five miles. Where the river gushes from a rugged canyon at the Continental Divide, they turned to the north, taking a Ute trail that is now rather closely followed by Highway 84. This brought them back to the Chama River just above Tierra Amarilla, a short distance south of the Colorado-New Mexico line. Here the headwaters of the river bore off to the east, around the end of the San Juan Mountains, but Escalante's celestial observations showed them to be at the exact latitude of Monterey.

Leaving the Chama, they turned to the west, crossing the Continental Divide by way of a trail that led over a natural pass, and close to a small lake that Escalante named Laguna Olivares—now Horse Lake. This was on the old Ute slave route, and there is little doubt that the trails, as was usually the case with Indian trails through mountainous country, converged at the natural passes and river fords, then diverged at either side of the hazard. The Escalante party probably chose the trail leading in the most westerly direction, for the journal shows them to have held a course very close to the present state line for a distance of about sixty miles.

Then the Ute slave trails turned to the northwest, leading in the general direction of the only feasible crossing of the Colorado River Gorge, at the site of Moab, Utah. That the Escalante party was fol-

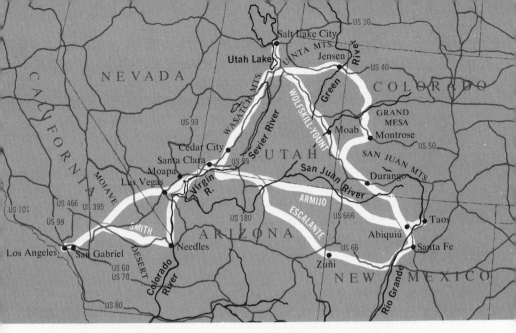

The Old Spanish Trail: routes of Father Escalante, Jedediah Smith, William Wolfskill and George Yount, and Antonio Armijo. The Spanish ran a profitable business capturing young Indians and taking them to Mexico City for sale as slaves. Their route was chiefly responsible for the eastern section of the trail.

lowing one of these trails is most certain, since it also turned to the northwest, passing through present Durango, on to Dolores and down the course of the Dolores River. There, unquestionably, the Indian trail was lost at the point where it left the river, for the Spaniards continued downstream until they became hopelessly imprisoned in the twisting labyrinth of rock-walled Summit Canyon. Often making no more than two or three miles in a day, they reached Gypsum Canyon on August 19. Since it led in from the east, they turned in that direction, hoping to find friendly Utes who could direct them back to the lost trail.

This was the extent of the Escalante exploration of the route which, more than half a century later, was to become known as the Old Spanish Trail. The Ute Indians of Colorado and Utah were at that time quite separated, walled off from each other by the deep canyons of the Dolores, Colorado, and Green rivers. The Escalante party continued eastward to the vicinity of Montrose, Colorado, where it made contact with the Utes. These Indians knew their way around the deep canyons, but not through them, so led and directed the Spaniards down the Uncompahgre River to the present site of Delta, eastward to the vicinity of Hotchkiss, and northward across the Grand Mesa. At a small village there, they were fortunate enough to find two visiting Laguna Utes, whose home was at Utah Lake. The Laguna Indians guided the Escalante party far to the northwest, crossing the Colorado River below Grand Valley, the White near Rangely, and the Green at Jensen, Utah. From Jensen their course followed very closely the route of U.S. Highway 40 to Strawberry Lake. From there they turned to the southwest, crossed the Wasatch Mountains, and followed Spanish Fork Canyon down to Utah Lake, south of Provo.

After a few days' rest, and guided by local Indians, the Spaniards moved southward along the route now followed by U.S. Highway 91, reaching the Sevier River on September 29. The Sevier is one of the most unusual rivers in the United States. It rises in southwestern Utah, flows northward for nearly a hundred and fifty miles, then turns to the west, and flows again toward the south, to be swallowed by the desert surrounding Sevier Lake. The Escalante party spent nearly a week exploring the country adjacent to the westward bend of the Sevier, then was caught in a howling snowstorm which lasted two days.

Through an error in calculation, Father Escalante believed they had again reached the latitude of Monterey, but computed the distance to the Pacific coast as being between four and five hundred miles. Since their supplies were nearly exhausted, the explorers decided to turn homeward.

Father Escalante's description of the country traversed by the expedition was flawless, and his speculation as to what lay beyond resulted, a half century later, in opening the trail he had envisaged. Noting that the Sevier was a considerable river at the point where it turned to the west, he presumed that it flowed straight on to the Pacific, and entered his speculation in his journal.

Having decided to return to Santa Fe, the Escalante party traveled southward along the western margin of the Wasatch Mountains. They crossed the route which would eventually become the Old

Spanish Trail, discovered the headwaters of the Virgin River, and continued almost straight south past Zion National Park. Turning eastward, they forded the Colorado at the point since known as the Crossing of the Fathers, and returned to Santa Fe by way of the Hopi villages, Zuñi, Acoma Pueblo, and Albuquerque. They arrived on January 2, 1777, having traveled and mapped nearly two thousand miles of trail through an unknown land in five months.

Following the Escalante expedition, the California missions began to prosper and become self-sufficient, so the Church made no further effort to open a trail between Santa Fe and the Pacific coast. There is, however, little doubt that the eastern portion of the route was in fairly constant use thereafter, both by Indians and Spanish traders, though there are few authentic records of trading expeditions. One of the earliest records is of the half-breed, Manuel Mestas, who for nearly fifty years was a Ute interpreter. In 1805, when seventy years old, he went as far as Utah Lake to recover horses the Indians had stolen from the Santa Fe area.

Another record is of the Arze-García trading venture of 1813. This party went well beyond Utah Lake, probably for the purpose of capturing Paiute slaves—as soon became a regular custom of the Spanish traders—for they reported trouble with the Indians on the Rio Sebero—the Sevier River. On their way back to Santa Fe they found Chief Wasatch of the Utes waiting to trade with them "as was his custom" at the Moab ford of the Colorado River. This would indicate that as early as 1805 there were many Spanish traders using the trail. In any event, the Arze-García venture was disappointing. They returned home with but twelve Indian slaves and a hundred and nine pelts, which they referred to as "but a few."

American mountain men did far more than the Spanish to establish the Old Spanish Trail. William Wolfskill and Ewing Young came to Santa Fe with the earliest trader caravans from Missouri, and were largely responsible for Taos becoming headquarters of the mountain men. During the winter of 1822-23 Wolfskill trapped the lower Rio Grande, but because of the warm climate beaver furs were not in prime condition. The following fall he and Ewing Young led expeditions across the Continental Divide, by way of the Ute slave trail, to trap streams flowing into the Colorado. When, in June, 1824, they returned to Taos, they learned from new arrivals over the Santa Fe

Trail that other trappers, far to the northwest, were finding beaver more plentiful and the furs of superior quality.

In August of that year several large parties of trappers left Taos and "traveled to the northwest thirty days' journey," before setting up winter headquarters. They certainly crossed the Colorado River at Moab, Utah, and the Green at the present town of Green River, since these were the most southerly points at which the deep canyons of the rivers could be crossed by pack trains. Although in going out and returning to Taos, these parties, and the hundreds that followed in succeeding years, may have used divergent trails between the Rio Grande and the Colorado, they all constituted the route which the mountain men called the Old Spanish Trail.

JEDEDIAH SMITH AND THE BUENA VENTURA

No one can say to which of the mountain men belongs the most credit for establishing the eastern half of the Old Spanish Trail, but there is no question as to the western half; the credit belongs almost entirely to Jedediah Smith.

Jedediah Smith was born near Binghamton, New York, on January 6, 1799, one of a family of fourteen children. Although his parents were pioneers, moving westward with the frontier, Jed was taught at an early age to read the Bible, write, and cipher. At thirteen he was employed as clerk on a British fur-trading vessel on the Great Lakes, throwing him into contact with Canadian trappers and arousing his eagerness to explore the wilderness. Upon hearing, in March, 1822, that General William Ashley, Lieutenant Governor of Missouri, was organizing the first American expedition to trap beaver in the Rocky Mountains, Smith left his job and set out for St. Louis. It was early May before he arrived, only to find that the expedition, under Major Andrew Henry, had left for the mountains in mid-April. However, because of Jed's experience with the British firm, General Ashley offered him a job as his personal clerk.

Even though disappointed at having missed the opportunity upon which he had set his heart, Smith was not discouraged. He accepted the offer and immediately went about preparing for the next opportunity that might present itself. St. Louis was then the fur capital of the United States, its population fairly evenly divided between French, Spanish, and American frontiersmen, some of the French having trapped the Missouri to its headwaters high in the Rockies. During the following months Smith learned to speak French and Spanish, hunted out the men who had penetrated deepest into the mountains, won their friendship, listened to their tales, and learned the secrets that they alone knew. He gathered every atlas, frontier journal, or map he could lay hands upon, and studied them until he knew their every detail. Among them were Carey's General Atlas, published in Philadelphia in 1818, and maps and journals prepared by Meriwether Lewis, Zebulon Pike, Father Escalante, the Hudson's Bay Company, and numerous sea captains.

Jedediah Smith had amazing ability to carry in his mind an accurate picture of any map he had studied, or any territory through which he had traveled. From the Hudson's Bay and Lewis maps and journals, he learned the courses of the Missouri and Columbia rivers, their main tributaries, and formed mental pictures of the mountainous regions through which they flowed. From those prepared by Pike and Father Escalante, he was able to envisage the eastern and central Rockies, though the course of streams was limited to the stretches

Beaver trappers of the old West. From Pioneers in the Settlement of America, *William A. Crafts.*

followed by the explorers. From sea captains' maps he learned the shape of the Pacific coast, the location of harbors, and of the Spanish missions in California.

But there was little to be learned of the Southwest. The only available map was in Carey's General Atlas, and though published as authentic, it was entirely imaginary. Based upon Father Escalante's speculation that the Sevier River probably discharged into the Pacific, and upon knowledge that a large river flowed into San Francisco Bay from the east, the map maker had invented the Buena Ventura River. He depicted it in the shape of a great tree, its trunk planted on San Francisco Bay, and its widely spreading branches reaching out to the mountains of western Utah. Otherwise, the map was simply an outline of the California coast and an oblong of blank space.

Jed Smith's opportunity came sooner than he had expected. In the late fall of 1822 Major Henry sent two keelboats back from the upper Yellowstone, bringing beaver pelts that sold for $24,000. The amazing success of this first American beaver trapping venture sparked a stampede for the mountains. Frontiersmen rushed to St. Louis in droves. Those with sufficient funds to outfit expeditions formed trapper bands, and by February, 1823, a fleet of keelboats was being poled up the Missouri. In March General Ashley himself set out for the headwaters of the river with a party of a hundred young trappers, Jed Smith among them.

All those who went to the mountains with the Henry and Ashley expeditions of 1822 and 1823 were rugged, self-reliant, and courageous young frontiersmen in their late teens and early twenties. Among them five stood out sharply because of their natural aptitudes, so Ashley chose them as captains of his trapper bands. They were Jim Bridger, Tom Fitzpatrick, David Jackson, Jedediah Smith, and William Sublette.

No American trapper captain went into the mountains as well qualified as Jedediah Smith, for he was not only a gifted explorer and natural leader of men, but carried a store of knowledge that no other man possessed. For three years he led his band throughout the northern region of the Rockies, trapping the streams as far westward as central Idaho, and returning to rendezvous each summer with bulging fur packs. By the end of the 1825-26 season General Ashley had become extremely wealthy from his trapping venture, decided to devote his entire attention to politics, and sold out to Smith, Sublette, and Jackson.

Politics was not the only reason for General Ashley's selling out: the thickest cream had already been skimmed from the pan, American trappers from St. Louis were overrunning the tributaries of the Missouri. Those from Taos had pushed as far to the northwest as Great Salt Lake, stripping the beaver streams of western Colorado and eastern Utah. Rivalry for the remaining pelts had become fierce between the American and British firms. The Hudson's Bay Company held absolute control of the Columbia River territory, had doubled the number of its trappers, and each spring and fall was sending them farther to the southeast.

Jed Smith realized the situation even more fully than Ashley evidently had. With beaver already becoming scarce in the easily accessible streams, the days of fabulous profits were past, and the Hudson's Bay Company had two enormous advantages over Smith, Sublette, and Jackson. Beaver pelts were prime only from October to May, and in the northern Rockies no trapping could be done during the dead of winter, since the streams were frozen and the beaver secure within their rock-hard lodges. American trappers must sit idle in winter camp for at least three months, under constant danger of losing their fur packs to marauding Indians, or their horses to starvation and freezing. In the Columbia River territory the winters were mild enough that the Hudson's Bay Company could keep its men trapping all winter, and there was no danger of losing animals by freezing and starvation.

The greatest advantage of the Hudson's Bay Company, however, was in transportation. General Ashley had held his summer rendezvous on the Green River in southwestern Wyoming, more than fifteen hundred miles from St. Louis. Even though keelboats were used, the distance to navigable rivers was six hundred miles, over rugged mountains through hostile Indian country, making it necessary that pelts be taken out and supplies brought in by heavily guarded pack trains. This was not only dangerous and costly in wages, but required an enormous investment in horses and equipment. With its headquarters at Fort Vancouver, the Hudson's Bay Company had little or no transportation problem. Its fur packs could easily and cheaply be boated down the Columbia and its tributaries in small quantities, and supplies brought back in the same manner, reducing the risk of loss to hostile Indians.

The map of the Southwest that Jed Smith had seen in Carey's Atlas was still clear in his mind, and appeared to provide a solution to his problem. He reasoned that so large a river as the Buena Ventura must be teeming with beaver, and would furnish a cheap means of rapid transportation. Furthermore, at least three months of idle time would be saved each year, for the winters in the Southwest would certainly be mild enough to permit trapping. All that seemed necessary was for Smith, Jackson, and Sublette to explore the region first, hold it against the Hudson's Bay Company, and negotiate with the California Mexicans for a Pacific headquarters at the mouth of the river. There the fur packs could be consigned to Yankee trading vessels, and shipped inexpensively to New York or Europe.

Since Jed Smith was better qualified than either of his partners, both as an explorer and linguist, it was decided that he should undertake the exploration. On August 22, 1826, he set out from Great Salt Lake with a party of fifteen men, promising to rejoin his partners, if possible, at the south end of Bear Lake during the summer of 1827. For transport, he took fifty horses, half of them loaded with camp supplies, beaver traps, flour, meal, dried meat, and merchandise for trading with the Indians. From the present site of Salt Lake City he set off into, "the country S.W. which was entirely unknown to me, and of which I could collect no satisfactory information from the Indians who inhabit this country on its N.E. borders."

Actually, he did not set off to the southwest, but followed the Jordan River due south, circled the eastern shore of Utah Lake, and continued along approximately the route followed by the Escalante party a half-century before. Here there were, doubtlessly, several trails, since the valley was the natural route between the Sevier River and Utah Lake, and had been used by the Indians for centuries. In all probability Smith took a trail holding closer to the western rampart of the Wasatch Mountains than that followed by the Escalante party, for he reached the Sevier well above the point where it turns to the west. He named it the Ashley River, and erroneously presumed that it flowed straight on northward, emptying into Utah Lake.

Expecting to discover the headwaters of the Buena Ventura any day, Jed Smith started the exploration which would determine the route of the Old Spanish Trail's western half. Although the journal covering his first expedition to California has become lost, a map, evidently copied from his sketches, was prepared in 1839 by David H. Burr, Geographer for the United States House of Representatives. Also, the journal of Smith's second expedition, over approximately the same route, was unearthed in researches made by the late Maurice Sullivan. From Burr's map and references made in the second journal, the route of the first expedition has been closely traced by Dr. LeRoy R. and Ann W. Hafen.

After following the river upstream for some sixty miles, Smith reached the point where it gushes from the mountains through a narrow, seemingly impassable canyon. There he turned westward up the broader Clear Creek Canyon, crossed a low divide, and traveled southward along the Beaver River to the point where it loops back to the north. Here he again reached the route of the Escalante party and, possibly by the same Indian trails, continued southward to the east branch of the Virgin River—which he named the "Adams River in compliment of our President"—in the vicinity of Hurricane, Utah. There the Escalante party had continued on to the south, but Smith turned to the southwest along the Virgin. For several days he traveled in the stream bed, through its rugged canyon across the extreme northwestern corner of Arizona.

From the Arizona-Nevada line, Smith followed the Virgin down to its confluence with the Colorado, which he called the Seedskeeder (Siskadee), believing it to be the lower reaches of the Green. There he crossed the Colorado and traveled for four days down the eastern side, through country "remarkably barren, rocky, and mountainous," reaching the Mohave villages near the present site of Needles, California on October 5.

Here were the villages Father Garcés had visited in 1776, and it was the ancestors of these Mohaves who had guided him across the deserts to the California missions. Jed Smith found the Mohaves still friendly and cooperative. In a letter which has been preserved, he wrote, ". . . At this place a valley opens out about 5 to 15 miles in width, which on the river banks is timbered and fertile. I here found a nation of Indians who call themselves *Ammuchabas;* they cultivate the soil, and raise corn, beans, pumpkins, watermelons and muskmelons in abundance, and also a little wheat and cotton. I was now nearly destitute of horses, and had learned what it was to do without

[167]

food; I therefore remained there fifteen days and recruited my men, and I was enabled also to exchange my horses and purchase a few more of a few runaway Indians who stole some horses of the Spaniards. I here got information of the Spanish countries (California), obtained two good guides, and recrossed the Seedskeeder which I afterwards found emptied into the Gulf of California by the name of the Collarado. . . . I travelled a west course fifteen days, over a country of complete barrens, generally travelling from morning until night without water."

This is typical of Smith's journal, for he wasted few words in dwelling on his hardships, but they must have been many, for three quarters of the country he had traversed is bleak and barren. It is probable that some horses of which he was destitute had been eaten, since he had only eighteen left when, on November 27, 1826, he arrived at San Gabriel Mission, becoming the first American to reach California by an overland route.

Having failed to discover the headwaters of the Buena Ventura, Smith had crossed the desert with the expectation of arranging for a headquarters at its mouth, then following the stream back to its source. But Americans were unwelcome in California. The fledgling Mexican Government, self-conscious of its inability to defend its northern paradise on the Pacific, was prematurely fearful of an invasion from the east. As soon as Governor José María de Echeandía learned that an American party was in his province he demanded that its leader be brought to San Diego immediately. There Smith was held prisoner until January 18, on the pretext that the Governor could not release him without authority from Mexico City. It was only at the insistence of Yankee trading vessel captains, with whom the Governor wished to maintain friendly relations, that Smith was freed and permitted to continue his exploration.

With a fresh supply of horses and provisions, and still expecting to discover the Buena Ventura River, Smith led his little party across the Tehachapi Mountains and northward through the San Joaquin Valley. Upon reaching the Stanislaus River, he tried to make a crossing at a point about twenty-five miles north of Yosemite National Park. The snow on the summit was too deep to get the horses through, five of them starved to death, and he was obliged to turn back.

Until May 20, Smith and his men explored the foothills of the

Sierra Nevada along the San Joaquin Valley, trapping the streams and searching for a canyon through which the legendary Buena Ventura flowed to the Pacific. Then, in order to keep his promise to his partners, and in hope of discovering the Buena Ventura on the eastern side of the range, he prepared to make a second attempt at crossing the summit. Realizing the danger to be great, he was unwilling to risk the lives of his entire party, so established a camp on the Stanislaus River. Promising to return in the fall if still alive he set off with five horses, two mules, and the two hardiest men in the band.

The feat accomplished by Jedediah Smith and his two companions during the following month is unique in the history of the United States, and quite probably in the history of the world. With no instruments, no Indian guides, and no wild animal trails to follow, they scaled the Sierra Nevada, often through snowdrifts as much as eight feet deep, crossed the widest expanse of barren desert on this continent, and came out exactly where Smith had planned: at the southern tip of Great Salt Lake. He reported the history-making journey in his usual matter-of-fact manner, "After travelling twenty days I struck the southwest corner of Great Salt Lake, travelling over a country completely barren and destitute of game. We frequently travelled without water, sometimes for two days over sandy deserts where there was no sign of vegetation. When we arrived at the Salt Lake, we had but one horse and one mule remaining, the balance of my horses I was compelled to eat as they gave out." Needless to say, the nonexistent Buena Ventura River was not discovered.

In mid-June, 1827, Smith reached Bear Lake in southeastern Idaho for the promised rendezvous with his partners. A month later he again set out for California, this time with a party of eighteen men. He followed his route of the previous summer as far as the east branch of the Virgin River. There he explored a route which avoided the rugged canyon across the corner of Arizona, and would provide a badly needed oasis on the Old Spanish Trail. Not far below Hurricane, Utah, he turned to the northwest and discovered the semi-tropical Santa Clara Valley. He found the Shivwits Indians raising corn, beans, pumpkins, and melons, as they still do. And there was abundant grazing for his nearly exhausted horses.

After recruiting his men and animals a few days among the friendly Shivwitses, Smith crossed a low divide to the southwest, reached the

Virgin River near the Arizona-Nevada line, and followed his 1826 trail to the Mohave villages. The Indians, who had been so friendly and helpful on his first visit, acted strangely. At sight of the white men they ran away, but were finally induced to come into camp and trade. Among them was Francisco, one of the two who had acted as guides across the California desert in 1826. When Smith asked him the reason for the Mohaves' fear, he said that, "a party of Spaniards and Americans from the Province of Sonora by the way of the Gila, had been there . . . quarreled and separated, one party going up the Colorado and the other in another direction."

Unfortunately, Francisco was telling Smith only what the Mohaves wanted him to know. The full story is told—probably with embellishments—in James Ohio Pattie's *Personal Narrative*. In the winter of 1826-27 Pattie and a mixed party had trapped down the Gila to its mouth, then turned up the Colorado reaching the Mohave villages in March. The Mohave chief, in sign language, demanded a horse in exchange for beaver the trappers had taken from the river. The demand was refused, and Pattie writes: "On the morning of the 7th, the chief returned on horse back, and in the same sulky tone again demanded a horse. The captain bade him off, in a language and with a tone alike understood by all people. He started off on full gallop, and as he passed one of our horses, that was tied a few yards from camp, he fired a spear through the animal. He had not the pleasure to exult in his revenge for more than fifty yards, before he fell pierced by four bullets. . . . [The Indians] raised a war whoop, and made a charge upon us. At the distance of one hundred and fifty yards we gave them a volley of rifle balls. This brought them to a halt, and a moment after to a retreat, more rapid than their advance had been. We sallied out after them, and gave them a second round, which induced all, that were not forever stopped, to fly at top of their speed. We had killed sixteen of their number. We returned to our camp, packed, and started, having made a determination not to allow any more Indians to enter our camp." This action, typical of the treatment accorded Indians by the Spanish and some American mountain men, made bitter enemies of the Mohaves, and altered the eventual route of the Old Spanish Trail.

It was six months after the Pattie massacre that Smith reached the Mohave villages. Following their initial fear and strangeness, the Indians acted friendly, but he distrusted their behavior, so stopped only long enough to build a raft for his supplies, trade for a few horses, corn and beans, and make the new chief a handsome present.

The Indians showed no hostility until the raft was in midstream, with the horses swimming behind. They then swarmed onto the river in dugout canoes, drove the horses back, and killed ten of the helpless white men before the raft could reach the farther bank. There Smith and his eight remaining men held them off until dark, then escaped into the desert with only their rifles and fifteen pounds of dried meat. The crossing to San Gabriel Mission, which on the preceding expedition had required fifteen days on horseback, was made in nine and a half on foot, most of it under cover of darkness. Smith was again imprisoned by the Mexican Governor and released at the insistence of Yankee sea captains, but only after the posting of a thirty-thousand-dollar bond and his promise to leave the country within two months.

EVOLUTION OF THE ROUTE

Following Jed Smith's second California expedition, a considerable part of the Old Spanish route came into use, although there was no hard-and-fast trail. In the winter of 1827-28 George Yount and his trapping band went nearly as far as the Mohave villages, but turned back when they heard from a Yuma Indian of the Smith massacre.

In the fall of 1829 several American trapping parties are known to have used the western portion of the trail. Ewing Young, with a party including Kit Carson, followed it from the Colorado to San Gabriel Mission. Thomas (Peg Leg) Smith was in a party that trapped the Virgin River and its Santa Clara branch, then took Jed Smith's trail of 1827 and disposed of their fur packs in Los Angeles.

As far as is known, the first party ever to traverse the entire length of the Old Spanish Trail was that of William Wolfskill and George Yount. After Ewing Young's return to Taos from his 1829-30 trapping expedition to California, he entered into partnership with Wolfskill for the purpose of trapping there the following season. They planned to dispose of their pelts at San Francisco Bay, invest the proceeds in large California mules, and drive them back to Santa Fe. Young and his party went ahead, probably trapping down the Gila.

[171]

Wolfskill was delayed in getting away from Taos—no doubt due to his thriving business of supplying Taos lightning to the outgoing trapper parties—but in the early fall of 1830 he joined with George Yount in making up a party of twenty-one men. It was the last of September before they left Taos, riding horses and driving a string of pack mules loaded with beaver traps, gaudy merchandise for trading with the Indians, and the usual camp supplies for a trip of two months. At Abiquiú, which later became the eastern gateway to the Old Spanish Trail, they stopped to buy four fat steers, which they drove along as a fresh meat supply.

The Wolfskill-Yount party crossed the Colorado and Green rivers at the well-known Moab and Green River fords, then traveled northward as far as the Uinta Mountains before turning westward to the Wasatch Range. It is, however, evident that they were quite familiar with this area, for instead of crossing the entire range to Utah Lake, they turned southward through an interior valley to the Sevier River.

Although there was no journal kept by the Wolfskill-Yount party to show the exact route followed, Yount later recounted his experiences on the journey, and a portion of the manuscript has been preserved. It not only indicates this to have been the first traversing of the entire trail, but that it began the evolution which would eventually shorten the original route by nearly two hundred and fifty miles. It reads in part: "Profiting by previous journeyings through the plains of the west, they at this time were enabled much to shorten the distance, and to accomplish the passage to this river sooner than ever before."

It also indicates that although Yount had previously been as far as the Mohave villages, he was not familiar with Smith's route of 1827 beyond the point where it left the Sevier River, and that he was attempting to follow it by description.

By starting their journey so late in the year, and by going so far to the north, it was November before the Wolfskill-Yount party reached the Sevier, and they were obliged to make their way up the river through snow two or three feet deep. This not only slowed their progress, but made described landmarks difficult to recognize. Instead of leaving the Sevier where it emerges from the mountains through a rugged canyon, they lost their way by turning to the left when they should have gone to the right. Strangely, by becoming lost, they pioneered some seventy-five miles of the eventually established trail. They continued upriver to the present site of Spry, Utah, then veered westward to intercept the Smith route near Cedar City. Some later party went on to the west from this point, turned south along the Santa Clara Valley to pick up Smith's trail thus avoiding one of the worst sections of the original route.

Although considerably longer than the Gila Trail, the Old Spanish Trail became the regular route for commerce which developed between New Mexico and California during the 1830's and 1840's. The reasons for its popularity were those which Father Escalante had foreseen in 1775: the avoidance of depredations by the Apaches and Navajos, and a passage far enough north that there would be grazing and water for the animals. This does not mean that any considerable portion of the trail lay through verdant country and the homeland of friendly Indians; far from it. The section through eastern Utah was over a high, roughly broken wasteland, almost entirely devoid of vegetation, and with few springs or water holes. The passage through the Wasatch Mountains was rugged and the canyon of the Sevier barely passable in many places. The final quarter was the most dangerous stretch of trail in the West, lying across three hundred miles of blistering desert, completely destitute of game, and nearly so of grass and water.

The Utes were not always friendly. One subtribe or another was often on the warpath, ambushing river fords and extorting tribute in horses or merchandise before letting the travelers pass. The Paiutes were the hyenas of the western deserts and mountains, skulking the course of every caravan or party on the trail. The main body of a train was reasonably safe from the cowardly, animal-like predators, but if a man or animal straggled or became separated from the band, his chance of survival was small. If a man, he would be stripped of his clothing, and his body left where it fell. If a horse or mule, it would be stripped of its pack, its hide ripped away, and the flesh gnawed from the bones as if by wolves.

No one knows who pioneered the shortened route which, in the early 1830's, became the established course of the Old Spanish Trail. On the section between Santa Fe and the Green River there was almost no change from the route followed by the early slave traders, since this course was dictated by the only points at which the Colorado and Green river canyons could be crossed.

Between the Green and Sevier the course was changed radically, and reduced to less than half its original distance. This, no doubt, came about by trappers moving from one major stream to another, since the mountain men always chose the shortest route that provided grazing and water for their pack animals. The shortened trail climbed to the high plateau westward of the Green, up the headwaters of the San Rafael River, and turned south at the base of the Wasatch Mountains to the lower branch of Muddy Creek. There it crossed the eastern hump of the Wasatches through a low pass, reaching the Sevier in the vicinity of Salina, Utah.

A large portion of the finally established desert trail was pioneered by Antonio Armijo, no doubt to avoid the Mohave villages, and certainly under the guidance of Indians who were thoroughly familiar with the entire desert area of southern Nevada and southeastern California. Armijo was the first to take a merchandise caravan from New Mexico to California. Fortunately, his sketchy diary and a brief account of his journey have been preserved.

In early November, 1829, Armijo set out from Abiquiú with a party of thirty men and a train of mules loaded with goods manufactured in New Mexico, mostly hand-loomed blankets and serapes. The Mexicans, no doubt, rode horses and drove along a considerable number of spares, together with a few sheep, goats, or cattle to supply fresh meat for the journey. It was too late in the season to take the Old Spanish Trail, for at that time its upper loop extended as far north as the Uinta Mountains. So, instead of turning north where the Chama River flows out of its mountain canyon above Abiquiú, Armijo held straight on to the west across the Continental Divide. He then turned to the northwest, up the Canyon Largo branch of the San Juan River, and left New Mexico at the Four Corners—the only point where four states now join. In the longest entry made in his diary Armijo notes, "At the San Juan River . . . we found six Navajos but nothing happened. . . . We took with us an Indian paid . . . with eleven mares for his trip, in order that he might guide us as far as he knew, and so that he would protect us from the depredations which members of his nation are wont to commit."

Also, the Armijo party must have had a copy of the map prepared by Father Escalante on his return to Santa Fe in 1776, for they traveled in a fairly direct line to the Crossing of the Fathers. There they led their animals up from the canyon over rough steps gouged into the smooth sandstone by the Escalante party of fifty-five years previously. After crossing the Colorado it is quite evident that Armijo had Indian guides from a more westerly tribe, for he mentions that, "some of them were frightened by the presence of horses which they did not seem to know about." Nevertheless, some one of them was familiar with the Smith trail of 1827, since the party turned northwest to reach it on the Santa Clara branch of the Virgin River.

Up to this point the movement of the Armijo party was of no consequence in establishing the ultimate route of the Old Spanish Trail, but from there on it was of vast importance. The caravan followed the Smith trail southwest along the Virgin to its confluence with the Colorado, but there turned due west to the present site of Las Vegas, Nevada.

The manner in which the new course across the trackless deserts was discovered is hinted in Armijo's diary notations. On the Colorado he wrote: "January 1 [1880]. Citizen Rafael Rivera is missing from the reconnaissance party of the day before . . . January 5. Stopping: reconnaissance party returned and did not find Rivera. January 7. Citizen Rivera returned and announced that he had discovered the villages of the *Cucha Payuches* and *Hayatas*." This would be the Paiutes at the warm springs near Las Vegas.

For the next thirteen days the entries are short and terse: "At *Salado* [Salty] Arroyo, with nothing new. At a dry lake. At the little spring of the turtle. At the pass without water. At the Little Salty Springs. At the River of the Payuches, where a village was found: nothing happened for it was gentle. Down the same river. At the Alkali River. A day's journey without water. At the lake of the Miracle. At the little spring of the badlands. A day's journey without any water."

Then, on January 21, comes the key entry: "At the arroyo of the *Hayatas*, at the end of which comes in the trail from Moqui, traveled by the Moquis with the object of trading shells with said *Hayatas*."

Armijo's only way of knowing this would be that he had a guide who had been in the sea shell commerce which for centuries had been carried on between the Pacific Coast Indians and those along the Colorado and Virgin rivers. Only such a guide would have been able to lead the way from one to another of the few widely spaced sources of water along the route. In January the rivers referred to might have had a trickle of brackish water in them, and in summer it could usually be found by digging deep into the sandy beds.

Even with an expert guide, the long desert crossing—double in length the route taken by Father Garcés, Jed Smith, and Ewing Young—was rugged and hazardous, as shown by the succeeding entries in Armijo's diary: "Up the same arroyo. Ditto. Along this arroyo; we ate a horse. Ditto. Ditto. Ditto: we ate a mule belonging to Miguel Valdes."

The arroyo was the dry bed of the Mohave River, and it is apparent from the entry of January 27 that a relief party had been sent ahead when the California mountains came into view: "Along said arroyo we met the reconnaissance party with supplies and men from the ranch of San Bernardino."

Armijo's entries, though containing little or no description, are enough to show that the party followed the route which thereafter became the course of the Old Spanish Trail. It left the Las Vegas springs in a southwesterly direction, crossed the Spring Mountains at a low pass, and continued almost due westward nearly to the Amargosa Range. There it turned to the southwest, past the southern end of Death Valley, through Avawatz and Granite passes, then on to rejoin the Garcés-Smith trail just east of Barstow, California.

The Californians were delighted with the bright New Mexican woven goods, and even more delighted that Armijo was willing to trade them for horses and mules, by that time so numerous they were considered almost worthless. Within less than a month the merchandise had been traded for several hundred horses and large California mules. The final entry in the diary reads: "I returned on March the first by the same route with no more mishap than the loss of tired animals, until I entered the Navajo country, by which nation I was robbed of some of my animals, and I arrived in this jurisdiction of Xemey [Jemez] today the 25th of April, 1830—Antonio Armijo."

The final entry had as much effect upon the Old Spanish Trail as the discovery of the short-cut route across the deserts: it was too dangerous and costly to move horses, mules, or other valuable merchandise over any trail through Navajo or Apache territory. Nevertheless, the profit from the venture had been enormous, for New Mexican woven goods brought fabulous prices in mules and horses at the California end of the trail. And the demand for big mules was so great on the Santa Fe Trail that an animal worth no more than ten dollars in Los Angeles, easily sold for fifty in Santa Fe Plaza.

Although Armijo, a Mexican, pioneered the commerce between New Mexico and California, American frontiersmen soon flocked into the horse and mule business—not always honestly. And, to avoid depredations by the Navajos and Apaches, all the traffic moved over the Old Spanish Trail.

The last significant change in the route was made soon afterward, and whoever made it was certainly daring, but his identity is unknown. As finally established, the route left the Virgin River at the northern tip of what is now the Lake Mead National Recreational Area. There it extended due west to the Muddy River at a point near Moapa, Nevada, then southwest in a fifty-five-mile waterless crossing of the desert to Las Vegas. This was the longest absolutely waterless *jornada* on the entire twelve-hundred-mile route.

At first the commerce carried on by the Mexicans between Santa Fe and Los Angeles was by small caravans, such as Armijo's. But as the number of parties on the Old Spanish Trail increased, the Ute chieftains became more demanding in their extortion at the fords and passes, and the skulking Paiutes haunted the trail continually, pilfering night camps and killing stragglers. Year by year more of the small traders banded together, forming large caravans for their mutual protection on the trail. By the time the trade reached its peak, in 1847-48, a single great caravan moved westward each fall, after the heavy runoff from melting snows in the mountains, then returned in spring before the rivers were again in flood.

Lieutenant George Brewerton, who traveled the Old Spanish Trail from Los Angeles to Santa Fe with Kit Carson in April, 1848, wrote an excellent description of the spring caravan: "This caravan consisted of some two or three hundred Mexican traders who go once a year to the California coast with a supply of blankets and other articles of New Mexican manufacture; and having disposed of their goods, invest the proceeds in Californian mules and horses, which they drive back across the desert. . . . This caravan had left Pueblo de los Angeles some time before us, a circumstance which did us great injury, as their large *caballada* [containing nearly a thousand head] ate up or destroyed the grass and consumed the water at the few camping grounds upon the route.

"We finally overtook and passed this party, after some eight days' travel in the Desert. Their appearance was grotesque in the extreme. Imagine upward of two hundred Mexicans dressed in every variety of costume, from the embroidered jacket of the wealthy Californian, with its silver bell-shaped buttons, to the scanty habiliments of the skin-clad Indian, and you may form some idea of their dress. . . . I could not help thinking while observing their arms and equipments, that a few resolute men might have captured their property, and driven the traders like a flock of sheep. Many of these people had no fire-arms, being only provided with the short bow and arrows usually carried by New Mexican herdsmen. Others were armed with old English muskets, condemned long ago as unserviceable.

"Near this motley crowd we sojourned for one night, and I was struck with its picturesque appearance. Their pack-saddles and bales had been taken off and carefully piled, so as not only to protect them from damp, but to form a sort of barricade or fort for their owner. From one side to the other of these little corrals of goods a Mexican blanket was stretched, under which the trader lay smoking his cigarrito, while his Mexican servant or slave—for they are little better—prepared his coffee and *atole*."

The merchandise being taken back to Santa Fe was mostly silk and other Oriental goods, which had reached the California coast by way of Yankee Clippers in the China trade. The number of horses and mules driven by this caravan was small compared to some of the caballadas of earlier years. In 1842 a party of "194 New Mexicans made their departure from Cajon Pass with 4150 animals legally acquired."

THE ROBBERS' ROAD

In an effort to preserve the commerce on the Old Spanish Trail for his own people, the Governor of New Mexico issued an order as early as 1832, prohibiting anyone from entering into the trade without securing a license issued by himself. The mountain men paid as little attention to this order as to national boundaries, and some of them paid even less heed to the ownership of horses and mules which they drove east from California.

A newspaper account, published at the time of Peg Leg Smith's death, tells of what may have been the first California horse and mule raid by American mountain men. When Peg Leg and the band with which he was trapping in 1829 came to Los Angeles with their fur packs, they were given a rough reception and ordered out of the country. They did as they were ordered, "taking with them, however, a band of three or four hundred horses, in spite of efforts of the Californians to prevent the act."

In 1840 the last rendezvous of the beaver trappers was held, and some of the more unscrupulous mountain men turned to horse and mule thievery. That year Peg Leg Smith and Wakara, a notorious Ute chief, are credited with making a raid on San Luis Obispo and running off twelve hundred of the best saddle horses in California. Some sources credit this raid to Old Bill Williams, and say that some three thousand horses and mules were stolen. The latter number is fairly well confirmed, and it is probable that both Smith and Williams were in the raiding party, for both later claimed to have been.

The Californians quickly gathered a posse of seventy-five men and two hundred and twenty-five horses. Spurring for Cajon Pass, they picked up the trail and followed it across the desert at the best possible speed. Not far beyond Barstow, they saw a great cloud of dust ahead. Knowing it to be raised by the stolen stock, they mounted fresh horses and gave chase. But the Americans, numbering only twenty-five, were watching their back trail and saw the dust raised by the posse. Whipping their plunder into a wild stampede, they raced on past the next water hole, but pulled a trick which has all the ear marks of Old Bill Williams. As the thieves passed the water hole they divided their force; half of them howling, shouting, and flogging the tiring herd along, while the other half hid in the nearby reeds.

The Californians, as expected, stopped to refresh themselves. They had barely left their horses and gone to drink when the hidden thieves spurred out of the reeds, drove away every horse in the caballada, and left the Californians to get home as best they could. Before the next water was reached the Americans had lost nearly half the herd through thirst and exhaustion. Lieutenant Brewerton reported that, when crossing the desert in 1848, this section of the trail was literally lined with bleached skeletons. The animals that survived were driven over the Old Spanish Trail to western Colorado. To avoid the Mexican settlements along the Rio Grande, they were detoured through the San Luis Valley to Bent's Fort on the Santa Fe Trail. There they were sold to traders from the Missouri Valley, with no questions asked regarding ownership.

How many thousand stolen horses and mules were driven over the Old Spanish Trail is unknown, but they were many, and more than a few famous American mountain men took part in the thievery. Jim Beckwourth, the noted mulatto scout, trapper, and Indian fighter was among them. Joe Walker, after guiding a Frémont party to California in 1845, returned to his Pueblo, Colorado, camp with a herd of four or five hundred excellent horses, which he doubtlessly considered "contraband of war." Some of these he sold to Kearney's Army of the West when it reached Bent's Fort in 1846, on its way for the conquest of New Mexico and California.

Strangely, the first and last uses of the Old Spanish Trail were as a slave trail, and there were numerous American mountain men— some of them quite famous—who turned to the slave trade when silk hats became popular and the market for beaver pelts collapsed. Dr. J. H. Lyman traveled over the trail in 1841, and reported of the Paiutes in western Utah: "The New Mexicans capture them for slaves; the neighboring Indians do the same; and even the bold and usually high-minded old beaver-hunter sometimes descends from his legitimate labor among the mountain streams, to this mean traffic. The price of these slaves in the markets of New Mexico varies with the age and other qualities of person. Those from ten to fifteen years old sell from fifty dollars to one hundred dollars, which is by no means an extravagant price, if we take into consideration the herculean task of cleansing them fit for market."

Slave trading by the mountain men is not known to have been carried on after the outbreak of the Mexican War, but the Mexicans continued the practice until 1852, when the Utah legislature enacted an anti-slave-trade law. The law, of course, had little effect upon the Indians, and the Utes carried on a Paiute slave trade with the Navajos and other plains and desert tribes until the mid-1860's. The Mexican War also marked the end of the American traffic in stolen California horses and mules, but the Ute chief, Wakara, continued his depredations until his death in 1855.

The last great caravan traveled over the Old Spanish Trail in the spring of 1848. Kit Carson passed it on the deserts while carrying the death sentence of the commerce in his saddle bags. It was a dispatch from the U.S. Military Commander of California, notifying the New Mexico Commander that traders entering California would thereafter be required to pay a duty on their goods. Since the duty was twenty percent, it put an abrupt end to the traffic.

But Carson carried news far more important than the imposition of a duty on the commerce. Also in his saddle bags was a copy of the *California Star*, published in San Francisco on April 1, 1848, containing the first news of the gold discovery to reach the East.

The gold rush had as devastating an effect upon travel over the Old Spanish Trail as the impost on merchandise. The distance was too great, and the route too rugged for the passage of wagons. Most of the Argonauts from the northern states followed the Oregon Trail across the Rockies, and the Humboldt River route to California. Those from the southern states chose the Cooke wagon road over the Gila route, and most of the Old Spanish Trail fell into disuse.

In 1847 the first Mormon settlers arrived at Great Salt Lake, and the Mormon Battalion reached California. Soon after the passing of the 1848 caravan, the Mormons took a wagon over the Old Spanish Trail from the vicinity of Little Salt Lake to Los Angeles. Gradually the wagon route was improved and extended northward to Salt Lake City, and for nearly a quarter of a century remained the most important thoroughfare in the far Southwest. But the name of Old Spanish Trail was relegated to history; the wagon road was known as The Mormon Trail. It, too, has passed into oblivion, though its route is fairly closely paralleled by U.S. Highway 91 and the Union Pacific Railroad, while high above roar jet liners on the Los Angeles-Salt Lake flyway.

5

The Santa Fe Trail

EXPLORERS, TRAPPERS, AND TRADERS

The Santa Fe Trail is famous as the first American thoroughfare west of the Missouri River. But like all other trails over which the westward expansion was made, it was simply a route. Its course followed a multiplicity of age-old Indian trails westward along the Kansas, Smoky Hill, and Arkansas rivers. It is generally believed that Santa Fe was the first trading center in the Rockies, but this is a mistake. Taos Pueblo, seventy-five miles to the north, had been an important trading center for generations before the Spaniards arrived. There the Utes brought their Digger Indian slaves, and in coming to trade for them, the plains Indians wore deep trails between the Arkansas River and the Rio Grande. One of these ancient routes became the western section of the Santa Fe Trail.

Just as England taxed the Bostonians' tea, Spain taxed her colonists on all merchandise brought into her territories. She was extremely jealous of the trade and ruthless in her taxation. Goods from the United States were allowed to enter Mexico only through the port of Veracruz, and to reach Santa Fe this merchandise had to be transported two thousand miles on pack mules. The cost of transportation, the tax, and the Spanish merchants' unreasonable profits, resulted in fantastic selling prices. For instance, calico costing a few cents a yard in Boston, sold in Santa Fe for anywhere from two to three dollars a yard.

Zebulon Pike was the first American to bring back word of the exorbitant Santa Fe prices. In 1806 the United States Government sent him to explore the Louisiana Purchase, the western boundary of which was clearly stated to be the Continental Divide, but the southern boundary was indefinite, and Spain claimed it to be the Arkansas River. Pike followed the Arkansas into the foothills of the Rockies, then turned southward to the headwaters of the Rio Grande, where the Spanish arrested him as a spy invading their territory. They held him prisoner for a few days at Santa Fe, then sent him to Chihuahua for trial. Pike was not ill-treated, but following his exploration Americans were looked upon with suspicion by the Spanish Government.

It was 1807 before Pike was released, and probably several years later before the news he had brought trickled westward from Washington to Missouri. At the frontier town of Franklin, the most westerly American settlement, Robert McKnight and his brothers had a trading post where they carried on a thriving business with the Indians. When Robert heard of the fabulous prices goods were bringing in Santa Fe, he decided to go there with a merchandise caravan, and convinced James Baird and William Chambers to join him in the venture. They set out in April, 1812, with seven men and a small train of pack mules. Since they were using Pike's report as a guide, it is probable that they traveled along the Arkansas nearly to the present site of Pueblo, Colorado, then followed the age-old Indian trail up Huerfano Creek to the summit of the Sangre de Cristo range, and down the Rio Grande to Taos and Santa Fe. Upon reaching Santa Fe they were arrested, their stock of merchandise and mules confiscated, and they were sent to prison at Chihuahua, where they were held until Mexico won its independence in 1821.

By the time McKnight set out on his disastrous trading trip Pike's report of the great buffalo herds on the Kansas prairies had spurred parties of frontier huntsmen to push westward. One of these was led by Joseph Philibert. In the spring of 1814 he left St. Louis with eight or ten mounted hunters leading pack horses. They rode up the Missouri to its northward turn, then followed old trails leading more directly to the great bend of the Arkansas than those along the Kansas and Smoky Hill rivers. Hunting westward along the Arkansas, they reached the foothills of the Rockies in late fall, their supplies running low, and their pack horses loaded with buffalo robes. In order to make an early hunt the following spring, Philibert decided to leave

[183]

most of his men in camp at the mouth of Huerfano Creek while he
returned to St. Louis with the robes and brought back supplies, together with bright colored cloth and trinkets for trading with the
Indians.

Philibert made his return journey without difficulty, and disposed
of his robes to the Chouteau Brothers fur-trading firm. Auguste
Pierre Chouteau, one of the younger brothers, was much impressed
by the size and value of the robe packs, and proposed that he, Jules
De Mun, and Philibert join forces and organize a much larger hunting
and trapping expedition. The agreement was made, and in the spring
of 1815 the party marched westward along the Arkansas. When they
reached Huerfano Creek they found the camp of the previous fall
deserted, and learned from nearby Indians that the men had been
forced by starvation to make their way to Taos.

Knowing of McKnight's imprisonment, Philibert and Chouteau
were afraid to take their costly pack train into Spanish territory. Instead, they sent De Mun with an Indian guide to reach Taos and
discover the fate of the men. He found that they had passed the
winter in comfort, being fed and treated hospitably by the Pueblo
Indians and the few Mexicans living in the settlement. For some
unimaginable reason, De Mun decided to continue on to Santa Fe and

explain to the Spanish Governor the cause of their being in his territory. To his surprise, Governor Mainez received him with courtesy, and raised no objection to the American hunters having come into Spanish territory. Much relieved, De Mun gathered up the men at Taos and returned to his partners on the Arkansas, unwittingly setting the stage for American invasion of the Southwest.

Great buffalo herds covered the prairies that stretched northward from the Arkansas, but the creeks and rivers flowing into it from the Sangre de Cristo Mountains to the south were teeming with beaver, and Auguste Chouteau was wise in the ways of the fur business. Either a well-dressed buffalo robe or beaver pelt would bring six dollars on the St. Louis market, and one robe was as bulky to transport as a score of beaver pelts. The Philibert-Chouteau party began working its way up Huerfano Creek, trapping beaver as it went. The trapping was excellent. After reaching the summit of the Sangre de Cristos, the trappers sampled the headwaters of the Rio Grande enough to find that they were alive with beaver, then went on to Taos, where the men probably did a little bragging to their Mexican friends of the previous winter. After a hearty welcome they crossed the range again, and began trapping the headwaters of the Purgatoire River, dropping back to Taos whenever they found themselves running short of supplies.

By fall the beaver packs were bulging, and worth more than $30,-000, but unfortunately affable Governor Mainez had been replaced by the American-hating Pedro Maria de Allande. On the trappers' next visit to Taos they were arrested, their fur packs, horses, traps and guns confiscated, and they were thrown in the *calabozo*. After forty days of being threatened by the Governor that they were to be shot as spies, they were turned loose, given a horse apiece, and told to get out. De Mun and Philibert returned to St. Louis, but Chouteau remained in Kansas to become an important figure in the history of both the Santa Fe and Overland trails.

For six years following the Philibert-Chouteau confiscation American frontiersmen continued hunting along the western reaches of the Arkansas. Although they knew a fortune in beaver pelts to be in the mountain streams to the south, they kept to the north side of the river, and developed a trade more profitable than buffalo hunting. Mules were scarce and high priced in Missouri, but the Mexicans along the Rio Grande had plenty, and Indians were never averse to stealing. As soon as they discovered that American hunters would exchange trinkets and bright cloth for mules, they raided the Mexican herds mercilessly, drove the stolen animals to the north bank of the Arkansas, and traded them to whichever hunter would give them the most cloth and trinkets.

FATHER OF THE SANTA FE TRAIL

In the late summer of 1821, William Becknell of Franklin put a notice in the *Missouri Intelligencer* that he was making up a party to go "westward for the purpose of trading for horses and mules and catching wild animals of every description." On September 1, his party crossed the Missouri and set out along the now well-traveled route to the Great Bend of the Arkansas, each leading a pack horse loaded with the sort of merchandise for which Indians liked to trade. It was late in the season for trading, the Indians had disposed of all their stolen stock, and were hunting in Spanish territory, so the Becknell party reached the present location of La Junta, Colorado, without having done any business. In desperation, Becknell turned southward and followed an age-old Indian trail up Timpas Creek, across Raton Pass, and down to the headwaters of the Canadian River near present-day Maxwell, New Mexico. The next day the traders were surprised by a small troop of Mexican soldiers, and fully expected to be arrested. But the soldiers were delighted to see them, told them that Mexico had won its independence, that the Spanish Governor was gone, and urged them to take their goods to Santa Fe. Becknell reached the pueblo on November 16, opened a caravan trade that was to continue for more than forty years, and earned the title of "Father of the Santa Fe Trail."

Although the merchandise Becknell and his associates had brought was intended for trade with the Indians, it sold quickly at tremendous profit, and the payment was made in Spanish silver dollars. Most of the men decided to spend the winter in Santa Fe—and their easy profits on the Mexican *señoritas*. But Becknell and a man named McLaughlin loaded their saddle bags with silver and hurried back to Franklin, reaching that little frontier town on January 29, 1822. As an indication of the profit made, Fanny Marshall had lent her brother sixty dollars toward the amount necessary to buy his pack

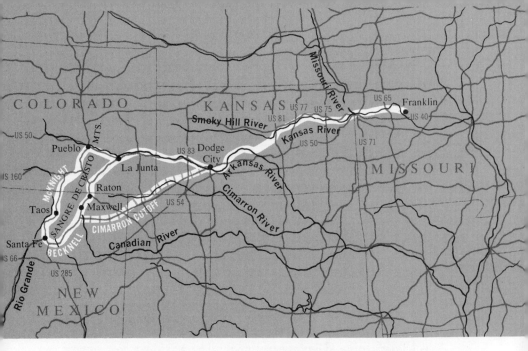

The Santa Fe Trail: routes of Robert McKnight and William Becknell. Becknell opened trade to Santa Fe and then pioneered the Cimarron Cutoff, taking the first wagons over the trail. He was called "Father of the Santa Fe Trail."

horse and trade goods; she received nine hundred dollars as her share of the profits.

News that New Mexico was open to the Americans spread like a contagion along the frontier, and from far and near traders and trappers began gathering at Franklin. The trappers were for the most part the rough, tough soldiers of fortune who, as the mountain men, were to push the American frontier westward to the Pacific. The traders were men who had made their living by trading with the Indians along the Mississippi and Missouri, none of them having more than a few horses, a few packs of cheap merchandise, and a few dollars. Although Becknell's percentage of profit on his 1821 venture had been great, only a small amount of the goods had been his, so he was unable to finance as large a caravan as he wanted to take to Santa Fe in 1822. Consequently, he joined forces with other small merchants who were anxious to get into the Santa Fe trade.

[187]

Becknell's caravan, numbering twenty-one men, left Arrow Rock, across the Missouri from Franklin, on May 22. There is no record of the value of the caravan's cargo, how many pack horses there may have been, or how many of the men were financially interested in the venture. But it was the most important caravan ever to move over the Santa Fe Trail, for Becknell and two of his associates took their merchandise on wagons, the first to roll westward from the Missouri. It is quite likely that all the men not financially interested were trappers, for it is known that Ewing Young was among them.

Except for spring mud along the Missouri, the Becknell party had no trouble until it reached eastern Kansas, and the men were allowed to string out when a halt was necessary for pulling a wagon out of a mud hole. Not long after leaving the river, two of the men were riding far out in front when they were surprised by a small band of Osage Indians. They were severely beaten, robbed of their horses, guns, and clothing, and carried off to the Indian village. But, fortunately, Auguste Chouteau had established a trading post among the Osages, and was present when the captives were brought into the village. He at once secured their release, had their property given back, and accompanied them to the caravan. The incident was slight, but had great influence upon the manner in which caravans were conducted on the trail. Thereafter, a captain was appointed for each party, no spreading out was permitted, and guards were posted during the nights.

Mud, thickets, and flooded creeks were troublesome to the Becknell party in Missouri and eastern Kansas. Farther west the country became treeless prairie, somewhat hilly at first, then rising gradually and flattening out into great plains of short grass. There was abundant grazing for the animals, and wagon wheels rolled as easily as upon a roadway, the only difficulty being the necessity of cutting down a few steep creek banks.

Becknell followed the usual route through central Kansas to the great bend of the Arkansas, then continued southwest along the river to a point about five miles beyond where Dodge City now stands. It is known that he had hunted and traded with Indians in the area for several years, and he may have learned from them of the Cimarron River, farther to the south. The Cimarron rises just below the Colorado-New Mexico boundary, and flows eastward through the panhandle of Oklahoma nearly to the corner of Kansas. There it turns to the northeast and, like the Arkansas, forms a great bend, the apex of which is fifty miles to the southwest of Dodge City.

Whether or not Becknell had knowledge of the Cimarron, he did know that it would be almost impossible to get his wagons over Raton Pass, and that he could save about a hundred miles of travel if he could discover a direct route across the deserts to Santa Fe. Choosing a place where the Arkansas was more than a quarter mile wide but only three or four feet deep, he made his crossing and struck off to the southwest, with no landmarks and only a pocket compass by which to set his course. The only water carried was in the men's canteens, heat waves shimmered above the scorched land, and in sandy places the wagon wheels cut deeply, slowing progress and wearing down the mules. Becknell sent scouts far out ahead and to either side, but no sign of water was found, and in all directions flat semibarren land stretched away to the horizon. Before evening of the first day the canteens were empty and the wagon mules beginning to give out from heat and hard pulling.

Becknell went on through the night, setting his course by the north star and keeping the men afoot to save the horses and mules as much as possible. By noon of the second day the caravan was barely crawling, with horses, mules, and men nearing the point of complete exhaustion from heat and thirst. As the afternoon dragged on one animal after another fell and was unable to rise. The men bled them, drank the blood, and staggered on. When they had nearly lost hope and two or three men had fallen out, a lone buffalo was seen coming from the east. As he approached the men went wild with excitement; his belly was distended with water, and there was mud, not yet entirely dry, on his legs. He was shot, slimy water from his paunch drunk greedily by the men still able to keep their feet, and a canteen of it taken back to those who had fallen.

Becknell had set his course amazingly well, for when the buffalo's track was followed back it led, within a few miles, to the bend of the Cimarron. With water reached, the worst of the hardship was past, for the river led in an almost straight line toward Santa Fe for a distance of ninety miles. Although it, like many desert streams, was often dry in summer, water could usually be found by digging into the sandy bed. Between the headwaters of the Cimarron and the Canadian rivers lay another sixty-mile stretch of arid desert, but crossed by a few creek beds in which water could be found by digging. Becknell turned southward beyond the Canadian, picked up his trail of the previous year, and followed it around the southern end of the Sange de Cristo Mountains to Santa Fe, having traveled 870 miles since leaving Franklin.

Sources vary widely as to the value of merchandise carried by the Becknell caravan of 1822, but it was sold at an enormous profit, and Becknell returned to Franklin by the route he had blazed, which was thereafter known as the Cimarron Cutoff.

Another party to set out for the Santa Fe trade in 1822 left its mark on the trail. When, after nine years' imprisonment, Robert McKnight and his men were released, McKnight remained in New Mexico, and for some years operated the copper mines near the headwaters of the Gila River. But James Baird and William Chambers returned to St. Louis. Baird was successful in persuading some merchants to finance them in a trading venture, but it was fall before they had gathered their stock of goods and pack animals at Franklin. Prudent men would have waited until spring, but Baird and Chambers were greedy for the huge profit that could be made if they reached Santa Fe by Christmas, so set out at once.

They had reached the point where Becknell had crossed the Arkansas when they were caught in a raging blizzard. Unable to travel, they made camp on a small island in the river, where they could best protect themselves from Indian attacks, but their pack animals wandered away and died. Being rugged frontiersmen, Baird and Chambers managed to keep alive until spring. As soon as the ground thawed, they dug deep holes on the island, lined them with grass, cached their merchandise packs, tramped the dirt firmly over them, and built fires so that ashes would hide signs of their digging from the Indians. Making their way afoot to Taos, they secured pack mules, returned, dug up their packs, and went on to Santa Fe. For more than twenty years the holes remained visible from the bank of the river, marked the crossing place for the Cimarron Cutoff, and was known as The Caches.

Except for Baird and Chambers, there is record of only one caravan reaching Santa Fe in 1823. This was a cooperative venture led by Stephen Cooper and is of importance for two reasons. When he returned to Franklin in October he not only brought the first fur packs shipped over the Santa Fe Trail, but four hundred mules, jennies, and the Spanish jacks that sired the first Missouri mules.

Along the Santa Fe Trail, as elsewhere throughout the West, the Indians were friendly until the white men taught them to be otherwise. The early hunters in southwestern Kansas encouraged the Indians to steal horses and mules from the Spaniards, and to trade a whole herd for a ten-dollar pack of trinkets and bright calico. The Indians soon learned that it was easier to waylay a small party and take the packs than to make the long journey into New Mexico and steal mules to trade for them. The beaver trappers who went over the Santa Fe Trail with the earliest traders were tough, ruthless frontiersmen, many of whom believed the only good Indian to be a dead one. On their way to the mountains they made many a good Indian, and made the Cheyennes, Comanches, and Kiowas the dreaded enemies of the traders.

By 1824 Auguste Chouteau had, through understanding and honest dealing, won the confidence and control of the Osage Indians along

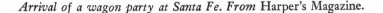

Arrival of a wagon party at Santa Fe. From Harper's Magazine.

the Missouri Valley section of the trail, but on the prairies of Kansas and the deserts of New Mexico no small party was safe from attack. As a result, it became necesssary for small merchants wishing to enter the Santa Fe trade to join together in large well-armed caravans.

On April 1, 1824, a meeting was held in Franklin for the purpose of organizing a Santa Fe caravan. It was not to be a cooperative venture. Each trader was to supply his own merchandise, pack animals or vehicles, and a guard for each eight animals or two wagons. The rendezvous was to be on May 5, and each man was to come equipped with a good rifle, a pistol, four pounds of powder, eight pounds of lead, and twenty days' provisions. Although the journey was expected to require ten to twelve weeks, buffalo meat would furnish most of the rations as soon as the plains were reached.

It was May 16 before the caravan set out, consisting of eighty-one men, one hundred and fifty-six horses and mules, twenty-five vehicles, and a small wheeled cannon for frightening away the Indians. Among the traders were M. M. Marmaduke who later became the Governor of Missouri, and Augustus Storrs who was appointed consul to Santa Fe in 1825. It is estimated that the total investment in merchandise was thirty-five thousand dollars. The caravan followed the Cimarron Cutoff route and reached Santa Fe on July 28. The merchandise, consisting mostly of cotton goods, a few woolens, small tools, needles, thread, buttons, trinkets, etc., was quickly sold at a profit of better than one hundred and fifty-five thousand dollars. With one hundred and eighty thousand dollars in silver and gold, and fur packs worth ten thousand dollars, the traders hurried back to Franklin in less than sixty days. Marmaduke and Storrs, both influential men in Missouri, rushed news of the fabulous profit to Senator Benton in Washington. It soon spread throughout the United States, making Missouri the most popular state on the frontier.

Thomas Hart Benton was the most rabid expansionist in the Senate. In the Santa Fe trade he saw not only an opportunity to push the boundaries of the United States westward, but an excellent opportunity to expand the population, commerce, and wealth of his own state. At Benton's request, Augustus Storrs prepared a statement of the "origin, present state, and future prospects of trade and intercourse between Missouri and the Internal Provinces of Mexico." The report would have done justice to a Madison Avenue copywriter. After delineating the course of the trail, Storrs noted that, "The face of the country, through which the route passes, is open, level, and free to the base of the Rocky Mountains . . . there is not a single hill of consequence, or which presents difficulties to the progress of a wagon." He wrote of the "high and perfectly level plain to the Semarone," but avoided mentioning the lack of water. After recommending that a road be surveyed at Government expense, he suggested that peace treaties be negotiated with the nine Indian tribes through whose hunting grounds the trail passed.

Benton at once proposed a bill for building a road from the Missouri to the point of the Cimarron Cutoff on the Arkansas. From there to Santa Fe and Taos, with the approval of the Mexican Government, the best possible route was to be surveyed and markers set up. The bill passed both houses of Congress, and was signed by President Monroe two days before the expiration of his term. It carried an appropriation of thirty thousand dollars; ten thousand dollars for surveying and establishing the road, and twenty thousand dollars for buying rights of way from the Indians. Upon taking office, President Adams promptly appointed a Road Committee, including the Lieutenant Governors of Missouri and Illinois, and named Joseph Brown as surveyor.

When, on July 4, 1825, the surveying party set out from Franklin there was a great celebration—the most valuable part of the entire project. There was, of course, no actual intention of building a road. Brown's function was simply to discover, survey, and mark the most feasible wagon route to Taos and Santa Fe. He did his work as well as he could under the circumstances, finding the most practicable places for fording streams, describing the best possible line of travel from one ford to another, and marking the course with mounds of earth, since there were no stones on the prairies. Unfortunately, his detailed descriptions of the route were tucked away in some pigeon-hole at Washington and lost for a generation, and within a year the wind had blown away the mounds of earth with which he had marked the trail.

The survey was barely started before the commissioners set out to pay twenty thousand dollars for the rights of way from the Indians. On August 10 they made a treaty with the chief of Auguste Chouteau's peaceful Osages at a beautiful grove, a hundred and forty miles southwest of present Kansas City. The commissoners promised the chief eight hundred dollars in merchandise for perpetual safe passage through his hunting grounds, and in honor of the occasion named the meeting place Council Grove. Fifty-five miles farther to the south-west they made a like treaty with the friendly Kansas Indians, then found a good excuse for turning back without visiting the dangerous prairie tribes: these people were nomadic, hunting over a vast area on both sides of the Arkansas, so it would be impossible to prove whether they were under the jurisdiction of the United States or Mexico, and it would be improper to make an American treaty with Mexican Indians. The only result of the commission's activity was the establishment of Council Grove as the great rendezvous point for caravans moving westward over the Santa Fe Trail.

The 1825 caravan was much like that of 1824, except that double the amount of merchandise was taken to Santa Fe, and the profit was far less than that of the previous year. The Mexican Government required an import tax equal to sixty percent of the cost of the goods to be paid before the merchandise could be sold. This drove out some of the smaller merchants, but those who continued in the trade in-creased the amount of goods taken, so as to maintain their profit level in spite of the tax. In 1824 eighty traders had carried goods which cost no more than thirty-five thousand dollars. In 1826 seventy traders carried goods costing ninety thousand dollars. In 1827 the number dropped to fifty with an equal amount of merchandise.

At the time Becknell set out on his first trading trip to Santa Fe, Franklin was the most westerly town on the American frontier, but as the trade increased towns sprang up farther along the river, and in 1825 the first settlers arrived at Independence. During the next few years small caravans started out from various river ports early in May, traveled separately through the peaceful land of the Osage Indians, and met for rendezvous at Council Grove.

There, for mutual protection against the fierce prairie tribes, a single annual caravan was organized, and a captain chosen by vote of all the men, whether independent traders or hired hands. The captain appointed a wagon boss, a pack train boss, a chief scout, lieu-tenants for the various divisions, and a wrangler for the loose stock that was always driven along for replacements. Rules were laid down, the position of each division of the caravan set, and each man as-signed his hours for night guard duty. Westward from Council Grove, the caravans usually traveled in three or four parallel col-umns, since there was no roadway and compactness made them more easily defensible. At night the wagons, carts, and carriages were formed in a square, pack animals unloaded, and the packs stacked up to form a breastwork in case of Indian attack. In the late afternoon and early evening the stock was grazed as far out as a mile from the camp, but as darkness fell it was brought in, corralled inside the square for the night, or picketed close at hand to avoid possibility of a stampede by the Indians.

When Santa Fe was reached the caravans split up, some traders selling their merchandise from their wagons or packs, some renting little adobe buildings where they could set up shop, and some operating from corrals. For a few years following the imposition of the import tax the shrewder merchants preferred to trade their goods for horses and mules, since an animal costing fifteen or twenty dollars in Santa Fe would bring upwards of a hundred in Missouri. Because of this method of operation, all the traders were seldom ready to return at the same time. For this reason the caravans usually returned to Missouri in two or more divisions, fur packs and Mexican silver being carried in the otherwise empty wagons, and the herd driven along behind.

In August, 1828, the advance division started homeward across the New Mexico deserts, some fifty or sixty men driving a herd of a thousand horses and mules behind a dozen or so wagons. The heat was almost intolerable, there was no breeze, and the dust rising from four thousand shuffling hoofs was so thick that a man could scarcely see a hundred feet ahead. As the party reached what is now the western end of the Oklahoma Panhandle, Daniel Munroe and a young man named McNees rode far ahead to find water. They found it in a little nameless creek, drank heartily, lay down on the bank, and went to sleep. When the caravan came up, McNees was dead and Munroe dying. Tracks showed that a small band of Indians had surprised them in their sleep, and shot them with their own guns. In panic, the traders scooped out a shallow grave in the sand, buried McNees, loaded Munroe onto one of the wagons, and pushed on as rapidly as the straggling herd could be driven.

By the time the Cimarron was reached, Munroe had died, and a stop was made for burying his body. It had barely been covered when six or seven Comanches rode into sight on the far side of the river. These certainly were not the Indians who had killed Munroe and McNees, or they would not have approached a force of fifty or more heavily armed white men without apparent fear. But the white men were both panicked and angry. As soon as the Indians came within range they were met with a fusillade of gunfire. Only one of them escaped to take word of the massacre back to their camp. Soon shrieking Comanches raced their ponies into the valley from all directions. The band was not large enough to give battle to so strong a force of white men, but in true Comanche fashion it circled the caravan, shrieking, yelling, and waving blankets until it had stampeded and driven away almost the entire herd of a thousand horses and mules.

Two weeks later the second division reached the Cimarron, made up mostly of traders who had sold their goods for silver. Somewhat more than fifty thousand Mexican silver dollars were being transported in four or five wagons, behind which twenty-five men drove a herd of a hundred and fifty choice Mexican mules and horses. The Comanches had evidently been watching the progress of the party across the deserts, and had set an ambush for it at the location of the massacre. Although far outnumbered by the Indians, the little caravan was able to break out of the ambush, though the captain was killed and scalped.

The Comanches, like most other plains Indians, had no taste for open battle with well-armed white men, but they were superb horsemen, and harried their less skillful white enemies as wolf packs harried the buffalo herds. Across the Oklahoma Panhandle the Indians kept up a continual harassment, staying just out of gunshot in daylight, then sneaking in at night to stampede and drive away stock. By the time the corner of Kansas was reached, every horse and mule had been driven away. During daylight the traders stood off the Comanches by forting up in the wagons, but they were cut off from water and there was no possibility of holding out. When darkness fell they sneaked away to the north, each man carrying a little food and about a thousand silver dollars.

The Comanches evidently believed that it was only necessary to keep the white men from reaching water at the Cimarron, and that if they tried to escape to the north they would die of thirst before reaching the Arkansas. In any event, the men were not molested as they crept away. Staggering on without sleep or water for forty-eight hours, they made their way straight northward, reaching the Arkansas at Chouteau's Island, near the present Colorado-Kansas boundary. There was no possibility of carrying the silver any farther, so they cached it on the island and set out on the four-hundred-mile walk to Independence.

Until the bend of the Arkansas was passed the party had no great difficulty, for there was plenty of buffalo, no Indians were encountered, and the fall weather remained mild. Beyond the bend there were no buffalo, game became scarce, and the weather turned cold and stormy. Long before reaching the Missouri the men were nearing the point of starvation, and the less rugged became too weak to carry their firearms. East of Council Grove the five strongest went ahead to seek help, but found none until within fifteen miles of Independence. As rescuers hurried back along the trail they found exhausted men strung out for a distance of fifty miles, one of them blinded by starvation and fighting off wolves with a stick.

Several of the merchants who had suffered at the hands of the Comanches were influential men in Missouri, and when they returned, robbed and half-dead, immediate demands were made for military protection of travelers on the Santa Fe Trail. Benton delivered hours of oratory in the Senate, and when, on March 4, 1829, Andrew Jackson was inaugurated President, he directed that four companies of soldiers be assigned. The troops were to escort a caravan from the Missouri to the Mexican border beyond the bend of the Arkansas each spring, wait for it there, and escort it back in the fall.

There were two great faults in the plan. First, the Comanche attacks had taken place in territory claimed by Mexico, and it well might be considered an act of aggression if American troops crossed the Arkansas without permission from the Mexican Government. Secondly, the troops assigned were infantry, since there was yet no cavalry in the United States Army, and foot soldiers would have little chance in battle against mounted Indian warriors.

Most of the Missouri merchants decided that, considering the import tax, the inadequacy of military protection, and the growing hostility of the Indians, the risks of the Santa Fe trade were greater than any possibility of large profits. In 1829 the number of traders who joined the spring caravan dropped from eighty to twenty, but among them were the Bent brothers, whose names would be linked inseparably with the history of the Santa Fe Trail.

The first American beaver trapping expeditions went into the Rocky Mountains the year after Becknell's opening of the Santa Fe trade. That year General Ashley sent his famous party including Jedediah Smith, Tom Fitzpatrick, and Jim Bridger into the northern Rockies. Among the early trapper captains going over the Santa Fe Trail, all of whom made Taos their headquarters, were Ewing Young, Joe Walker, Old Bill Williams, and Ceran St. Vrain—son of one of the leading French fur-trading families of St. Louis.

THE BENT BROTHERS

For several years before the Ashley expedition, the Missouri Fur Company had been trading for pelts with the Indians, far up the Missouri. Among its members was twenty-one-year-old Charles Bent, the highly intelligent son of a St. Louis judge, a fearless pioneer, and contented only in the wilds of the frontier. He was small, black-haired, and though a descendant of the Massachusetts Pilgrims, so dark skinned that he was usually mistaken for a French Canadian, whose language, together with several Indian dialects, he spoke fluently. The trappers' coming to the mountains seriously curtailed fur trade with the Indians, and shortly before Ashley sold out to Smith, Sublette, and Jackson the Missouri Fur Company failed. Charles Bent and Joshua Pilcher then organized their own trapping party, and Charles was joined by his teen-aged brother William, also a natural frontiersman with amazing ability to learn the languages and win the confidence of Indians.

In the severe winter of 1827-28 the Pilcher-Bent party lost all its horses in a blizzard, was obliged to cache its packs, and encamped on the Green River in western Wyoming. In the same camp there was a party led by Ceran St. Vrain, which had also lost its horses in the blizzard. It is quite probable that during the winter encampment Charles Bent and St. Vrain laid plans to quit trapping and go into the Santa Fe trade. In any case, St. Vrain returned to Taos in the fall of 1828, and the Bent brothers to St. Louis. There the brothers disposed of their furs, bought trade goods, wagons and mules, and arrived at Independence on or about William Bent's twentieth birthday to join the 1829 Santa Fe caravan.

One by one the other eighteen traders arrived until, at the end of May, thirty-eight wagons, loaded with merchandise costing sixty thousand dollars, surrounded the few log cabins and warehouses of Independence. In all, there were seventy-nine men, including several who had survived the tragedy of the previous fall and cached their silver on Chouteau's Island. At the election Charles Bent, a natural leader, was unanimously chosen captain of the caravan.

The wagons had been ready to roll for more than a week before the promised escort of two hundred soldiers arrived from Fort Leavenworth. It was led by Major Riley, and second in command was Philip St. George Cooke, then only a second lieutenant two years out of West Point. The delay had been caused by Major Riley's mistake of crossing the Missouri and getting his little army mired in the bogs along the eastern bank. The traders were thoroughly disgusted, and several threatened to abandon the caravan, for the escort appeared to be more of a hindrance than a protection: not only were the infantrymen the riffraff of the frontier, commanded by an officer who knew no better than to lead them into swamps, but their supply wagons were being drawn by slow moving oxen. The next morning, however, the caravan rolled out onto the long trail. In the lead rode Major Riley, followed by the infantry, the ox-drawn supply wagons, the mule-drawn traders' wagons, and a wrangler driving the loose stock.

Presumably some of the disgruntled traders had made it evident to Riley that they considered his escort a hindrance rather than a protection. Otherwise, there can be little excuse for his conduct. From the outset it became apparent that the slow-footed oxen would have no difficulty in keeping ahead of the fast-stepping mules, for the mules had to be rested after each hard pull, while the oxen continued to plod on. No doubt in an attempt to strike back, Riley pulled away from the traders' wagons enough that by the time Council Grove was reached the night camps of the soldiers and merchants were several miles apart. Charles Bent protested, but since he had no authority over the escort, he could only push the traders' division of the caravan along as rapidly as possible.

All went well through the hunting grounds of the friendly Osages, and for a short distance beyond Council Grove. Then one morning, from long experience gained in the mountains, Charles Bent recognized the first sign of hostile Indians. He galloped his horse to the soldiers' camp to warn the less experienced Riley, but the warning was too late. During the night Indians had stampeded the few horses brought along as officers' mounts, and driven six of them away. The major had scattered his infantrymen far and wide to run down the thieves, but not so much as a hoof mark had been found. The experience was well worth the few horses, for Bent had little trouble in convincing Riley that all the wagons should roll in a compact column, and that the place for infantrymen was at the front and rear of the column.

In addition, Charles Bent learned a lesson that would set the pattern for a great deal of the future travel throughout the West: oxen could not only out-travel mules in rough country, but also were evidently safe from Indian raids. Since no attempt had been made to steal Riley's oxen, Bent reasoned that plains Indians preferred buffalo meat, and would be tempted to steal only such animals as could be stampeded and driven away at high speed. He determined to try oxen in the Santa Fe trade. Before many years had passed they outnumbered mules better than four to one, and continued to do so throughout the early settlement of the West.

With the caravan united, no further Indian trouble was encountered along the Arkansas. At The Caches, Charles Bent prepared for the crossing, while Major Riley chose a camp site for awaiting the fall return. But the traders who had originally railed loudest against the escort lost their courage, and demanded that it remain with the caravan across the Cimarron Desert. When Riley refused, stating that he had no authority to enter Mexican territory, they insisted on continuing along the north bank of the Arkansas to Chouteau's Island. Bent was unable to dissuade them by pointing out that such a course would lengthen the journey by at least two days, and that if the Comanches intended an attack the place of crossing would make no difference.

On July 10, Chouteau's Island was reached, the owners retrieved the thirty-odd thousand silver dollars cached there the preceding fall, and again the timid refused to cross into Mexican territory without the escort. Again Riley refused, but agreed to let the caravan take along a small cannon. With it to give the frightened traders a spark of courage, Bent persuaded them to continue.

The route Becknell had pioneered across the flat plain between the Arkansas and Cimarron was bad enough, but the crossing from Chouteau's Island was infinitely worse. The river flowed through shifting channels, over hidden potholes and beds of quicksand, and the land stretched away to the southward in a series of rolling sand hills and gullies. A full day of back-breaking, mule-killing labor was required to get the thirty-eight wagons across. Next morning the start was made for the Cimarron; every barrel, keg, and canteen filled with water. By late afternoon only nine miles had been traveled, and the caravan was toiling through a circular basin, toward a narrow gulch at its south end. In this dangerous situation Charles Bent kept the wagons as closely together as possible and sent three men to scout the gulch ahead, one beyond the east rim of the basin, and his brother William to the west.

William Bent was riding a mule that had been bought at Independence. Its slit ears showed it to have once been in the hands of the Comanches, and no mule passed through their hands without learning to hate them. With nothing but rolling sand hills visible in any direction, the plodding mule suddenly raised his head, swung his muzzle toward the west, and snorted. He could not have told young Bent a clearer story. There were Comanches to the west, and since there was no breeze to bring their scent from that direction they were close at hand.

Shouting and firing his rifle as a warning to the caravan, William set spurs to his mule barely before the Comanche war shriek rose from a gully less than a hundred yards to his right. Within moments scores of racing ponies boiled into sight, naked warriors lying flat against their necks, howling and letting fly a storm of arrows.

In the basin Jacob Coates and Bill Waldo, both veteran frontiersmen, raced their horses up the rim toward the sound. As they came over the edge the Indians swerved aside momentarily, unable to believe that any but a strong party would charge out to meet them. Instantly another wildly yelling band swept into the far end of the gulch. Instead of holding their ground, the men who had been sent to scout ahead whirled and raced for the wagons. The two on fast horses escaped, but Samuel Lamme, on a stiff-legged mule, fell behind and was riddled with arrows. His body had hardly hit the ground before half a dozen warriors were on top of it, stripping away his scalp. Then the two bands joined and raced shrieking toward the caravan.

Almost without exception, the traders panicked, but the Bent brothers knew the Indian aversion for charging into rifle fire. Shouting for the teamsters to pull their wagons into a circle, Charles and William leaped to the ground and ran toward the oncoming Indians, yelling the mountain men's battle cry. They were followed by eight or ten frontiersmen guards, firing and reloading as they ran. The show of fight was enough to turn the attack. The Comanches swung wide and circled the basin, howling like wolves in an attempt to stampede the mules, taunting, and waving Lamme's bloody scalp. While William and the few who had courage enough to join him held the Indians off, Charles managed to get the wagons pulled into a tight circle, with the draft mules and loose stock inside.

When trenches had been dug and breastworks thrown up, William and the frontiersmen backed toward the crude fortification, and the Comanches closed their circle tighter, slowing their ponies to the tireless lope of a prairie mustang. The pattern was a familiar one to men who had fought the Indians of the plains. The Comanches knew the range of muzzle-loading rifles, were circling just beyond it, and would keep up their siege until their ring was broken or thirst had won the battle for them.

Although the Indians of the Great Plains had relatively few fire-arms by 1829, they and their ponies were sufficiently familiar with rifle fire that, except at close range, they had little fear of it. But cannon fire was entirely unknown to them, and all Indians were inclined to ascribe anything unknown to the supernatural. Aware of this, Charles Bent had the little cannon pointed toward the back trail, loaded it heavily with powder and small shot that would scatter, and called for volunteers to ride for help from the troops. Waiting until deep twilight, he mounted the volunteers on the fastest horses in camp, then touched a spark to the cannon fuse. At the roar a gaping hole was ripped in the Indian circle. Frightened ponies stampeded, bucking and throwing their equally panicked riders, who scrambled to their feet and ran from the roaring demon they could not under-stand. Before the panic was over and the Comanches had returned to continue their siege from a safer distance the volunteers were well on their way to the Arkansas.

By daylight the troops arrived and the Comanches broke their widened circle, but continued their harassment from a greater dis-tance, small parties racing in now and again in an attempt to stampede and scatter the stock. Again the caravan crept southward across the arid desert, with the Comanches following well beyond range of the white men's demon. The water barrels ran dry, the infantrymen staggered as they slogged through the sand, and thirst-crazed horses, mules, and oxen died by the score. At the end of the second day a sinkhole of stagnant water was found, so alkaline from evaporation that putrid minnows floated on the surface.

Riley called a halt and refused to take his troops farther into Mexican territory, and again the timid among the traders balked at going on without an escort, but had little choice. In trying to return to the Arkansas they would almost certainly lose the rest of their animals, then be marooned until the caravan came back in the fall. The upshot was that all the traders went on, while Riley returned to his camp on Chouteau's Island.

The troops had barely turned back before a hundred frightened Mexicans came whipping their jaded burros into the traders' camp. They had been out killing buffalo and drying the meat when attacked by the Comanches who were harassing the caravan. Although the Mexicans were out of ammunition and of no help in holding off the Indians, they knew where water could be found, and a few of the most daring agreed to make a break for Taos.

Day after day the beleaguered caravan crept on, across the wilderness to the Cimarron, through the Oklahoma Panhandle, and out onto the New Mexico deserts. By day the terrified Mexicans flocked around the wagons like sheep and at night crawled beneath them, while the few frontiersmen in the party held the Comanches at bay with rifle fire and an occasional blast from the little cannon.

Meanwhile one of the Mexicans reached Taos with news of the caravan's predicament. St. Vrain and Ewing Young gathered forty trappers, nineteen-year-old Kit Carson among them, and set off immediately across the Sangre de Cristo Mountains and out onto the desert. But the Comanches, gathering strength as the siege continued, now numbered several hundred warriors, and had no intention of letting their rich prize escape. Fighting like demons, they drove the trappers back toward the Sangre de Cristos, while young Carson raced to Taos for reinforcements. Fifty-five men turned out, bringing the number of mountain men to nearly a hundred, a force too formidable for any tribe of bow-and-arrow Indians to withstand. After a short, disastrous skirmish the Comanches retreated, to head back for the Arkansas and harass the less formidable infantrymen.

Out of the rescue of the 1829 caravan grew friendships which were to have an immense effect upon the westward expansion of the United States. Before Santa Fe was reached Charles Bent and Ceran

St. Vrain had formed a partnership which would dominate the commerce between the United States and Mexico, make them the most influential men in New Mexico, and lead to its eventual conquest without the firing of a shot. An equally strong friendship developed between William Bent and Kit Carson, neither yet of age, but destined to have a greater influence than any other two men upon the success of the Santa Fe Trail, the subduing of the plains Indians, and the opening of the West.

Following the rescue in the deserts, the caravan turned aside from the route of previous years. To have the protection of the mountain men it crossed the Sangre de Cristo Range to Taos, opening the first wagon road in the Rocky Mountains, a route which became the Taos branch of the Santa Fe Trail.

At Taos the friends separated, St. Vrain remaining, and Charles Bent going on to Santa Fe with the other traders, over the old Spanish road along the Rio Grande. At the same time Young set off on a beaver-trapping expedition to the Gila River, taking Carson with him as camp boy. William Bent may or may not have gone to Santa Fe with Charles. If so, he soon returned to Taos, for that fall he joined a party of beaver trappers setting out for the headwaters of the Arkansas.

Since the merchandise brought to Santa Fe by the beleaguered caravan of 1829 was less than half the amount brought the previous year, it found a ready market at exorbitant prices, and the profits made by the traders were extraordinary. Furthermore, Charles Bent made a close friend of the *jefe politico* at Santa Fe, and through him secured a force of two hundred Mexican troops to escort the returning wagons back to the Arkansas. The return was made by way of Taos, where St. Vrain and some thirty mountain men joined the caravan to take their fur packs to the St. Louis market.

Again, on the waterless *jornada* between the Cimarron and Chouteau's Island, the caravan was attacked by a band of several hundred Indians, but this time Arapahos instead of Comanches. The poorly armed Mexican troops sallied out for battle, but the Indians drove them back, killing the captain and a few soldiers. At this point the mountain men joined the skirmish and quickly turned it into a rout. They killed a score or more of the attackers, and convinced Charles Bent that mountain men were the only dependable escort for caravans crossing the hunting grounds of plains Indians. His conviction was strengthened when Chouteau's Island was reached. From the time of Riley's return, his camp had been harassed by roving bands of buffalo hunters from all the plains tribes, and at best the infantrymen could only hold them at bay. Four of Riley's men had been killed, numerous wounded, and most of his stock had been killed or driven away. Bent was obliged to lend him mules to get his camp equipment back to Fort Leavenworth.

Following Riley's sad experience the United States Government decided to discontinue escorts on the Santa Fe Trail until such time as mounted troops were available. But in spite of the lack of escort and the danger of Indian attack, sixty traders with seventy wagons and merchandise costing one hundred and twenty thousand dollars joined the 1830 caravan. Prominent among them were Charles Bent and Ceran St. Vrain, and at their insistence eighty rugged frontiersmen and mountain men were taken along as teamsters and guards. This caravan pioneered a new route across the Kansas plains, which thereafter became the mainline of the Cimarron Cutoff. It left the Arkansas seventeen miles beyond the point where Becknell had turned off, and again joined his trail near present Satanta. This route had numerous advantages. Although slightly longer than the Becknell route, there were a few landmarks by which to set a course for the bend of the Cimarron, there was less sand, and the waterless trek was reduced by about a half day's journey. Although several Indian attacks were attempted, each was turned into a rout by the well-mounted frontier guards, and the caravan went through with little difficulty.

The success of the 1830 caravan led to 1831's seeing the greatest traffic on the Santa Fe Trail of the first two decades of its existence, as well as another of the many great tragedies of the early West. That year a quarter of a million dollars' worth of merchandise was freighted over the trail by three hundred and twenty men, more than seventy of them independent traders, and it is probable that oxen were used for the first time for this purpose. The flood of trade goods was so great that the Santa Fe market became glutted, prices dropped to less than half that paid the previous year, and many a trader went back to Missouri without having made his expenses. But the firm of Bent-St. Vrain prospered, sending its wagons down the old Spanish road along the Rio Grande, and as far into Mexico as Chihuahua.

How many separate caravans went over the Santa Fe Trail in 1831 is unknown, but two that left Missouri before that of Bent, St. Vrain & Company made history. In one was Josiah Gregg, who kept a diary and later wrote *Commerce of the Prairies,* an American classic describing the trail and caravan life in passing over it. In the second were four of the most famous mountain men—Jedediah Smith, William Sublette, David Jackson, and Tom Fitzpatrick.

Following the trappers' rendezvous of 1830 Smith, Sublette, and Jackson had sold out to the Rocky Mountain Fur Company, of which Fitzpatrick was a member, probably agreeing to bring supplies for the following season as far as Santa Fe. In any case, the partners entered the Santa Fe trade in 1831. Tom Fitzpatrick met them at Independence, and they set out with a caravan of twenty-three wagons, loaded with trappers' supplies and trade goods. They crossed the Arkansas River near present Fort Dodge, planning to follow Becknell's original Cimarron Cutoff route.

No four men in the world had pioneered more trails through unknown mountains and wildernesses, but they became lost on the flat, arid plain where there were no landmarks. With their water supply gone, mules dying by the score, and men falling in their tracks, Jed Smith and Tom Fitzpatrick rode ahead to find the Cimarron. Fitzpatrick's horse soon gave out and Smith rode on alone. Months later an Indian told the story of his death. A band of shrieking Comanches had surrounded him and panicked his thirst-crazed horse. Before Smith could bring it under control the Indians swarmed in and lanced him to death, but not until he had killed their chief. His grieving companions made their way to Taos, where Fitzpatrick gathered a party of trappers, and headed back into the Rockies. Among the men was Carson, just returned from California with Ewing Young, and soon to become famous throughout the mountains as leader of the Carson Men.

The Bent, St. Vrain & Company caravan went through without trouble. Leaving his partner to dispose of the goods, Charles Bent set out with a few well-mounted frontiersmen for a fast trip back to Missouri. By August he was in St. Louis buying goods, and in early September left Independence with another large caravan, the first ever to be pulled over the Santa Fe Trail entirely by oxen. The year 1831 not only marked the beginning of ox-drawn caravans, but the withdrawal of the peddler merchants from the Santa Fe trade.

Thereafter the commerce was largely on a wholesale basis, with the firm of Bent, St. Vrain & Company dominating the field.

BENT'S FORT AND THE RIVER PORTS

While Charles Bent and Ceran St. Vrain had been establishing themselves as the leading American merchants in northern Mexico, William had been off on a venture of his own. From the time he had first gone to the mountains as a teen-aged boy, his greatest interest had been in Indians, and in dealing with them. The beaver-trapping party he had joined in the fall of 1829 worked the streams flowing into the Arkansas from the Sangre de Cristo and Front ranges of the Rockies, and made its base camp at the present site of Pueblo, Colorado.

Probably in the spring of 1830, William Bent returned to the base camp of the year before, not to trap beaver, but to trade with the plains Indians for buffalo robes. Little is known of his early operations, except that he built a log trading post, his business prospered, and he made a lifelong friend of the Cheyenne chief, Yellow Wolf.

Legend has it that Yellow Wolf urged young Bent to move his trading post seventy-five miles down the Arkansas, to the vicinity of present-day La Junta, since trails of all the prairie tribes crossed there and he would have a larger trade. This may be so, but it is much more probable that William chose the location because it was in the heart of the buffalo hunting area, near the only available timber east of the foothills, and at the point where the old Indian trail that Becknell had originally followed left the Arkansas. There was, however, great danger in such a move, for the location was the traditional battleground of the fiercest prairie tribes—the Comanches, Kiowas, and Jicarilla Apaches from south of the Arkansas; the Cheyennes, Arapahos, and Pawnees from the north. A trading post could be successful there only if strongly fortified and garrisoned.

There has been considerable disagreement among historians as to when Bent's Fort was built, and who its owners were. Recent research makes it almost certain that the original venture was a partnership between the Bent brothers and St. Vrain, though William was the sole operator. The entire plan must have been worked out during the summer of 1832, and it is evident that the Bent brothers had been extremely successful before that time. In November of that year they arrived at Independence with a large drove of Mexican mules, a cargo of silver bullion, and fur packs and buffalo robes reported by the local newspaper to be worth one hundred and ninety thousand dollars. In the spring of 1833 William returned with a caravan of equipment and armament for the fort, and it is known to have been completed in 1834.

Bent's Fort was built on the north side of the Arkansas River, and flew the only American flag west of the Missouri. The main structure was 178 by 137 feet, with solid adobe walls four feet thick and fourteen feet high, the upper portion loopholed for defenders' rifles. Projecting from diagonal corners were turrets, providing a clear view of the outer side of the walls, and enabling defenders to repulse any attempt to scale them. The only entrance was a square tunnel, large enough for a prairie schooner to pass through, and closed at each end by a ponderous plank door armored with heavy sheet-iron. On either side were windows where Indians could come to trade without being admitted to the main fort. Above the tunnel rose a square watchtower, where swivel cannons were mounted, powerful enough to command the river and surrounding prairies for a distance of a mile or more. At the center of the structure there was a great courtyard, with space for a caravan of wagons. Surrounding it were living quarters, kitchens, arsenal, workshops, storage rooms for a hundred tons of buffalo robes and fur packs, and warehouses capable of holding a two years' supply of provisions and trade goods.

William Bent, like Theodore Roosevelt, believed that the best way to avoid war was to "walk softly and carry a big stick." His fort, with seldom less than a hundred defenders, was the stoutest stick west of the Missouri, but he walked softly among the Indians, winning their confidence by honest dealing, marrying a chief's daughter, and continually widening his trade circle. By the time the fort was completed his influence among the plains tribes had become so great that there was never danger of attack.

Becknell's original route had fallen into disuse, as it was impossible to get wagons over it, but during the building of the fort it was cleared and roughly graded into a usable wagon road. Its opening and the establishment of the fort, split travel over the Santa Fe Trail roughly in half. With the Kiowas and Comanches almost constantly on the warpath, the Cimarron Cutoff was safe only for large, heavily guarded caravans, and the loss of animals was always great in crossing the arid deserts. Although nearly a hundred miles longer, the route by way of Bent's Fort was safer from Indian attack, and since it followed the Arkansas River, Timpas Creek, and the foothills of the Sangre de Cristo Mountains all the way there was less loss of stock from thirst. The result was that the great annual caravans continued to cross the cutoff, but most of the other traffic went by way of the fort.

The Bent brothers could not have chosen a better time to quit trapping and turn their attention to the Mexican and Indian trade of the Southwest. By 1834 the streams of the Rockies were rapidly being trapped out, and within five years most of the trapper bands had left the mountains, many of the men becoming buffalo hunters on the prairies.

By 1833 buffalo hunting had become a thriving industry, the Mexican trade was booming, the Santa Fe Trail worn into a deep-rutted road, and Bent's Fort had become the frontier headquarters. There travelers stopped to rest their teams before making the hard pull over Raton Pass. White hunters brought rough-dried hides to market, and Indian bands came from far and near to pitch their wig-

Bent's Fort. From Doniphan's Expedition, *John T. Hughes. Courtesy of The New York Public Library, Rare Book Division.*

wams outside the walls and trade their velvet-soft buffalo robes for the white man's goods. Whoever came—Indian, trader, hunter, or traveler on the trail—he was William Bent's guest.

To feed his guests, together with his hundred or more regular employees, required at least a thousand pounds of buffalo meat a day. But buffalo were becoming scarce in the area, and meat could no longer be hunted from day to day. When the herds migrated in spring and fall a crew of hunters had to follow them to the north and south, killing hundreds, drying the meat, and packing it back to the fort on mules. Each year this hunting became more dangerous, particularly to the south of the Arkansas, for the Kiowas and Comanches considered the buffalo theirs. Although these southern tribes came peaceably to the fort to trade, their hatred for the whites increased as the buffalo herds thinned. Attacks on caravans crossing the Cimarron Cutoff became more vicious, and few bands of white hunters dared to invade Comanche or Kiowa territory.

When, in 1838, beaver trapping became unprofitable, Kit Carson brought his already famous Carson Men to Bent's Fort and contracted to keep it supplied with buffalo meat. Since hunting to the north of the Arkansas might incur ill feeling among the friendly Cheyennes and Arapahos, Carson set out with five of his men to scout for herds in the southeastern corner of Colorado, the center of the Comanche hunting grounds. They were attacked by a war party of two hundred warriors when on an arid plain with no cover from which to fight. Carson leaped from his mule, slashed its throat, and shouted for his men to come in close and do the same. The men had barely time to throw themselves prone behind their still kicking mules before the Indians charged, but their ponies panicked at the smell of fresh blood, swerved to either side and raced past. Three Carson Men fired, and three Comanches fell. In a frenzy of rage the Comanches fought their ponies into a tightly packed, trampling mass and charged again and again. The carcasses of the dead mules bristled with arrows, but at the last moment each charge split, and each time three Carson Men fired. With more than twenty of their number killed, the Comanches took up their death circle, just beyond rifle range and at a jogging trot.

Comanches were among the most superstitious Indians on the prairies. They would never go into battle without a medicine man, and if his incantations failed to bring victory it was considered a sure sign that his medicine had lost its power. He must either commit suicide or be shamed by the entire tribe and lead a dog's life.

With the Comanches in their death circle, the only hope for the hunters was that Carson could bluff the Indians into thinking his medicine stronger than that of their medicine man. One of his men, who had been captured by the Comanches as a boy, spoke their language perfectly. Carson had him shout insults at the medicine man, telling him his medicine was antelope milk as compared to Carson's. When darkness came, Kit would scatter his strong medicine on the night wind, and the weeping squaws would come in the morning to gather the Comanche dead.

The strategy worked, for the medicine man was in a desperately tight spot. Dancing, chanting, and waving charms, he worked himself and the warriors into a frenzy. Then, leaping on his pony, he raced ahead of them toward the barricade.

Holding his men back, Carson stepped out a few paces to meet the charge. As the Indians raced into rifle range he took careful aim at the medicine man's throat, waited for the ponies to get close enough to smell blood, squeezed the trigger, and dropped flat as a storm of arrows whizzed above him. At the instant the ponies panicked he leaped to his feet again, giving the Comanches the impression that their arrows had hit but not harmed him. They had no stomach for testing the strength of his medicine on the night wind, and streaked back toward the Cimarron.

The legend of Carson's strong medicine spread like prairie fire among the plains tribes, extended beyond himself to the Carson Men, and had great effect upon the safety of travel over the Santa Fe Trail. It was seldom that the leader of a war party would knowingly attack a caravan or party guarded by Carson Men, whether or not Kit was present. When not hunting buffalo for Bent's Fort, they were kept busy guarding traders on the Santa Fe Trail.

In 1839 a significant change in the Santa Fe trade occurred. Mexican Governors were always susceptible to bribes, but in 1839 Governor Armijo put matters on a more businesslike basis. He announced that he would allow no American goods to enter New Mexico unless he received a rakeoff of $500 on each wagon load, regardless of its size. This squeezed the small merchants out of the Santa Fe trade, and the large firms were forced to change their method of operations. Where most of the wagons had been no larger than could be pulled by four mules or oxen, it was now necessary that each vehicle carry the greatest possible load. To accomplish this, enormous prairie schooners were built and put into Santa Fe trade, some of them requiring as many as thirty oxen. The Armijo gouge was beneficial to the Bent brothers. It not only increased their caravan business, but the additional tax drove countless Mexicans into trading their hides and furs for American goods at Bent's Fort.

By 1842 Independence had become second only to St. Louis as a river port, for it was the starting point of both the Santa Fe and Oregon trails. Each spring greater numbers of emigrants were setting out for the Northwest, and each year the traffic over the Santa Fe Trail was expanding. At the height of the spring season the town was overrun with emigrants, river men, trappers, buffalo hunters, traders, and teamsters, fighting over the scant grazing for their thousands of horses, mules, and oxen.

The Bent brothers, with seldom less than five hundred head of livestock at Independence, decided they must have their own headquarters, far enough from town to keep their teamsters away from the saloons and gay houses, and to relieve the grazing shortage. They chose a location called Westport Landing—now Kansas City—where there was a natural rock levee and cargoes could be transferred directly between wagons and riverboats. Within a year Westport Landing, rather than Independence, had become the eastern terminus of the Santa Fe Trail.

For the next four years larger and larger caravans rolled over the Santa Fe Trail with little difficulty, and protected only by the Carson Men. Charles Bent and Ceran St. Vrain became firmly established as the leading merchants in New Mexico, and William extended his influence throughout the Great Plains, making Bent's Fort the largest American trading center west of St. Louis.

THEN CAME THE SOLDIERS

At the outbreak of the Mexican War the Santa Fe Trail became the military road of the West, seeing its greatest concentration of traffic during the spring and summer of 1846. In May the annual spring caravan left the Missouri with four hundred and fourteen prairie schooners, about eight thousand draft animals, and more than five hundred men. At the same time Colonel Stephen Watts Kearny was at Fort

Leavenworth recruiting his Army of the West. His instructions from the War Department were to march over the Santa Fe Trail, conquer New Mexico, establish a government there, and move on for the conquest of California, but to interfere as little as possible with the spring caravan.

Early in June, Kearny began sending supply trains ahead at intervals of three or four days, each made up of from twenty-five to thirty wagons. The main supply caravan, consisting of a hundred wagons, set out near the end of the month, and on June 30 Kearny left Fort Leavenworth with a baggage train of three hundred wagons, an artillery battalion, and 1750 mounted dragoons. The dragoons were Missouri volunteers, the flotsam of the frontier, and described by Ruxton, the great historian of the early West, as, "the dirtiest, rowdiest crew I have ever seen collected together."

The Army of the West was scarcely under way before it became more or less disorganized. There was no roadway between Fort Leavenworth and Elm Grove, the point at which Kearny decided to intercept the Santa Fe Trail. The first day's march was made through pouring rain, then the weather turned hot and humid. Before Elm Grove was reached on July 4, the Army was strung out for twenty miles or more, sweating mules and horses wallowing in a sea of mud, while swearing dragoons tugged at ropes to help pull the wagons and artillery out of the mire.

When the hard-packed wheel ruts of the Santa Fe Trail were reached the Army of the West pushed forward, singing and shouting, more in joy that the mud had been passed than in celebration of Independence Day. For the rowdy, undisciplined volunteers, the expedition became more of a lark than a march to war. They were for the first time heading for "wild Injun and buffala country," and every dragoon's trigger finger became itchy as the column neared the bend of the Arkansas. There the first great herd of buffalo was seen, estimated to have been more than half a million, and the few Regular Army officers were unable to enforce discipline. Although hunters had been sent ahead to supply meat for the troops, the dragoons shot thousands of buffalo for sport, and left their carcasses to rot on the prairies. Indians who came within musket range were sniped at, and those at a distance were frightened away by cannon fire.

Roistering and enjoying themselves, the dragoons caught up with and passed the advance supply wagons, then the great caravan, and arrived at Bent's Fort during the last week of July. Camp was pitched eight miles east of the fort, and Kearny went forward to confer with the Bent brothers. It was their belief that, although Governor Armijo had recruited troops for defense, there would be no great resistance by the New Mexicans. They pointed out that the people of Santa Fe had little direct contact with the Mexican capital, had for the past decade looked to the United States for their trade, and considered the Americans their friends.

Kearny remained skeptical, and took no action until July 31. At that time James Magoffin arrived from Washington with secret orders from President Polk. He conferred with Kearny, and requested a detachment of ten dragoons to escort him to Santa Fe under a flag of truce. Shortly after the conference, the colonel sent for Captain Philip St. George Cooke, instructed him to accompany Magoffin to Santa Fe, and gave him a letter to be delivered to Governor Armijo. The letter stated that the United States was annexing all of New Mexico lying east of the Rio Grande, and warned the Governor against trying to resist the formidable Army of the West.

Possibly because of rumors that Armijo had been reinforced and planned an ambush in the vicinity of Raton Pass, Kearny did not send Cooke and Magoffin ahead, but started his march of invasion on August 2. The temperature rose to 112°, the summer had been dry in the Sangre de Cristos, and Timpas Creek, a brawling torrent in spring and fall, was reduced to a brackish trickle. Without knowing where he might meet Armijo and his forces, Kearny was unable to send his supply wagons ahead. The dragoons and their horses drank what little water there was, and the supply train fell far behind, thirst-crazed mules dying by the hundreds. Leaving the trail pockmarked with abandoned wagons and dead mules, the teamsters drove on as best they could, trying to keep the dragoons supplied. But before Raton Pass was reached the men were on one-third rations, and in the sweltering heat they were dying by the dozen from dysentery and exhaustion.

Magoffin and Cooke hurried ahead under a flag of truce, but the Army of the West could barely creep, Kearny hoping not to meet the enemy until the mountains had been crossed and what was left of his supply train brought up. The march to the Mora branch of the

Canadian River required twelve days. Nothing had been heard from Magoffin or Cooke, but Kearny received a message from Governor Armijo, "If you take the country it will be because you are strongest in battle. I suggest to you to stop at the Sapillo, and I will march to the Vegas. We will meet and negotiate on the plains between them."

Since the message was ambiguous, the Army of the West marched on to Las Vegas, but there was no sign of a Mexican army, and no one had been sent to negotiate. Posting a strong guard, Colonel Kearny went to bed. At midnight he was awakened by officers who had just ridden in from Bent's Fort, bringing news of his promotion to the rank of lieutenant general. But while the general was being congratulated on his promotion, the glory of conquering New Mexico was being taken from him.

What James Magoffin's secret orders from President Polk may have been, how he carried them out, and whether or not he divulged any part of them to Kearny is unknown. From the results, however, certain conclusions have been drawn. California was of tremendous value and western New Mexico of practically none, but Kearny's orders were to take New Mexico first, then move on for the capture of California. It is more than probable that the President feared France or England might seize California if Kearny were long delayed in the conquest of New Mexico. Doubtlessly, Magoffin's secret orders were to undermine Armijo by disaffecting Mexican Army officers, using western New Mexico as a bribe if necessary. It is also probable that Magoffin had divulged this information to Kearny at Bent's Fort, causing him to claim only the annexation of eastern New Mexico in his letter to Armijo.

Colonel Diego Archuleta, brilliant and ambitious, was General Armijo's second in command. It is known that Cooke and Magoffin arrived in Santa Fe under a flag of truce on August 12. They were received at the Governor's palace, and Cooke remained there to await Armijo's reply, but Magoffin disappeared. It is almost certain that he went directly to Archuleta, making him the proposal that if he abandoned Armijo the United States would annex only to the Rio Grande, and would then permit him to establish himself as Governor of the territory to the west. Archuleta evidently accepted, for he disaffected, leaving Armijo in a defenseless position. The

[215]

Governor ordered what troops remained loyal to set up a defense in Apache Canyon, between the Pecos River and Santa Fe, then fled to Chihuahua.

Still having heard nothing from Cooke, and unaware of what had taken place in Santa Fe, Lieutenant General Kearny led his limping and half-starved Army of the West out of Las Vegas. As he approached the Pecos River, scouts brought word that Armijo was waiting in Apache Canyon, where fifty poorly equipped soldiers could turn back a well-armed and supplied army. Kearny prepared as best he could for battle, and marched forward to storm the pass, but there were no defenders. On August 18 he marched triumphantly into Santa Fe without firing a shot. A great celebration in his honor was staged by the citizens, and Lieutenant Governor Vigil—Charles Bent's brother-in-law—joyfully surrendered New Mexico to the conquerors.

It is possible that Magoffin failed to inform Kearny of his deal with Archuleta. It is also possible that the newly commissioned lieutenant general was disappointed at being deprived of an opportunity for a glorious victory. In any event, he proclaimed annexation of the entire state, leaving Archuleta no territory in which he might establish himself as Governor.

Now that New Mexico had been annexed without an opportunity for military victory, Kearny was anxious to move on for the conquest of California, but he must first establish a civil government and await the arrival of additional occupation forces. After a month spent in attending lavish dinner parties, and making speeches in which he promised the citizens free elections and protection by the armed might of the United States, Kearny appointed Charles Bent Governor of New Mexico, and Vigil Lieutenant Governor. The appointment of Vigil, the only holdover from the Armijo Government, was injudicious. Archuleta, a far more brilliant and capable man, had anticipated the appointment in payment for his defection, and was furious when Kearny ignored him.

In making his report of the annexation to Washington, Kearny had written, "The inhabitants of the country were found to be highly satisfied and contented with the change of government, and apparently vied with each other to see who could show us the greatest hospitality and kindness."

While the general was being wined and dined by the elite, his dragoons were reveling in the hospitality and kindness of the Santa Fe *señoras* and *señoritas*, of whom one of Doniphan's officers wrote, "They do not seem to know what virtue or industry is, and being almost the slave of the husband, are very fond of the attention of strangers."

The Mexican men took a dim view of their women's kindnesses to the drunken, swaggering Missourians, and their original hospitality soon turned into a deep and lasting hatred of all Americans. When Kearny set out for the conquest of California, there were thirty-five hundred rowdy American soldiers in Santa Fe, and, stirred by disgruntled and angry Don Diego Archuleta, trouble was rapidly brewing.

Through all the years that Taos had been the headquarters of the American mountain men they had had no trouble with the Pueblo Indians, for rough and tough as they were, the trappers had respected the gentle Pueblo men and left their women alone. But as soon as dragoons were brought into New Mexico they attempted to molest the Indian women, and the Pueblos grew bitter toward Americans. Taking advantage of this hostility and the fact that Carson and his men were in California with Frémont, Don Diego Archuleta led a band of his native followers to Taos. They plied the Indians with whiskey, and stirred them into a general uprising against the Americans, planned for Christmas Eve. The plot was discovered, and Archuleta escaped to Chihuahua with his followers, but the Pueblo Indians remained sullen and angry.

Charles Bent had made his home in Taos since the time of his marriage, and continued it there after his appointment as Governor, traveling as often as possible from Santa Fe to visit his family. He was in Taos on January 18, 1847, when the Indians suddenly revolted, flocked from their pueblo into the little town, and were joined by a rabble of Mexican peons.

Throughout the night the anger of the mob increased as jugs of Taos lightning passed from hand to hand and rabble-rousing Mexicans inflamed the Indians with tirades against the Americanos. Charles Bent, his wife, and Carson's wife who was living with them, had plenty of chance to escape to Santa Fe, but Bent, who had always been on the friendliest terms with the Pueblo Indians and Taos Mexicans, could not believe they would do him or his family harm. When, on the morning of the 19th, an angry mob gathered in front of his house, he went to the door to reason with them, but mob hysteria had risen beyond the point of reason. He was shot down, scalped while still alive, and his body riddled with knife wounds. The women and children escaped only because of the bravery and loyalty of the household servants.

Twenty other Americans were killed in the rebellion, and though the leaders were tried and executed the smoldering embers of hatred had been fanned into a blaze. The plains Indians had been angered by the dragoons on their way west. Rebellion spread throughout the entire region, and no caravan passed over the Santa Fe Trail without being attacked. Forty-seven Americans were killed, three hundred and thirty wagons looted and burned, and more than sixty-five hundred head of stock butchered or run off. From the time William Bent had first begun trading with the Indians, his influence had kept the Cheyennes and Arapahos at peace with the white men, but the rebellion soon spread to them, too. Trade was brought to a standstill, and for the first time Bent's Fort was attacked. Troops on the Santa Fe Trail were no safer than caravans. Lieutenant Love, commanding a company of dragoons and carrying three hundred thousand dollars to pay the troops at Santa Fe, was attacked, had five men killed, six wounded, and lost a large number of horses.

To keep the plains Indians under any reasonable control was to cost the United States more than forty million dollars during the next fifteen years, but the Santa Fe Trail had to be kept open for supplying not only the troops but the twenty thousand newly acquired American citizens of New Mexico. Forts were built along the route, and strong troops of cavalry patrolled the trail. Government supply wagons and merchants' caravans continued to roll, but with Charles Bent's death and the uprising of the Cheyennes and Arapahos the heyday of Bent, St. Vrain & Company drew rapidly to a close. In August, 1849, William stripped the fort of everything valuable, touched a match to the arsenal, and blew the great landmark of the western prairies into a heap of rubble. Although the California gold rush was reaching its climax, there was little trade to be had from it. Only about eight thousand Argonauts went west by way of the Santa Fe Trail, due to the danger of Indian attacks.

In 1850 monthly mail and passenger service was established between Independence and Santa Fe, and was glowingly announced in the *Missouri Commonwealth*: "The stages are gotten up in elegant style, and are each arranged to convey eight passengers. The bodies are beautifully painted and made water-tight, with a view of using them as boats in ferrying streams. The team consists of six mules to each coach. The mail is guarded by eight men, armed as follows: Each man has at his side, fastened in the stage, one Colt's revolving rifle, in a holster below, one of Colt's long revolvers, and in his belt a small Colt's revolver, besides a hunting knife, so that these eight men are ready, in case of attack, to discharge 136 shots without having to reload. This is equal to a small army armed as in ancient times, and from the look of the escort, ready as they were either for offensive or defensive warfare with the savages, we have no fear for the safety of the mails." Passengers felt less confidence for their own safety and were scarce for several years.

Although relatively few Forty-Niners went to California by way of the Santa Fe Trail, the gold rush sparked the great westward expansion, and in spite of Indian depredations traffic over the trail increased rapidly. By 1855 the Santa Fe trade alone amounted to five million dollars. In 1865 three thousand merchandise wagons rolled westward over the trail, in addition to a continual stream of Army traffic. In 1866 the number of merchandise wagons increased to more than five thousand. Towns and way stations lined the route far westward into Kansas. The great buffalo herds were gone from the prairies, streams had been bridged, and Concord coaches sped east and west night and day, carrying thousands of passengers and hundreds of tons of mail and express, but by the end of the year the Santa Fe Trail had passed its peak.

In 1863 the first steel rails had pushed westward from Wyandotte, Kansas, across the river from Kansas City. Hindered by Indian attacks, the progress was slow, but by 1866 the rails had been extended to Junction City, a hundred miles west of the Missouri, and to meet them the Santa Fe Trail veered northeastward from the great bend of the Arkansas. Year by year the rails crept toward the southwest, and the Santa Fe Trail terminated at each new railhead. By 1872 the rails had reached the point where, a half century before, Becknell had crossed the Arkansas to pioneer the Cimarron Cutoff. There Dodge City, the cowboy capital of the West, was laid out, shipping in its first year nearly a quarter million cattle driven north from Texas, an equal number of buffalo hides from the Great Plains, and countless tons of merchandise coming and going over the shortened Santa Fe Trail.

For a year the railhead terminus of the trail was at Kit Carson, Colorado. Then the Kansas Pacific extended a branch southward to the approximate site of old Bent's Fort, and the Cimarron Cutoff fell into disuse. For a few more years freight wagons and stagecoaches rolled over the rugged stretch of road the Bent brothers had cleared while building their fort, following the age-old Indian trail that Becknell had traveled in 1821, up Timpas Creek and over Raton Pass. Then in 1879 Raton Tunnel was completed. On February 9, 1880, the first train rolled into Santa Fe, and the Santa Fe Trail withdrew into the annals of American history.

6

The Big Medicine Trail

THE FUR TRADE

Thomas Jefferson had been keenly interested in the fur-rich Northwest for more than twenty years before becoming President. His
original interest was aroused by John Ledyard, a brilliant Connecticut boy who had sailed with the famous British explorer, Captain
James Cook, in his futile search for the Northwest Passage.

In the spring of 1778, Cook had rounded South America, redis-
covered the Hawaiian Islands, and was sailing toward Alaska when
his ship was caught in a severe storm. After being driven eastward
for several days, he sighted land and found refuge in a harbor, later
known as Nootka Sound, on the western side of Vancouver Island.
He had no sooner entered the sound than his ship was surrounded by
scores of great canoes, skillfully handled and loaded to the gunwales
with happily shouting Indians. They were decked in a profusion of
well-tanned furs—bear, wolf, fox, skunk, marten, mink, and sea otter
—and many of them wore U-shaped pieces of iron or copper, looped
through incisions in their noses and earlobes.

Cook was more amazed at finding metal among these Indians than
at their great wealth in furs. He knew that no British ship had ever
before been in these waters, and was unaware that the Russians had
been so far south, or that a Spanish ship had anchored in Nootka
Sound three years earlier. Believing the nearest source of fabricated
metal to be a trading post at Hudson's Bay, he reasoned that these

Indians had either traveled that far east, or that the metal had been brought to the Pacific coast through trade between the intervening tribes.

As soon as the anchor had been dropped, the Indians swarmed aboard, overrunning the deck and trying to make off with any piece of loose metal they could lay hands upon. It soon became apparent that they valued nothing highly except metal, and would trade anything to get it—including young female slaves captured from other tribes. Captain Cook drew the line at slaves, but being bound for the Arctic where warm clothing and bedding would be needed, he let his men trade pieces of metal from the ship for a considerable number of sea-otter pelts.

When the storm abated, Cook claimed the entire region by right of original discovery for the British Crown, and sailed away to the north. Beyond Bering Strait, and at the gateway to the actual Northwest Passage, he was forced back by impassable ice floes, so he returned to the Hawaiian Islands, where he was killed in trying to recover a stolen landing cutter. Lieutenant James King then took command and turned back toward England by way of the Orient, stopping at Macao Roads in China for repairs. While there, he went up the river to Canton, taking along twenty rather poor sea-otter furs in hope of trading them for a few badly needed supplies. To his amazement, the Cantonese were enthralled by the soft, dark furs. The twenty pelts sold for eight hundred dollars, and the Cantonese begged King to bring more. The clamor was so great that an auction was arranged on shipboard, at which prime sea-otter pelts brought $120 each.

Following the auction, King's crew nearly mutinied in their demands that he return to Nootka Sound. When he refused, two of the sailors deserted, determined to find their way back and become wealthy from the sea-otter trade. John Ledyard realized the folly of the desertions, since trade by sea could be carried on only by men with sufficient capital to outfit and man a ship, but an idea began shaping itself in his mind. The Nootka Indians were primarily boatmen and, if their iron and copper had come from Hudson's Bay, there were probably rivers that could be navigated for most of the distance. There must, also, be streams flowing into Hudson's Bay from the southeast, their headwaters near those of the Connecticut

River. If so, a man with very little capital could get into the sea-otter fur trade, transporting bales of pelts from the Pacific Northwest to markets on the Atlantic coast by canoe.

Sea-otter furs became an obsession to John Ledyard, and he determined to discover a water route by which he could transport them across the continent, but his enlistment in the British Navy still had three years to run, and he learned in China that the United States was at war with England. Following the war, he succeeded in selling Thomas Jefferson, then Minister to France, on the potential value of the sea-otter fur trade to the United States, and the advantages of a transcontinental trade route between the Atlantic coast and the North Pacific. He then proposed and secured Jefferson's backing for one of the most fantastic schemes in history: he would cross Russia and Siberia to Kamchatka, find a means of reaching Vancouver Island, and discover a transcontinental water route back to New England. Afoot and in winter, Ledyard crossed Russia; he had reached central Siberia when he was arrested and turned back by the suspicious Russians. Heartbroken, he died a few years later, but his foresight was to have a profound effect upon the future history of the United States.

While John Ledyard was plodding across Russia, British sea captains were racing one another around South America and toward Vancouver Island, each intent upon reaching Canton with a cargo of sea-otter pelts before the market was glutted and the price fell. But Chinese demand for the soft, dark furs was insatiable. Profits from the sea-otter trade became enormous, and the Pacific Northwest the most coveted and controversial region on earth. Spain claimed exclusive ownership as far north as the present site of Anchorage, Alaska, by right of original discovery in 1775. Although the Spanish claim of prior discovery was legitimate, the British refused to recognize it, and completely dominated the Northwest fur trade, sailing their trading vessels into every bay or inlet from Puget Sound to the Gulf of Alaska.

To enforce its claim of sovereignty, Spain sent warships to Nootka Sound, seized two British vessels as prizes, and took them to Mexico, with their crews imprisoned below decks. But Spain had passed the heyday of her power. When threatened with retaliation by the British Navy, she capitulated. In the Nootka Sound Convention of

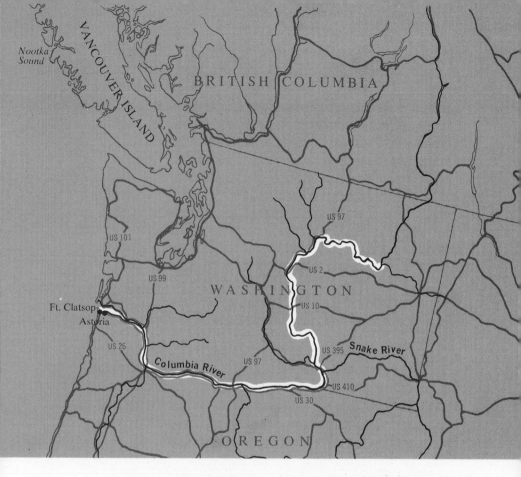

Area of the Northwest Fur Trade. Captain James Cook's accidental discovery of Nootka Sound and his reception by furladen Indians opened a sea-otter fur trade in the Northwest.

1790, she virtually abandoned her claim to exclusive ownership of the Pacific Northwest by granting British subjects the right to trade or settle on lands not currently occupied by Spanish subjects.

Although the British controlled the Northwest fur trade, a few Yankees had taken a small part in it. Among them was Captain Robert Gray, skipper of the trading ship *Columbia* out of Boston. It was customary for the British to gather pelts during the summer, then sail for China in late fall, and Gray had been reasonably successful trading northward from Vancouver Island while the British were absent. But the winter of 1791-92 was severe and most of the northern inlets froze solidly, forcing Gray to turn southward where sea otter were less plentiful.

Poking into every inlet, though with little success, Gray worked his way around Puget Sound and down the Pacific coast. By May 10, 1792, he had reached Cape Disappointment at the southern tip of Washington, having gathered only a few furs of poor quality. It had been known for more than ten years that a river of considerable size entered the Pacific at this point, but its mouth was barricaded by treacherous sand bars and high breakers which had blocked every attempt to cross them. Desperately in need of furs, Robert Gray determined to find a way across the barrier. Waiting for flood tide, at four o'clock on the morning of May 11, he sent a small boat ahead to take soundings, then followed cautiously with the *Columbia*, and soon found himself "in a large river of fresh water up which we steered."

Robert Gray had few peers as a sea captain and navigator, but his Yankee terseness and preoccupation with trade made him something less than a great explorer. He sailed only a few miles up the estuary, named the river for his ship, then anchored, and set about trading when "vast numbers of natives came alongside." The trade was brisk enough for him to complete his cargo in nine days, so he sailed away for China, though first rowing ashore to claim the entire watershed of the river as a possession of the United States. His matter-of-fact log shows that he changed anchorage once and that the water was ten fathoms deep, but gives no description of the land or the Indians, who had obviously never before seen white men. Fortunately, Gray had in his crew a seventeen-year-old boy, John Boit, who not only kept a journal but was highly observant, imaginative, and articulate. A few random sentences from his journal were of greater value than all the furs obtained in trade:

"The men at Columbia's River are strait limb'd, fine looking fellows, and the women are very pretty. They are all in a state of Nature except the Females, who wear a leaf Apron. The Indians are very numerous, and appear'd very civill (not even offering to steal). During our short stay we collected 150 Otter, 300 Beaver, and twice that number of land furs. The river abounds with excellent Salmon, and most other River fish, and the woods with plenty of Moose and Deer, the skins of which was brought us in great plenty.

"This River in my opinion, wou'd be a fine place to set up a Factory [a trading post]. We found plenty of Oak, Ash and Walnut trees, and clear ground in plenty, which with little labour might be made fit to raise such seeds as is necessary for the sustenance of inhabitants, and in short, a factory set up here and another at Hancock's River in the Queen Charlotte Isles, wou'd engross the whole trade of the NW Coast (with the help of a few small coasting vessels)."

LEWIS AND CLARK

Thomas Jefferson had never lost interest in John Ledyard's scheme for tapping the fur resources of the Northwest by way of a transcontinental water route. That interest was fanned to a flame by Gray's discovery of the Columbia River and John Boit's description of its advantages as an ideal place to locate a settlement, for Jefferson was an expansionist who had fully recognized the implications of the Nootka Sound Convention. Although not actually stated, the agreement made occupancy the basis of sovereignty in the Northwest, whether the settlers were British subjects or those of any other nation, and he believed the future security of the United States required possession of an outlet to the Pacific. Great Britain, however, had a much better opportunity to plant and supply settlements in the Northwest, since she already dominated the fur trade, and the distance by sea was no greater from London than from Boston. Furthermore, the claim of the United States to the Columbia watershed was obviously weak, since Gray had not explored the river above the estuary. But the French had explored and mapped the Missouri to its source at the Continental Divide, and Jefferson was familiar with their maps. He reasoned correctly that, since the Columbia was a mighty river flowing into the Pacific from the east, its source must be contiguous to that of the Missouri, and that the two rivers would provide the transcontinental water route Ledyard had envisaged. If so, it would reduce the distance to less than one fifth that by sea, providing an inexpensive means of transporting and supplying settlers.

Jefferson was anxious that the United States should immediately strengthen its claim to the Columbia watershed by actual exploration, and that it should, if possible, discover a water route connecting the Pacific with the Mississippi Valley. As Secretary of State, he could take no official action that would trespass on the French territory lying between the Mississippi River and Continental Divide, but he

Meriwether Lewis.

prevailed upon the American Philosophical Society to finance an expedition to the Columbia by way of the Missouri "for scientific research." A fund was subscribed, but, due to fear of involvement in the war between France and England, the expedition was never launched.

When, in 1801, Jefferson became President of the United States, no American had explored the Columbia River more than a few miles above its estuary, but the huge sea-otter herds of the Northwest had been destroyed and inland furs were coming into great demand. In searching for them, the Hudson's Bay Company had for several years been pushing its trappers farther and farther to the westward, but it was unknown to Jefferson whether or not they had crossed the Continental Divide and explored the upper reaches of the Columbia. Still intent upon strengthening the claim of the United States to the Columbia watershed, he asked Congress for authority to send a small scientific expedition to explore the Missouri and Columbia rivers "for the purpose of acquiring knowledge of the geography, plants, and animals of the interior."

Before congressional action had been taken upon the President's request, it became necessary for the United States to make the Louisiana Purchase, acquiring from France all her territory between the Mississippi River and the Continental Divide. The purchase had no sooner been made than Jefferson again asked Congress to author-

William Clark.

ize an expedition, this time for the purpose of exploring the newly acquired territory. The authority was granted, and the President chose Meriwether Lewis, his personal secretary, to carry out the project; but it is obvious that the sole purpose of the expedition was for the exploration of the Columbia River and discovery of a transcontinental water route.

Lewis chose for his second-in-command Lieutenant William Clark, a brother of the famous American frontiersman George Rogers Clark. During the winter of 1803-4, Lewis and Clark assembled at St. Louis supplies for a two-year expedition, and enlisted a crew of about fifty men, made up of young frontiersmen, soldiers, and French river men. On May 14, 1804, the explorers set out in a large keelboat and two pirogues, the soldiers riding along the banks to hunt game and ward off Indian attacks. Lewis carried French maps of the headwaters of the Missouri, but so little was known of the topography of the area that he took along wheels and axles for making the expected portage to the headwaters of the Columbia.

Progress was slow against the strong current of the Missouri, and winter had set in by the time the villages of the friendly Mandan Indians were reached, a short distance north of the present site of Bismarck, North Dakota. These villages were the frontier outpost, and for two or more generations had been visited by French traders and trappers. There Lewis and Clark made their winter camp, and met a shiftless French half-breed named Charbonneau whose eighteen-year-old Shoshoni wife, Sacagawea, had in childhood been stolen from her people in western Montana. Since no one in the Lewis and Clark expedition was adept at sign language, communication threatened to be a greater barrier than the unknown wilderness to the west. But Sacagawea could speak various Indian languages and converse with Charbonneau, who could speak in barely distinguishable English. On the promise that he would be required to do no work, Charbonneau agreed to accompany the expedition as interpreter.

In the spring of 1805, Lewis sent the soldiers back to St. Louis with reports for President Jefferson. At the same time he and Clark started upstream in two pirogues and six canoes, taking with them twenty-six men, a French-Canadian guide, Lewis's servant, Charbonneau, and Sacagawea with her baby on a cradle board. By early June they had reached Great Falls, Montana, but were unable to continue with the pirogues, and were obliged to cache a large part of their supplies. Above the falls the guide knew nothing of the country, but Sacagawea began recognizing scenes of her childhood, and it was believed that people from her tribe would soon be found who could guide the party to the headwaters of the Columbia. The hope failed to materialize. No Indians of any tribe were encountered, portages had to be made with increasing frequency, and two months were required to ascend the Missouri to its headwaters at the Idaho-Montana boundary.

On August 12, the party scaled the Continental Divide and discovered a band of Indians well supplied with horses. Sacagawea ran to meet them with tears rolling down her cheeks, sucking her fingers to show the Americans that these were her relatives. They supplied the expedition with thirty-eight horses, and led it northward for several days, then refused to go farther. As far as Charbonneau was concerned, Sacagawea could have turned back with her people, but she had come to admire Clark greatly, and at his request decided to go on. For three weeks the explorers groped their way northward to a point near present Missoula, Montana. Finding a well-worn Indian trail that led to the west, they followed it across the summit of the divide, then lost it among a jumble of barren black mountains. No game was found, the food supply became exhausted, and to stave off starvation the lost explorers were obliged to live on horse flesh. Staggering with exhaustion, they reached the Clearwater River at the present site of Orofino, Idaho, in early October.

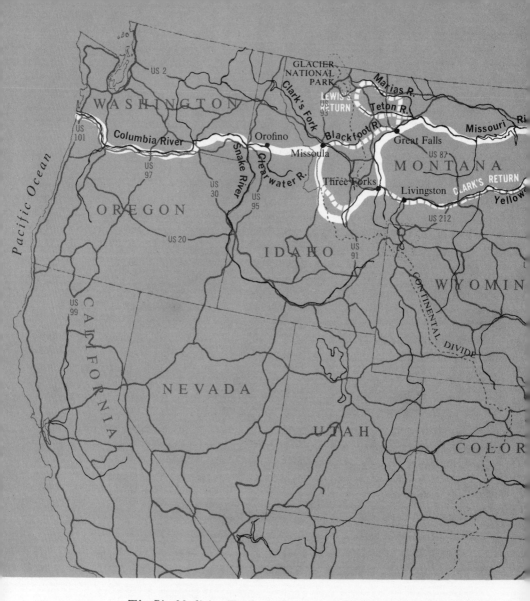

The Big Medicine Trail: the Lewis and Clark expedition. Although this was the natural route to the Northwest, Lewis's encounter with

The valley of the Clearwater was green and fertile, hundreds of excellent horses grazed in the meadows, and a village of neat brush wickiups stood beside the stream. Friendly, intelligent Indians dressed in white buckskin came out to meet the famished explorers. They

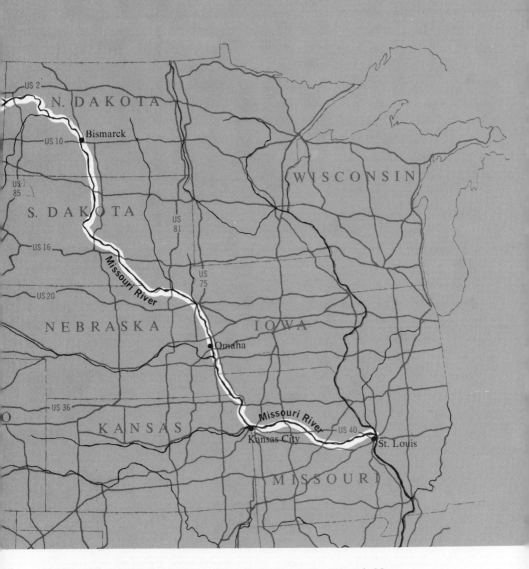

*the Blackfoot Indians closed it off before it was really opened. Most
of it remained undeveloped.*

called themselves Nez Percés, welcomed the whites, and brought
them roasted fish and bread made of camass-root flour. To questions
translated by Sacagawea, an old man told of having canoed down the
river for "many suns to a great lake of salt water."

Lewis and Clark spent several days at the Nez Percé village, while the men regained strength, felled trees, and hollowed them into canoes. A council was held with the chiefs, and in exchange for two guns and a keg of powder the Indians agreed to care for the expedition's horses until it should return. On October 7, 1805, the Lewis and Clark expedition set off down the Clearwater in six log canoes. Exactly a month later, they heard the roar of the Pacific through the fog that shrouded the mouth of the Columbia River.

Lewis and Clark built Fort Clatsop on the south bank of the river, spent the winter uneventfully among the friendly Indians, and in late March of 1806 started their return journey. At the Nez Percé village they found their horses well cared for. The Indians were happy to see them, loaded their packs with dried meat and camass flour, and guided them by a good trail across the Continental Divide to the vicinity of Missoula. Before turning back, they pointed up the Blackfoot branch of Clark's Fork River as the best route to the great falls of the Missouri. Lewis, with half the men, took the proposed route, while Clark turned southward to explore the Yellowstone River and then rejoin Lewis at its confluence with the Missouri. He held roughly to the outcoming route until reaching Three Forks, then turned eastward to the Yellowstone at the present site of Livingston, Montana. His passage down the river was made without difficulty, and he encountered only friendly Indians.

The route over which the Nez Percés had led the explorers back to Missoula and the one pointed out along the Blackfoot were easily travelable and led in an almost straight line from the Clearwater to the great falls of the Missouri, forming a perfect link between the navigable portions of the two great river systems. As a result, Lewis was able to make the return journey in a quarter of the time required for the outgoing trip, and reached Great Falls far ahead of schedule. Delighted with the success of his expedition, and with time on his hands, he decided to explore the plains country to the north, and, in doing so, closed to Americans the transcontinental route that Jefferson had sent him to discover.

From Great Falls, Lewis marched north to the Marias River, turned westward almost to the portals of present Glacier National Park, and had started back when he encountered a band of Blackfoot Indians. Whether or not the ensuing battle was avoidable, the Lewis party opened fire on the Indians and won the everlasting hatred of the

Blackfeet for all Americans. These Indians had long been in contact with the French-Canadian trappers of the Hudson's Bay Company, were well equipped with firearms, and their homeland was the territory surrounding the upper reaches of the Missouri and Yellowstone rivers. Since they were the most powerful and warlike tribe in the Northwest, their hatred closed both rivers to American travel.

Following his unfortunate battle with the Blackfeet, Lewis marched down the Teton River to the Missouri, built boats, and, as planned, met Clark at the confluence of the Yellowstone. Charbonneau, Sacagawea, and two of the men who had decided to stay on the frontier were left at the Mandan villages. The rest of the expedition floated rapidly down the Missouri and reached St. Louis on September 25, 1806.

As soon as Meriwether Lewis had sent off a report to President Jefferson, he and William Clark settled down to the serious business of editing their journals for publication. They were, however, a bit too painstaking, and did not complete the task for eight years. Sergeant Patrick Gass, one of their men, had also kept a journal, and Gass, though less particular about the excellence of his prose, was more practical. He had his journal in the hands of a publisher within

Meriwether Lewis telling the Indians that they were now under the protection of the Great White Father. From Journal of the Voyages and Travels of a Corps of Discovery, *Patrick Gass. Courtesy of The New York Public Library, Rare Book Division.*

less than a year, and several editions were quickly sold, firing the American imagination as nothing before had ever done. Frontiersmen soon began poling keelboats far up the Missouri to trade gaudy, white man's goods with the Indians for beaver pelts. The most ambitious of these was Manuel Lisa, forerunner of the Missouri Fur Company. One of his parties, under the command of Andrew Henry, worked its way far up the Yellowstone River where it was attacked by Blackfoot Indians. Henry and a few of his men escaped afoot, and were driven westward across the Continental Divide. On a branch of the Snake River, fifty miles west of Teton National Park, they built a log cabin and holed up for the winter. The cabin became known as Henry's Fort, the first American outpost on the western side of the Rockies.

THE ASTORIANS

The greatest effect of the Gass journal was upon the imagination of John Jacob Astor, who dominated the fur industry in the United States and whose clipper ships dominated the China trade. His only rivals were the British-controlled Hudson's Bay Company and the Scottish-controlled Northwest Fur Company, both of which had pushed their operations across Canada to the Pacific. From the journals of Patrick Gass and John Boit, Astor conceived a plan for outmaneuvering his two great rivals and gaining complete control of the fur industry in the Northwest.

In the last year of Jefferson's administration, Astor went to him with his plan. He proposed to establish trading posts at frequent intervals along the Missouri to the Rockies and down the Columbia to the Pacific. He would also build a large fortified headquarters post at the mouth of the Columbia, an ideal location from which to make shipments for the China trade. Furs from the upper Missouri and Columbia would be taken there cheaply and rapidly over the water route pioneered by Lewis and Clark. A fleet of small ships would ply along the Pacific coast from California to Alaska, circulating among the islands and up the rivers to trade for furs with the Indians. In this way Astor believed his rivals could be forced to abandon their operations in British Columbia. Jefferson was enthusiastic about the plan, seeing in it the possibility of gaining American sovereignty in the Northwest by developing industry there.

In June, 1810, the Pacific Fur Company was incorporated. The ship *Tonquin* was at once loaded with provisions, building materials, and trade goods at New York, and set sail for the mouth of the Columbia under the command of Alexander McKee. That fall Wilson Hunt set off from St. Louis with a large party of frontier trappers and river men, taking two barges and a keelboat heavily loaded with supplies, traps, and trade goods. They were to follow the Lewis and Clark route, trap the upper Missouri and Columbia, select sites for trading posts, and meet the *Tonquin* at the Columbia Estuary.

Hunt wintered at the present site of St. Joseph, Missouri. He had just started on, in the spring of 1811, when John Colter, one of the two members of the Lewis and Clark expedition who had remained at the Mandan villages, came down the river, nearly naked and on the verge of starvation. In 1807, he had gone back to the headwaters of the Missouri, discovered the area that later became Yellowstone National Park, and been captured by the Blackfeet. A month before his meeting with Hunt's party, Colter had made his escape and had ridden a tangle of driftwood fifteen hundred miles downstream on the spring freshet. He reported that the Blackfoot hatred for Americans was such that nothing short of an army could make its way through their homeland. There was only one way in which he believed the expedition could reach the headwaters of the Columbia. It would have to leave the Missouri at the Arikara village, located below the present site of Bismarck, and make its way overland, keeping well to the south of Blackfoot territory.

A few days later, Colter's opinion was confirmed by three Kentuckians who came paddling down the river. They had been in Andrew Henry's party that had been driven across the divide by the Blackfeet, and had made their way overland to the Arikara village. They were positive that the upper Missouri could not be traversed by Americans, but offered to guide the expedition overland to Henry's Fort, and assured Hunt that he could reach the Columbia from there by way of Snake River.

With little other choice open, Hunt engaged the Kentuckians as guides. The Arikara village was reached in mid-June, but the Indians were short of horses, and only eighty-two could be secured. These were loaded with trade goods, traps, and supplies, and, with the men afoot, the expedition set off across the prairies. The guides led the

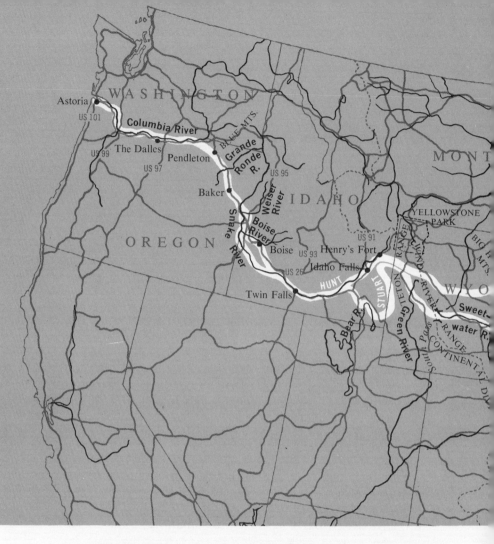

The Big Medicine Trail: routes of Wilson Hunt and Robert Stuart.
To avoid the hostile Blackfeet, Hunt was forced to find an alternate

way to the point where North and South Dakota now meet at the
Montana line. There they admitted they were lost, but were sure
that Blackfoot territory lay nearby to the north. For two months the
party groped its way to the south and west through the Wyoming
mountains, while the men became footsore and exhausted, supplies
ran low, and horses died from lack of forage. Then, from the top of
a pass, the guides recognized the towering peaks of the Teton Range,

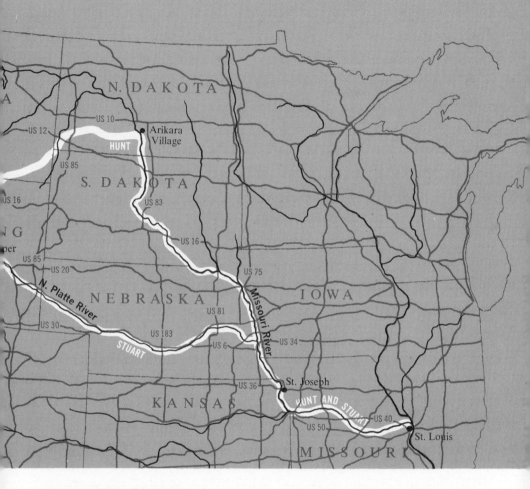

way to the Columbia River.

and in early October led the weary expedition to Henry's deserted fort.

After a day's rest, Hunt set his men to felling trees and hollowing them into canoes. But now that a tributary of the Columbia had been reached, he decided to start trapping operations. He assigned an ex-Army officer, Joseph Miller, to make the abandoned fort his headquarters. With the three guides who were familiar with the area,

Miller was to care for the horses and trap beaver until spring, then bring his fur packs downstream to the main fort at the mouth of the Columbia.

By October 20, fifteen canoes had been completed, were loaded with nearly five tons of trade goods, traps, and provisions, and the expedition set off down the Snake River. The current was swift, the canoes sped along with little effort, the river men sang lustily, and Hunt was equally joyful. Having lost so much time, he had feared that winter might maroon them in the high mountains, but at this rate of travel they should easily reach the mouth of the Columbia in three or four weeks.

The first difficulty was encountered at the rapids above Idaho Falls where two days, a canoe, and a half ton of trade goods were lost. They had two days of fast, smooth travel past the mouth of the Portneuf River, which flows into the Snake below the present location of Pocatello. The American Falls was reached, and below them the river swung away to the west, boiling through a canyon that was chiseled deep between the Snake River Plain and ranges of low, desolate mountains to the south. Only the amazing skill of the river men kept the canoes from swamping in the maelstrom below the falls, and each day the gorge narrowed and deepened. On October 28, near the present site of Twin Falls, a canoe loaded with most of the provisions capsized; one man was drowned, and four were barely rescued. Hunt sent scouts along the canyon rim, but they returned to report that the river was entirely impassable, that the canoes would have to be abandoned.

The situation was clearly desperate. Only five days' rations remained, winter was setting in. It was too late to turn back to Henry's Fort, and nearly a thousand miles to the mouth of the Columbia. In order to travel as rapidly as possible, nothing could be carried except food, warm clothing, arms, and ammunition. Hunt had caches dug, the trade goods, traps, and even his own journal buried. For three weeks the men struggled down the north bank of the river, through barren country entirely devoid of game, and were kept alive only by the few Indians they found fishing along the stream. In late November they reached the mouth of the Boise River, where the Snake turns northward through an awesome canyon to form the boundary between Oregon and Idaho. There Indians were found with a fair supply of scrawny horses, but Hunt's party had little to trade for them. They obtained a few, butchered one, and continued northward along the canyon rim.

Unable to travel more than a mile or two a day in their weakened condition, Hunt and his men reached the mouth of the Weiser River on Christmas Day. There they found a little village of friendly Shoshoni Indians, but their food supply for the winter consisted of only a few dogs and a small herd of emaciated horses. Regardless of their own poverty they took in the destitute whites and butchered horses and dogs to feed them. From these Indians, Hunt learned that the Columbia could be reached in winter only by crossing the Snake and following old Indian trails for twenty-one sleeps to the northwest. But with snow already deep, the trails could be followed only by Indians who were thoroughly familiar with the route. In exchange for a gun, a pistol, a few knives, and a little ammunition, the Indians agreed to furnish guides, five horses for food, and to care until spring for the men who were too weak to travel.

Three days were required for the strongest of the party to descend the Snake River canyon, cross the swift stream in a horsehide canoe, and climb out to the western rim. Then the guides led them to the northwest, the first white men to travel any part of the route that would become the Oregon Trail. The Indians turned up the canyon of Burnt River, skirted the eastern foothills of the Blue Mountains past the present site of Baker, Oregon, and continued northwest into the fertile valley of the Grande Ronde. There a few more horses were obtained at a Shoshoni village and new guides secured. These led the way across the forest-covered Blue Mountains and down to the present location of Pendleton on the Umatilla River. The Cayuse Indians in the Umatilla Valley were prosperous and generous. Hundreds of horses grazed in the meadows, and the lodges were well supplied with dried buffalo meat and camass-root flour. For five days the half-starved whites rested with the Indians, feasting and regaining their strength. When they went on, they were well mounted and supplied with provisions. At The Dalles, Hunt traded his horses for canoes, and on February 15, 1812, he and his party, saved only by the generosity of Indians, reached Fort Astoria on the Columbia Estuary.

The sea division of the Astor enterprise had fared little better than the overland party. At first all had gone well. Fort Astoria was built, and the *Tonquin* sailed northward to trade for furs at Nootka Sound, but the Indians, cheated and abused by other white traders, swarmed aboard. Most of the crew, including Alexander McKee, were massacred, and the remainder trapped in the hold of the vessel. Having no possibility of escape, they blew up the powder magazine, killing all hands and sinking the ship with its cargo of trade goods.

Loss of the trade goods in the *Tonquin*, in addition to those cached by the overland party, left the Pacific Fur Company in a desperate situation. Hunt decided to send a report of the double tragedy to Astor as quickly as possible. Six couriers, under the leadership of twenty-year-old Robert Stuart, were started off in the late spring of 1812. Stuart's instructions were to follow Snake River to the caches, retrieve Hunt's journal, and make his way to St. Louis by the shortest possible route.

ROBERT STUART ON THE BIG MEDICINE TRAIL

Robert Stuart, though young, was a natural frontiersman. He ascended the Columbia by canoe, traded with the Cayuse Indians for twenty horses, and had no difficulty in following well-worn Indian trails across northwestern Oregon to the Snake River. He kept to the west side of the canyon until he found an easy crossing place opposite the mouth of the Boise River, followed that stream eastward past the present site of Boise, Idaho, then turned southeast over the desert to the lower bend of the Snake. He had barely reached the river when he found Joseph Miller and the three Kentuckians whom Hunt had left at Henry's Fort the previous fall. Their trapping had been amazingly successful. They had twice gathered beaver pelts worth several thousand dollars, but both times had been robbed by Crow Indians, and were trying to make their way to the Columbia. All four had become disgusted with fur trapping, and decided to accompany Stuart to St. Louis.

Unprofitable as Miller's trapping had been, it was of great importance to the history of the West, for in his wandering he had discovered one of the key links of the Oregon Trail. After reaching the caches, Miller led Stuart along the Snake to the Portneuf River, southward up its valley where Pocatello now stands, over a low divide, and down to the broad green valley of Bear River. Near the southeast corner of Idaho, the couriers were attacked by a war party of Crow Indians, and driven to the north along the present Wyoming-

Idaho boundary. Stuart and his men rode at the limit of their horses' endurance for sixty miles or more. Then, believing themselves out of danger, they made camp and turned the jaded horses out to graze. At dawn, next morning, the Crows swooped down upon the camp in a whooping, shrieking attack, plundered it, and drove the horses away. Afoot, Stuart had little choice but to strike out for Henry's Fort, hoping to find there some of the horses left by Hunt the previous fall. A month was lost before the half-starved party made its way to the abandoned fort, only to find that the horses had all been stolen or had drifted away.

Again, Stuart had little choice. Although it was still early October, snow was falling in the high mountains, and unless he got out to the plains soon his men would be marooned and die of starvation. He decided to try following Hunt's trail back to the Arikara village on the Missouri. The pass through the Tetons was found without difficulty, but on the eastern side of the range the wrong Indian trail was picked up, leading into the rugged Gros Ventre Mountains. With their only food for two weeks being one wolf and an emaciated old buffalo bull, the little party stumbled onto the headwaters of the Green River, sixty miles south of Yellowstone Park. They were so near starvation that two of them verged on insanity, and Stuart had nearly abandoned hope when they came upon the camp of six Snake Indians returning from a buffalo hunt. The Indians were well supplied with dried meat, and generous with it, but their horses were few and worn down from hard travel with scant forage.

For several days the couriers stayed with the Indians, resting and regaining their strength. Their only means of communication was sign language, but Stuart was adept at it. When he asked for directions to a pass at the north end of the Wind River Mountains, the Indians made signs that the snow would be too deep for a crossing. One of them scratched an outline of the range on the ground, drew a mark around its southern end, and made gestures to indicate a broad, low pass that would be free of snow.

For an ax, a pistol, and a little ammunition, the Indians sold Stuart a thin old horse and a six-day supply of dried buffalo meat. On October 19 the couriers set out toward the southeast and, with their strength restored, traveled rapidly on short rations. Half their meat supply was still left when they reached the southern end of the Wind River Range, about a hundred miles due east of the point at which they had been turned northward by the Crow attack. The mountains flattened into a series of low hills, rising gently to the eastern horizon, and a deeply worn Indian trail led over them. There could be no doubt that this was the southern pass the Snake Indians had indicated. Stuart turned toward it, crossed the Continental Divide without realizing it, and came down to the Sweetwater River, flowing to the east.

In the valley of the Sweetwater, the couriers found game plentiful, and made their way downstream to the North Platte without difficulty. Near Red Buttes, a few miles above the present site of Casper, Wyoming, Stuart found a nook in the mountains that was surrounded by cedars and protected from winter storms. Mountain sheep and deer wintered in the valley, and buffalo were plentiful on the flatlands below. The couriers built a log cabin among the cedars and wintered comfortably. In the spring of 1813, they continued their journey down the Platte to the Missouri afoot, and on to St. Louis by canoe.

With the exception of a hundred-mile gap between Bear River and South Pass, Stuart had blazed the route that would become the general course of the Overland Trail, and was fully aware that he had discovered the most direct overland route to the Columbia. He painstakingly wrote a report of his journey and the exact route taken, noting that most of the distance could be traveled by wheeled vehicles. But his report received little attention, for in the War of 1812 the British had gained complete control of the Columbia River. Astor sold what remained of the Pacific Fur Company to his rivals, and for six years the Columbia was closed to Americans. By the time the treaty of 1818 was negotiated, again opening the Oregon region to settlement by citizens of the United States, Stuart's report and the route he pioneered had been nearly forgotten.

THE MOUNTAIN MEN

The general penetration of the Rockies by Americans was set off by the success of Ashley's first beaver-trapping venture. When, in the fall of 1822, his fur packs worth $24,000 were returned to St. Louis, hundreds of frontiersmen rushed to the mountains, most of them by keelboat up the Missouri River. Of all the hundreds, those to become most famous in pushing the American frontier westward

Jim Bridger. From The Old Santa
Fe Trail, *Colonel Henry Inman.*

were among the Ashley men: Jedediah Smith, Tom Fitzpatrick, Jim
Bridger, and the Sublettes—William and Milton—to be joined later by
Kit Carson.

In the fall of 1823, Smith and Fitzpatrick led their bands southward
from the Yellowstone, trapping the Big Horn River and its tributaries. By midwinter their fur packs were bulging and they had
reached the headwaters of the Big Horn in west-central Wyoming,
where the beaver streams were frozen solidly. To return to the
Yellowstone would require a trek of more than three hundred miles,
the furs could not be boated to St. Louis until the ice went out of
the upper Missouri in late spring, and in the meantime there would
be great danger of losing them to the Blackfeet. So as to reduce the
danger as much as possible, the trappers decided to pitch their winter
camp well to the south of Blackfoot territory, and make their return
to the Yellowstone in early spring. In search of a location with
abundant game, they crossed a low divide and reached the Sweetwater less than fifty miles east of South Pass.

Smith reasoned that since the Sweetwater flowed to the east it must

[243]

The Big Medicine Trail: routes of Jedediah Smith and Tom Fitz-

be a tributary of the Platte. If so, it should provide a short cut of seven or eight hundred miles to St. Louis, over which fur packs could be canoed, and which would entirely avoid danger from the Blackfeet. He and Fitzpatrick decided to cache their furs until spring,

patrick. The latter shortened the beaver-trappers' route to St. Louis.

and explore what they believed to be completely unknown country
to the west. They turned up the Sweetwater and crossed the Continental Divide by way of the age-old Indian trail, thus gaining credit
as the discoverers of South Pass, since few historians knew of Robert

Stuart's discovery in 1812. On the west side of the pass they followed Pacific and Sandy creeks down to the Green River, pioneering a section of the Oregon Trail which Stuart had not traveled. At the Green they separated to trap independently, agreeing to meet the following June at the cache buried on the Sweetwater. Their take of beaver pelts during the spring of 1824 was far beyond expectation, and their meeting at the cache made history as the first rendezvous held in the Rockies.

At the rendezvous it was decided that Fitzpatrick with a few men should take the fur packs to St. Louis, and return to the present site of Green River, Wyoming, with supplies for the following season. In the meantime, Smith and the balance of the men would hunt out the other Ashley trapping bands and guide them to the beaver-rich territory which is now western Wyoming.

A large buffalo-hide canoe was fashioned, loaded with pelts worth $30,000, and Fitzpatrick set off down the Sweetwater in late June. The stream was in freshet from melting snows, the heavily loaded canoe barely manageable among the submerged boulders, and on July 4 it was wrecked at a point where a great dome of rock stood in a meadow beside the Sweetwater. Fur packs bobbed away like corks on the racing water, part of them were lost, and the remainder saved only at the reckless risk of the men's lives.

Fitzpatrick realized that transporting valuable fur packs by canoe would be too hazardous until the rivers had been thoroughly explored. Because of the date, he named the dome Independence Rock, dug caches at its base, and buried the salvaged furs. To make the exploration he fashioned another canoe, but it was wrecked within thirty miles, at Fiery Narrows below the confluence of the Sweetwater and Platte. This time the men barely escaped with their lives, and lost most of their guns and ammunition. Having nothing to trade with the Indians for horses, Fitzpatrick and his men made their way afoot along the Platte to the prairies of western Nebraska. There the river, after being joined by the South Platte, became nearly a mile wide, but was too shallow for heavily loaded canoes. As a navigable water route, the Platte-Sweetwater system had proved to be impracticable. But its course to the central Rockies was little more than half the distance of that by way of the upper Missouri, and, like Stuart, Fitzpatrick believed the entire route could be traveled by wheeled vehicles. He reached Fort Atkinson, near the present site of

Council Bluffs, in early September, obtained pack horses on Ashley's credit, and returned with the fur packs in late October.

By November, Fitzpatrick had delivered the fur packs to St. Louis, told General Ashley of the rich fur country discovered beyond the Continental Divide, and urged him to transport supplies for the next season by wagon train. The general realized that wagon transportation would be far less expensive than the use of pack horses, but would not take the risk until he had assured himself of its practicability. With Fitzpatrick he took one wagon and two sets of harness to Fort Atkinson by keelboat, and set out for the mountains in late November, taking along twenty-five men, fifty pack horses loaded with supplies, and the wagon, drawn by four stout mules. Keeping to the south side of the Platte, and with the ground frozen solid, he had no difficulty until reaching the mountains in eastern Wyoming. From there on the wagon was a handicap, since the trail often had to be widened to allow passage, or detours made around gulches that could be easily crossed by pack animals. The experiment, however, proved that wagons could be taken over the route, and newspapers throughout the East ran glowing accounts of the first wheeled vehicle ever to be taken across the Continental Divide.

The bringing of a wagon to the heart of the beaver country was of no interest to the mountain men. But bringing supplies and taking back fur packs was of tremendous importance, for it saved each trapper band a four-thousand-mile round trip to St. Louis. The success of the 1825 rendezvous was so great that one was held every summer for the next decade and a half, usually in far-western Wyoming, and the route along the Sweetwater and Platte became the thoroughfare to and from civilization.

Within a few years the American mountain men had learned every stream and pass in the Rockies, as far west as central Idaho. Jim Bridger had built his famous fort in the southwestern corner of Wyoming, and had pushed westward through the Uinta Mountains to discover Great Salt Lake. Fitzpatrick had trapped every tributary of the Green River; Carson had penetrated far into the dangerous Blackfoot country of western Montana; and Jed Smith had bridged the remainder of the gap in the Oregon Trail left open by Robert Stuart. From Fort Bridger he had worked his way up Black Fork Creek to present Granger, Wyoming, then continued up Ham's Fork to its source near the Wyoming-Idaho boundary. From there he crossed a low ridge to the west, reached Bear River at about the point where Stuart was turned north by the Crow attack, and descended the Portneuf to trap the headwater of Snake River. While the American trappers were pushing their way to the northwest, the Hudson's Bay Company was pushing its men farther and farther to the southeast from the Columbia. By 1830 the entire route which would become the Oregon Trail was as well known to white men as it had been to the Indians when it was their Big Medicine Trail.

7

The Oregon Trail

THE IMMIGRANTS

Hall J. Kelley was a Boston schoolmaster with a deep-rooted hatred
of the British. Following the renewal, in 1827, of the treaty which
opened the Northwest to settlement by citizens of the United States,
he began bombarding Congress with demands that troops be sent to
"drive out the British tyrants." When his demands were ignored, he
circulated thousands of pamphlets, urging New England farmers to
gather at Boston with their families and household goods to join
him in migrating overland to Oregon, a region of "unparalleled
advantages." Kelley had, very evidently, read Robert Stuart's report
of discovering the Sweetwater-Platte route, Lewis and Clark's journal, and newspaper accounts of Ashley's taking a wagon over the
Continental Divide. Selecting the most glowing portions of these,
he added to them from his own fertile imagination, producing an
Oregon that would have put the Garden of Eden to shame, and
describing the broad highway leading to it through a land of abundance. The entire journey could easily be made in carriages, "by
way of a depression in the Rocky Mountains." All the Indians of
the West were friendly and generous, so the passage was perfectly
safe for women and children, and there was no need to take along
provisions, since the fertile plains were "teeming with buffalo."

No New Englanders left their rocky farms to journey with schoolmaster Kelley to the Promised Land, but his pamphlet aroused the

interest of a most unusual man: twenty-eight-year-old Nathaniel Wyeth. Imaginative, venturesome, forceful, and practical, Wyeth had already established himself as a successful businessman, cutting ice from ponds near Boston and shipping it to the West Indies. He hunted out and studied the Lewis and Clark journal, Gass's diary, available records of the Hudson's Bay Company, Robert Stuart's report, and newspaper articles regarding the exploits of the American mountain men. From these he gained a fairly good understanding of the difficulties to be encountered in crossing the continent, and realized that Kelley's scheme was simply a visionary's dream. He had no interest in driving out the British, but was much intrigued with the prospects of Oregon, and wrote in his journal, "I cannot divest myself of the opinion that I shall compete better with my fellow men in new and untried paths than in those to pursue which requires only patience and attention."

When Kelley's colonization plan failed to materialize, Wyeth decided to carry out the venture himself, but in a practical manner. He announced that he would enlist as many as fifty sturdy, single young men for the expedition, each of whom must have a trade, a profession, or be a successful farmer. Instead of representing the cross-country journey as Kelley had, Wyeth stressed its ruggedness and danger. To prepare for it, the men would be given three months' training on an island in Boston Harbor, where they would be toughened and taught frontiersmanship. He would arrange to finance the venture, and would send a ship ahead to the Columbia River, loaded with supplies, seed, cattle, and farming equipment. But each man would be required to sign a contract for his share of the investment, to be repaid over a period of five years from his farming profits after reaching Oregon.

Wyeth had no illusions about driving wagons and carriages from Boston to Oregon. He would send his wagons by ship and transport his expedition to St. Louis on canal barges and river packets, which were already in operation. Although the route from St. Louis followed rivers for nearly the entire distance, he understood that they were not always navigable, but his ingenious mind devised a means which he believed would overcome the difficulty. He invented and drew plans for a keelboat mounted on sturdy wheels.

The cost of chartering a ship to sail around Cape Horn would be great, but Wyeth conceived a plan for meeting the expense. From his study he had learned of the great demand for trade goods by the Indians of the Northwest, and the ship could fill out its cargo with such goods, on which a handsome profit should be made. With his well-laid plans and reputation as a successful businessman, Wyeth had no difficulty in raising whatever funds he could not supply himself. They were furnished by three Boston merchants, upon the agreement that they would share in the profits from the trade goods. His financing amply assured, Wyeth set about preparing for the undertaking, but Yankees were reluctant to join so hazardous an adventure, and only twenty-four enlisted. They included Nathaniel's brother Dr. Jacob Wyeth, geologist John Ball, a gunsmith, a blacksmith, two carpenters, two fishermen, and sixteen hardy young farmers.

By early March, 1832, three wagon-boats had been built, the men trained, and a small sailing vessel started on its voyage, loaded with implements, supplies, seed, a few milch cows, and a large cargo of trade goods. Wyeth and his party left Boston on March 11, and reached St. Louis on April 18. Upon arrival, he learned that William Sublette was in town, preparing to take a hundred-horse caravan of supplies to the summer rendezvous at Pierre's Hole, near Henry's deserted fort on the headwaters of Snake River.

Wyeth hunted out Sublette, gained his goodwill, and asked to join his party to the caravan. Sublette agreed, but insisted that the wagon-boats be abandoned, pointing out that they would be too heavy to haul over rugged trails and too cumbersome to handle in rapid streams. Furthermore, Sublette was planning to take a cutoff route to the mountains. He would leave the Missouri at Independence, follow the Santa Fe Trail to the vicinity of present Topeka, Kansas, then strike northwest to reach the Platte.

Wyeth had taken great pride in his wagon-boats, but he sold them for half their cost and took a packet to Independence, where he secured horses for pack animals and mounting his men. Independence was then a rough, tough frontier town, thronged with carousing mountain men, painted Indians, and cursing teamsters waiting to drive the spring caravan over the Santa Fe Trail. It was enough to frighten three of Wyeth's recruits into quitting the expedition and turning back. In early May, the rest set off with Sublette's caravan to pioneer the route which became the main line of the Oregon Trail between Independence and the Platte River. Sublette crossed the Kansas River west of Topeka, turned northward along the Big Blue

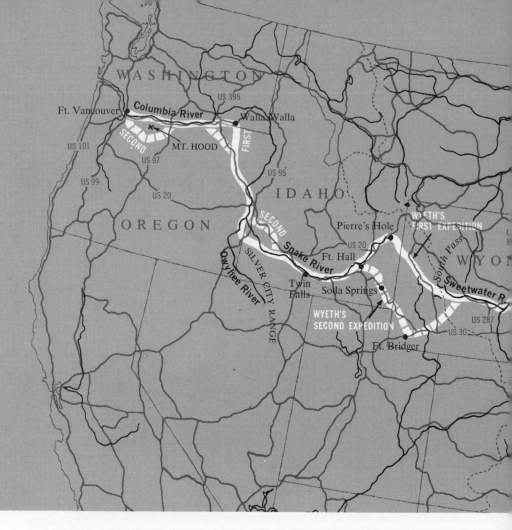

The Oregon Trail: routes of Nathaniel Wyeth's two immigrant

for some forty miles, then followed the Little Blue to its headwaters near Hastings, Nebraska, and came down to the wide valley of the Platte, opposite the present site of Kearney. There a war party of Pawnees overtook and passed the caravan, proudly waving a few bloody scalps just lifted from their enemies, the Kansas Indians. That was enough for three more of Wyeth's farmers. They set off down the Platte for St. Louis and home.

For twenty-seven days the combined caravan plodded westward

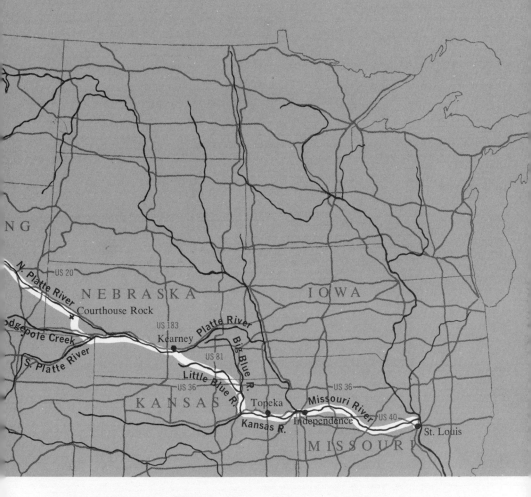

parties, the first to reach Oregon. Their trail became the main route.

along the south bank of the Platte, the Yankees continually amazed by the endless herds of buffalo that grazed along the valley. To avoid quicksand at the confluence, Sublette turned up the South Platte to the extreme northeast corner of Colorado, and followed Lodgepole Creek westward for about thirty miles. Then he turned north across a high divide, later known as Thirty-Mile Ridge, and reached the North Platte just below Courthouse Rock. This route also became the main line of the Oregon Trail, and Courthouse Rock one of its most famous landmarks. The trail from there to South Pass was that followed by both Stuart and Fitzpatrick, along the North Platte and Sweetwater. When the pass had been crossed, Sublette gave Wyeth his choice of going on with the caravan or striking out for Oregon by following the plainly marked trappers' trail southwest to Bridger's Fort, then turning northwest to the Bear, the Portneuf, and the Snake. The route Sublette described was to become the general course of the Oregon Trail, but Wyeth chose to continue with the rendezvous caravan.

Each year the mountain men's rendezvous had grown in size and dissipation, and that of 1832 was one of the largest and wildest. In mid-July the caravan reached Pierre's Hole, and the New Englanders were appalled at the stark barbarism of the scene. If this were a sample of the Far West, seven of Wyeth's men decided they wanted no more of it; they would return to St. Louis with William Sublette when he took back the fur packs. Wyeth, with the remaining eleven, joined Milton Sublette, who was leading a band of twenty men far down the Snake River to trap back upstream during late fall. Milton accompanied them to the vicinity of Twin Falls, Idaho, where he turned back, telling Wyeth to follow the river to its great canyon, then take any of the well-traveled Indian trails leading to the northwest.

Milton Sublette may have been unfamiliar with the Snake below Twin Falls, or may have neglected to tell Wyeth to cross to the north side after traveling some fifty or sixty miles. In any event, the Wyeth party kept to the south side of the river, where the terrain was broken by impassable gorges and canyons. Forced to leave the stream, they became lost in the mountains, ran out of provisions, and nearly starved before stumbling onto a village of friendly Shoshoni Indians on the Owyhee River of eastern Oregon. These Indians supplied them with dried salmon in exchange for a few fishhooks and trinkets, then guided them downstream to the Snake, and set them off on the age-old trail to the Columbia.

The trail was easily followed, but no Indians, either friendly or unfriendly, were found, and the Wyeth party was forced to live on horse meat. Instead of following the Umatilla River down to the Columbia, they continued northward on the Indian trail, and reached the present location of Walla Walla, Washington, on September 18, exhausted, ragged, and nearly starved. There they found a Hudson's

Bay Company trading post. The agent received them with all hospitality, fed them, supplied them with new clothing, and traded their worn-out horses for provisions and a river barge. On October 29, the barge drew up at the Hudson's Bay Company dock at Fort Vancouver, bringing the first American immigrants to Oregon.

The factor at Fort Vancouver, Dr. John McLoughlin, welcomed Wyeth cordially, but gave him news that was far from welcome. The ship sent around Cape Horn had been lost at sea, leaving Wyeth nearly bankrupt and his little colony with no equipment, livestock, provisions, or supplies. Many men would have despaired, but Nat Wyeth was not the despairing type. He determined to raise additional capital, recruit more colonists, and organize another expedition as soon as possible. Always resourceful, he believed he knew how it could be done. Dried salmon would sell for ten cents a pound in Boston, but, during the spring salmon run, any quantity of it could be secured from Indians along the Columbia in exchange for a few fish-hooks and trinkets. The profit on a shipload would not only cover the cost of charter but pay for a cargo of farming equipment and supplies. Furthermore, rendezvous trade goods were worth four times as much in the mountains as at Boston, due to the labor cost of transporting them. If he could recruit a large party of colonists, the transportation of trade goods would cost practically nothing, and the profit would pay the expenses of the overland journey.

In early February, 1833, Wyeth set out for Boston alone, met Milton Sublette on the Green River, and outlined his plan for bringing trade goods from Boston. Sublette agreed to buy three thousand dollars' worth, but only if they were delivered to Fort Bridger in time for the opening of the 1834 rendezvous.

Wyeth reached Boston in the late fall of 1833. The news that he had taken the remnant of his first expedition through safely to Oregon aroused great enthusiasm, particularly among the Methodists, who had long been anxious to plant missionaries among the heathen Indians of the Far West. The backers of the first venture, who had lost their entire investment, were far from enthusiastic, but Henry Hall, a Boston capitalist, agreed to finance a second venture. The brig *May Dacre* was chartered, loaded, and sailed for the Columbia in early winter. On February 7, 1834, Wyeth left Boston on his second colonizing expedition, taking with him rendezvous trade goods costing $800. There is no record of the exact number in his party, but it was far larger than the first. Among its members were two scientists, and several Methodist missionaries under the leadership of Jason Lee.

As before, Wyeth secured transportation to Independence by canal barge and river packet. The trade goods, camping gear, supplies, and provisions were loaded onto pack horses, and the colonists set out over the route taken on the previous expedition. But the start was made earlier in the spring, the weather was bad, and winter snows had been deep throughout the Rockies and Great Plains. The mud was deep, creeks and rivers overflowed their banks, and a day seldom passed without rain. Day after day was lost in waiting for streams to subside enough to be forded, and on many days no more than two or three miles could be traveled through the deep mud. The result was that Wyeth failed to reach Fort Bridger until the rendezvous was disbanding, and Milton Sublette refused to accept the trade goods.

Nat Wyeth was no man to grieve over adversities but quick to grasp any advantage, and he believed he had one. The first trader to arrive at rendezvous with his goods was assured of the greatest profit, and he planned to be first on the scene in 1835. He continued toward Oregon by the trappers' trail—up Bear River to Soda Springs, and down the Portneuf to the Snake. Ten miles north of Pocatello's present location, he set his colonists to building a stout log fort, which he named Fort Hall in honor of his backer. There he stored his trade goods, easily available to any rendezvous site along the Green River. Leaving a crew of twelve men to guard the merchandise and trap during the fall and spring seasons, he and the remainder of his colonists pushed on for the Columbia. They followed the trail pioneered by Stuart until reaching the river, then blazed the route which would become the Oregon Trail to the present site of Portland. It lay along the south side of the Columbia to The Dalles, then turned away from the river to circle Mount Hood and reach the Willamette Valley opposite Fort Vancouver.

Wyeth again found his hopes frustrated. The *May Dacre* had been struck by lightning at sea, and held up so long in making repairs that it missed the salmon run. Again his venture had been a financial failure, but he had opened the gateway of overland immigration to the Northwest, and it would never again be closed. He established his colony on an island at the mouth of the Willamette River; it prospered, and with each succeeding year more Americans arrived to clear farms and build homes farther up the valley.

THE MISSIONARIES

When the Methodists sent their missionaries west with Wyeth's second expedition, the American Board of Foreign Missions, supported by the Presbyterians and Congregationalists, bestirred itself immediately. At its convention in Ithaca, New York, it voted to send a party of six to the Columbia River Valley—two missionaries, their wives, a farmer, and a mechanic. Marcus Whitman, recently graduated from Fairfield Medical School applied for one of the missionary posts, but he was, unfortunately, single. Twenty-six-year-old Narcissa Prentiss, pretty, vivacious, deeply religious, and ideally talented for a frontier missionary's wife, virtually threw herself into Whitman's arms, and made him eligible for the post by marrying him. As a second couple, the Board chose Reverend Henry Spalding and his fragile, ineffectual wife, Eliza.

The Whitmans, Spaldings, a farmer, and a carpenter traveled to St. Louis during the winter of 1835-36, and outfitted there. By prearrangement, they were to join a rendezvous supply caravan led by Tom Fitzpatrick, which was to assemble at Belleview, a little frontier settlement near the confluence of the Platte and Missouri. Like most of the immigrants who followed them in later years, the Whitmans and Spaldings outfitted far too heavily. In addition to household furniture, trunks of clothing, boxes of religious books, provisions for several months, and elaborate camping equipment, they bought two wagons, fourteen horses, six pack mules, and seventeen cattle—most of them milch cows. In mid-May of 1836, they boarded a packet and traveled up the Missouri to Belleview.

The Fitzpatrick caravan of 1836 was one of the strangest ever to set off for the Rockies. The main body was made up of four hundred pack animals and seventy frontiersmen—rough, tough American mountain men, French-Canadian trappers, and Indian half-breeds. In ludicrous contrast was Sir William Drummond Stuart and his party of British sportsmen, bound for a "rousing buffalo hunt" on the prairies. The sportsmen were accompanied by an array of menservants, gunbearers, and dogs, and traveled in several ornate wagons, each drawn by six mules in glittering harness. To complete the motley assemblage, the missionaries trailed along behind, driving their milch cows and a few bawling calves.

At the outset the women were not only a curiosity to Fitzpatrick's rough crew but the object of more than a little ribald banter. Sister Spalding was shocked and appalled, but Narcissa Whitman glowed with exhilaration at the exciting adventure before her. A country judge's daughter, she was not unused to the profanity and rough talk of the frontiersmen, and showed no resentment of it. After a few days she won the admiration of the entire crew, and—within the limits of their ability and provocation—they watched their language in her presence. Whenever game was killed, the choicest cuts were brought to her tent, and the bearer's canteen was always filled with fresh milk.

The winter had been mild, the spring fairly dry, and travel was rather easy until the South Platte had been crossed. There the land began rising steeply toward the foothills of the Rockies. The wagons lagged behind, and, to cross Thirty-Mile Ridge, Whitman was obliged to jettison the least needed articles of furniture. Beyond Scotts Bluff the road became increasingly rugged. Long detours often had to be made around impassable gulches near the river, the draft animals weakened from overwork, and equipment which had seemed indispensable had to be discarded.

At Fort Laramie the British sportsmen left the caravan, and Fitzpatrick advised Whitman to abandon his wagons, transferring his goods to pack animals for the remainder of the journey. Whitman refused. If Ashley could cross the Continental Divide with a wagon, certainly a Christian gentleman could do the same. He had made up his mind to take his wagons through to the Columbia, and would not be deterred from his purpose. Fitzpatrick pointed out that there was no road, and that Ashley had been able to get his wagon through only by having a large crew and building road where necessary. Whitman finally agreed to leave one wagon, but was adamant about the other.

Beyond Fort Laramie the trail became more rugged as it ascended the eastern slope of the Rockies. Pack animals could easily climb it at the rate of two or three miles an hour, but it was unfit for wagon travel. Trees had to be cut, boulders pried aside, and detours made around deep gulches. Often the wagon tipped over two or three times in a single day, and most of the load had to be thrown out or transferred to pack animals, but Whitman was as stubborn as impractical. While Narcissa and the Spaldings rode with the caravan, he and the unfortunate farmer and carpenter fought the almost empty wagon up the valleys of the Platte and Sweetwater, and over South Pass to Bridger's Fort.

At the rendezvous the white women were as great an object of curiosity as they had been when first joining the caravan, and Narcissa made friends just as quickly. The mountain men, many of whom had not seen a white woman for several years, were fascinated by her beauty, and the Indians almost worshiped her. The squaws gathered in a throng, to touch their fingers to her white skin, marvel at her blue eyes, and admire her clothing.

Fortunately, Nathaniel Wyeth, after selling Fort Hall to the Hudson's Bay Company, had come to the rendezvous. Thomas McKay, adopted son of Dr. McLoughlin, was still at the fort, but would soon be returning to Walla Walla with a caravan. Wyeth gave Whitman a letter of introduction to McKay, and assured him that he could accompany the caravan to Oregon if he arrived at the fort in time, but urged that he abandon his wagon. Again Whitman refused, saying that if necessary he would make the journey unescorted: he had promised himself to open a road to the Columbia, and the wagon was going through. He was mistaken. By the time he reached Soda Springs, his draft animals were too exhausted to pull it farther.

Still determined to open a roadway to Oregon, Whitman discarded rear wheels and body, mounted a box on the front axle, and continued down the Portneuf to Fort Hall. The missionaries, nearly as exhausted as their draft animals, reached the fort just as McKay was setting out for Walla Walla. He welcomed them cordially, laid over a few days so they might rest and recuperate, then led the way down the south rim of Snake River Gorge. The caravan was continually slowed by the lumbering, makeshift cart, and at what is now Glenn's Ferry four mules were nearly drowned when the wheels capsized and tangled them in the harness.

McKay was thoroughly disgusted when Whitman insisted on going on with the useless cart. He wanted to be hospitable, but had lost all the time he could afford. Leaving three men for guides, he and his party rode away toward the Boise Basin. At the mouth of the Boise the guides also rebelled, threatening to leave the missionaries before trying to get the wheels across the Snake again. Whitman had no choice but to abandon his beloved vehicle and his ambition to open a wagon road to the Columbia. It was a sad disappointment, but also a great achievement, for he had proved that with no great amount of road-building the route was feasible for wagon travel.

Without the cumbersome vehicle, the party moved on at a good pace. On September 1, 1836, the first white women ever to have crossed the Rockies reached Fort Walla Walla, both in good health, and in barely more than three months from the time they had left the Missouri. Scarcely a month later, with help from the Hudson's Bay Company, the Whitmans and Spaldings had constructed buildings and established missions among the Nez Percé Indians, twenty miles farther up the Walla Walla Valley.

Yankee ships plied regularly between Boston and the Pacific coast, trading for hides and tallow at the Spanish ports in California, and captains often sailed up the Columbia for furs and dried salmon. No ship returned without a packet of letters from the American missionaries and colonists, but particularly from Narcissa Whitman, extolling the wonders of Oregon and the ease and safety of the overland journey. Marcus Whitman sent off voluminous reports to the Board of Foreign Missions, urging that more missionaries and colonists be sent and boasting that he had opened a wagon road to "the very shore of Oregon." He, however, failed to mention that it was the Snake River shore, nearly four hundred miles short of Fort Vancouver.

These letters and reports created great enthusiasm in New England church circles. Each spring an increasing number of small emigrant wagon trains plodded westward from Independence, over the route which had become known as the Oregon Trail. As each train passed, the roughest stretches along the trails were improved: chutes cut into gulch banks, boulders rolled aside, wider openings slashed through woods and thickets, and the roadway along steep hillsides leveled enough so that wagons would not tip over. By 1839 a very passable wagon route extended from Independence to the present site of Portland.

During the eight years following Wyeth's first colonization venture, most of the emigration to Oregon was by New England Protestants. Then, in the spring of 1840, the Jesuit Order sent the first Catholic missionary into the Rockies. He was Father Pierre Jean De Smet, short, fat, jovial, and fearless, with deep devotion to his calling

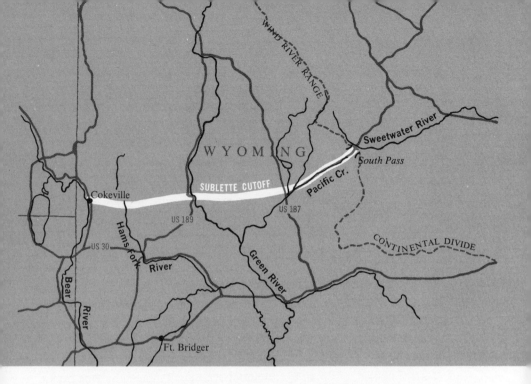

*The Oregon Trail: William Sublette's cutoff route. He pio-
neered this shorter route while escorting Wyeth's first immigrant party.*

and a marvelous sense of humor. Father De Smet, a Belgian, had for
ten years been a frontier missionary among the Potawatami Indians
at the present site of Council Bluffs, Iowa. In April, 1840, he accompanied Andrew Drips's supply caravan from Westport Landing, now
Kansas City, to the last rendezvous held by the beaver trappers.

Roly-poly Father De Smet became not only admired but beloved
by the mountain men before the rendezvous ended, but he, like
Father Garcés, preferred to travel alone among the Indians. From
the rendezvous he struck off with a band of Flathead Indians to the
general vicinity of Missoula, Montana. He visited any Indian en-
campments found along the way, making friends and acquainting
the natives with the Cross and the story of Christ. Late that fall he
crossed unharmed through the dangerous Blackfoot country, and
canoed down the Missouri to Council Bluffs.

In the spring of 1841, Father De Smet returned to the Rockies, taking with him the personnel for establishing the first Catholic missions in the northern Rockies: two priests, three lay brothers, a carpenter, a blacksmith, and a tinner. Traveling in carts pulled by two mules harnessed in tandem, they accompanied Tom Fitzpatrick's trapping party to the Bear River. After crossing South Pass, Fitzpatrick led them across the valley of the Green River by the route which would soon become famous as the Sublette Cutoff on the Oregon Trail. The route followed Pacific Creek down to the Big Sandy, then turned almost straight west, across nearly forty miles of waterless, sagebrush-covered desert to the Green. From there, it continued slightly southwest for thirty more waterless miles to Ham's Fork, and reached Bear River near the point where Wyoming, Utah, and Idaho join. Although rough on draft animals, it had advantages over the route by way of Fort Bridger, saving nearly seventy miles of travel and five creek fordings. It was taken by more than half the emigrant trains during the years that followed, the dry stretches usually being traveled at night.

Leaving Fitzpatrick at Bear River, Father De Smet and his party continued on, reaching Fort Vancouver June 8, 1842. There he found two other priests, brought across Canada by the Hudson's Bay Company. Their missions were thriving, so Father De Smet turned back to the mountains of northern Idaho and his beloved Flatheads. But his reports, letters, and journals stimulated a westward Catholic migration.

THE PATHFINDER

By the end of 1841, migration to Oregon had been considerable, but not enough to suit Senator Thomas Hart Benton of Missouri. He believed that many people had been frightened away by wildly exaggerated newspaper reports of danger from Indian attack. In casting about for a means of counteracting this unfavorable publicity, the Senator hit upon a brilliant scheme. His daughter had recently married a young second lieutenant in the Topographical Corps, John C. Frémont, who had ambitions to become a famous military leader and explorer, but whose greatest talent was for inspirational writing. As a stunt to demonstrate the absolute safety of the Oregon Trail, Benton conceived the idea of sending his twelve-year-old son as far as the Continental Divide, with Frémont to write the publicity. To

John C. Frémont.
From Harper's Magazine.

carry out his scheme at Government expense, he pushed through Congress an appropriation for "mapping the Oregon Trail to the western boundary of the United States," then had Frémont assigned to the task.

There was, of course, little reason for mapping the Oregon Trail, since there were no turnoffs and a blind man could have followed the deep wagon ruts. But Frémont arrived at St. Louis in the spring of 1842 with a German topographer and enough scientific and navigational instruments for an exploration of the North Pole. In addition, he brought a large inflatable India-rubber boat for proving the navigability of the Platte and Sweetwater rivers, and a lavish array of camping equipment. At St. Louis he bought specially constructed carts and wagons, packsaddles, and nearly a hundred horses, and employed twenty-one French-Canadian voyageurs. To add glamour to the expedition, he engaged two of the most famous mountain men— Lucien Maxwell as hunter, and Kit Carson as guide.

Because of his overelaborate preparations, it was mid-June before Frémont set out from Westport Landing with his impressive cavalcade. The trek to Fort Laramie would have been routine if Frémont had not tried to be a great explorer and prove the Platte River navigable. Days were lost while he made aimless side excursions in an effort to pioneer a shorter and better route. Others were wasted in trying to use the rubber boat as a ferry, and in dragging it over sand bars in the foot-deep Platte.

When the expedition reached Fort Laramie, Carson learned that there had been a battle the previous fall between a band of Sioux and a party of sixty American traders who had plied them with frontier whiskey and tried to rob them of their furs. Eight of the Sioux had been killed, and the tribe was reported to have gone on the warpath. Carson had no fear for himself, and little for the safety of the expedition, but, believing the danger great enough that the young son of a United States Senator should not be exposed to it, he advised Frémont to leave Randolph Benton in care of the factor until the expedition returned. Frémont insisted that the boy should remain with the expedition, that if the Sioux wanted a battle he and his voyageurs would teach them a lesson. It was Carson who did the teaching. Unable to read or write, he dictated his will to the factor. That was enough for the voyageurs. If the danger were so great that Kit Carson had made his will, they had no stomach to face it. Frémont was obliged to compromise: the boy was left at Fort Laramie and Carson convinced the voyageurs to go on.

The march to South Pass was as uneventful as that from Westport Landing to Fort Laramie, but the homeward journey had its moments of excitement. At the confluence of the Sweetwater and Platte, Frémont decided to launch his rubber boat and float triumphantly to the Missouri. The launching proved somewhat difficult in the swift water, but the rubber craft, being empty and flexible, rode easily over submerged boulders. Frémont was sure that it would be ideal for shooting rapids, and would unquestionably solve the problem of navigating swift mountain streams. Without further experiment, he had the scientific instruments, maps, journals, arms, bedding, and a good part of the provisions loaded into the boat. Carson, Maxwell, and a few of the men were sent ahead with the horses. Frémont, the topographer, and the rest of the voyageurs would ride the river, and they would all rendezvous at Fort Laramie.

With the voyageurs singing happily, the overloaded craft sped toward Fiery Narrows like an elephant on a rampage. At the mouth of the chasm it was caught and spun in a whirlpool, flinging sextant, telescope, and baggage overboard, then leaped into the flying spray of the cascades. Where the five-hundred-foot cliffs pinched closest together, the rubber steed sunfished, bucked wildly, and capsized. Battered and half drowned, Frémont and his men managed to save themselves and scale the canyon walls, but little else was salvaged.

The rest of the homeward journey was no more eventful than the westbound trek, but Frémont's account of the expedition was an inspirational masterpiece. At Government expense, Senator Benton had hundreds of thousands of copies printed and distributed throughout the East. The result was electrifying. Readers were convinced that the Oregon Trail was as safe and comfortable to travel as the streets of their own home towns; caravans were organized by the hundreds, and the great migration rolled westward from the Missouri with the greening of the grass in the spring of 1843.

The California Trail

JUST AS the Snake River determined the course of the Oregon Trail across Idaho, the Humboldt River determined the course of the California Trail across Nevada. The headwaters of the Humboldt, rising in the northeast corner of Nevada, were discovered by Peter Skene Ogden of the Hudson's Bay Company in 1828. Following the rendezvous of 1833, Captain Bonneville sent forty trappers, led by Joseph Walker, to hunt out new beaver streams west of Great Salt Lake. Joe Walker, like Frémont only in this one respect, had ambitions to be an explorer. He not only knew of Jed Smith's fame as the discoverer of an overland route to California, but of Ewing Young's success in trapping beaver there. Walker, no doubt, had his destination well in mind when he led his band westward from the rendezvous. He skirted the northern end of Great Salt Lake, then continued almost due westward for more than a hundred miles to Mary's River, the most northerly tributary of the Humboldt.

Although beaver were plentiful along the Mary's, Walker did not stop to trap, but hurried downstream, reached the Humboldt just west of present Wells, Nevada, and continued on to the southwest. For a hundred miles the river was clear and cold, with excellent beaver streams flowing in from isolated mountain ranges on either side. Then the lush grass that bordered the headwaters gave way to greasewood brush. There were no tributaries, the water became progressively brackish, and beaver scarce. Walker would certainly have turned back if his purpose had been to discover beaver streams, but he continued on.

Each day the desert became more arid, the water more brackish, the forage scarcer, the heat more intolerable, and the horses more emaciated. Naked Digger Indians skulked through the greasewood, pouncing like a pack of snarling jackals upon any horse that lagged behind or strayed, stripping hide and flesh from its bones with their teeth. As, day after day, the animals weakened, the Diggers grew more bold, and the pack increased until they outnumbered the trappers. Doubtlessly worried, and with his patience tried, Walker ordered his men to fire upon the defenseless Indians. In the massacre a score or more, including women and children, were killed, and the everlasting enmity of the Diggers aroused. Within the next thirty years, the Indians of the Nevada deserts would repay that treachery with far more than tenfold interest.

For a hundred miles, Walker followed the Humboldt southward, his men shooting at any Indian that was seen. With each mile the river slowed and dwindled from evaporation, until it became too bitter for either man or animal to drink. Then it spread into a shallow, alkaline lake and sank into the desert. By holding straight on to the south, Walker failed to discover Truckee River, which would have led him to the best pass across the central Sierra Nevada, later to become famous as Donner Pass.

Having only a vague idea of his whereabouts, Walker continued southward, for some strange reason crossed the stream that would be known as Carson River, and reached the northern loop of Walker River, forty miles east of present Carson City. With the solid rampart of the Sierra Nevada in view, Walker turned up the stream to the southwest, and followed it high into the mountains. Not knowing that he was retracing the general course pioneered by Jed Smith when returning from California in 1827, Walker crossed the summit of the Sierras, probably by way of Sonora Pass, and descended the Stanislaus River to the San Joaquin Valley. The party made its way to San Francisco Bay, and turned southward along the coast to Monterey, where it spent the winter of 1833-34. Walker's welcome by the Spanish officials was no more cordial than Smith's had been. In February he returned to the San Joaquin Valley, and followed it southward to the present site of Bakersfield. Doubtlessly knowing

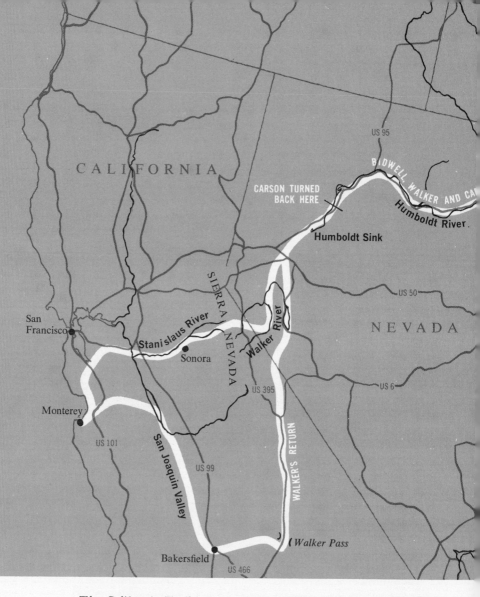

The California Trail: routes of Joseph Walker, Kit Carson, and John Bidwell. The course of the trail across Nevada was determined

of Smith's arrest at Mission San Gabriel, and wishing to avoid the risk, Walker turned eastward, climbed the Sierra Nevada through rugged Kern River Canyon, and crossed the summit at Walker Pass. Skirting the foothills northward, he picked up his trail of the previous

by the Humboldt River. Bidwell's party were the first immigrants to pass over it.

fall and returned to the rendezvous of 1834 by the route over which he had come.

In the fall of 1834, Kit Carson blazed the route which would connect the Humboldt with the Overland Trail. From Fort Hall he led his trapping band sixty miles down Snake River, then turned south-ward along Raft River to its headwaters, and westward to the point where Idaho, Utah, and Nevada now join. There he trapped the headwaters of Goose Creek and moved on to the southwest, trapping Thousand Springs Creek which flows down from three low mountain ranges and is swallowed by the desert lying between them. A desert-crossing of less than ten miles led to the source of Bishop's Creek, the most easterly tributary of the Humboldt. Carson and his men found beaver plentiful in the nine clear streams that flow into the Humboldt in northeastern Nevada, and moved on in search of more. They followed the river nearly to the sink, then turned back be-cause there was no grazing for the pack horses, no beaver in the brackish stream, and provisions were running low. Thereafter the mountain men trapped the headwaters of the Humboldt each season, following Carson's route from the Snake, but few parties went far-ther downstream than the present site of Battle Mountain, Nevada.

THE CALIFORNIA IMMIGRANTS

The first emigrants to pass over the California Trail were the Bid-well party. Twenty-five-year-old John Bidwell—handsome, intelli-gent, and imbued with the pioneer spirit—had come west in the fall of 1839 to teach school at Weston, Missouri. Soon after, he heard of the wonders of California through a letter from John Marsh, an early settler who had sailed around Cape Horn. The letter fired Bidwell's already smoldering enthusiasm, which proved so contagious that dur-ing the winter of 1840-41, he was successful in convincing five hun-dred Missourians to join his Western Emigration Society. In the early spring of 1841 they were to meet at Sapling Grove, each family with its own wagon, provisions, and camping equipment.

All went well until Thomas Farnham returned from leading a small party to Oregon. His reports of the hardships encountered on the overland journey were enough to discourage most of the Missourians. When Bidwell reached Sapling Grove he found only sixty-nine men, women, and children. Worse still, those who had arrived were pov-erty stricken, and most of them undecided as to whether they wanted to go to California or Oregon. There was less than a hundred dollars cash among the whole sixty-nine. Some were driving ox-drawn wag-ons, a few had come in carriages, others on horseback, and several were afoot. Knowing only that the starting point of the trail was at Independence, and that California and Oregon lay beyond the Rocky Mountains, the forlorn little party set out, and was fortunate enough to fall in with a band of mountain men led by Tom Fitzpatrick.

As with almost every emigrant organization that was to follow, discord and wrangling broke out in the Bidwell party soon after taking the trail. By the time it arrived at South Pass the party was divided into two feuding factions, one determined to go to Oregon and the other to California. At the northern bend of Bear River the feud reached a point where the two factions would no longer travel together, so Bidwell, with a group of thirty-two men, one woman, and one child decided to strike off for California. The only direction Fitzpatrick could give them was to follow the Bear to Great Salt Lake, skirt its northern end, and continue westward to pick up Carson's old trail to the Humboldt.

John Bidwell and his party followed Bear River to within ten miles of Great Salt Lake, but no one knows the exact route taken as they groped their way westward across the deserts and mountains. They were obliged to abandon their wagons, failed to find the trail, and did not discover the headwaters of the Humboldt until late September. With incredible suffering they made their way downstream to the sink, subsisting on the flesh of horses that gave out from starvation and exhaustion. Although there was no trail, they continued southward along the course Walker had taken, and reached the river that bears his name. As he had done, they followed the western branch of the river to its source, crossed the summit of the Sierra Nevada, and descended the Stanislaus River to the San Joaquin Valley. Considering that they had no knowledge of the geography of the West, no one to guide them, and no frontier experience, their achievement is one of the most amazing in American history.

With Frémont's report of his junket to South Pass having spurred the Oregon migration, Senator Benton pushed through Congress an appropriation for a second expedition. Its declared purpose was for the discovery of a more direct route to Oregon, but that was simply a subterfuge. The Senator's actual purpose was fourfold: to spy out the military strength of the British in Oregon and the Mexicans in California, and at the same time discover a direct route through the Rocky Mountains by which a migration of American citizens to California could be stimulated. In the early spring of 1843 Frémont

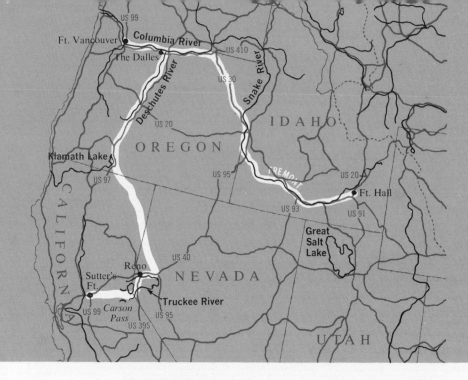

*The California Trail: John Frémont's expedition in search of
a shorter route. He failed, but his report inspired many people
to emigrate to California.*

was again in St. Louis outfitting an expedition, but this time he had
conquest in mind more than exploration. He enlisted thirty-nine experienced fighting men, mulcted Colonel Kearny out of a mounted
cannon from the U.S. arsenal, "for protection against the audacious
Indian tribes," and sent for Carson to bring his Carson Men and guide
him through the Rockies.

Carson met Frémont in Colorado during May, and told him there
was no direct route by which wagons could be taken through the
central Rockies, but the Pathfinder was determined to prove him
wrong. He spent so many weeks blundering into blind canyons and
exploring already well-known Great Salt Lake that winter caught
him at Fort Hall. Carson advised him to winter there or abandon the
cannon, but Frémont would do neither. He had planned to impress
the British at Fort Vancouver and the Mexicans at Monterey, and
would not be turned from his purpose. To drag the cannon to the

[272]

Columbia River Valley through deep snow killed dozens of mules, consumed all the provisions, and exhausted the men. Half-starved, ragged, and nearly frozen, they finally reached The Dalles. Frémont left Carson there with the expedition while he went down the Columbia by boat to reconnoiter Fort Vancouver. He returned with a few sacks of beans—and the opinion that one mounted cannon would impress the Mexicans much more than the British. Hiring two Indian guides, he set off for California.

The Indians guided Frémont southward along the Deschutes River and into the Klamath marshes of southern Oregon. There they became completely lost and abandoned the party. For days the men wallowed through the marshes, dragging the anchorlike cannon, while Frémont took celestial observations and plotted a direct course to Sutter's Fort. But the direct course led to Klamath Lake, and the Cascade Range blocked a passage around it to the west. An almost direct route, now followed by U.S. Highway 97, would have led around Mount Shasta to the Sacramento Valley, but Frémont, like Jed Smith, had seen maps showing the Buena Ventura River. He decided to stay on the eastern side of the mountains until he reached the Buena Ventura, then cross to California through its canyon.

In mid-January the expedition reached the Truckee River, east of present Reno, Nevada, but Frémont, still expecting to find the Buena Ventura, would not turn up the stream. By taking celestial observations he knew Sutter's Fort to be only a hundred miles away, almost straight westward, so two weeks were lost in searching for the Buena Ventura canyon. When, at the end of January, Carson discovered the river that bears his name, the situation had become desperate. The expedition was entirely out of provisions, so could neither go into winter quarters nor turn back, and hope of finding the mythical river had to be given up. On February 6 Kit discovered nine-thousand-foot-high Carson Pass, but the snow at the summit was nearly twenty feet deep, and the noon temperature below zero. The cannon and all packs had to be abandoned, and horses—solely for food—could be gotten across the mountains only by beating out a trail with wooden mauls. The crossing required a full month, and before the exhausted expedition reached Sutter's Fort two men had gone insane from hardship, frostbite, and starvation.

Frémont was in poor condition to impress anyone. Without Carson, he would have lost his own life and the lives of his men. He had found no new route through the Rockies and had not shortened the Oregon Trail by a single inch. Still, his report of the expedition was exciting and convincing. It inspired many an emigrant to pack his family and belongings into a covered wagon and head for California.

There are various claims as to who took the first wagons overland to California, but there can be little doubt that it was Joe Walker, although the area to which he took them was not then considered to be California. In the summer of 1843 Walker led the Chiles party, traveling with three mule-drawn wagons in addition to pack horses and saddle mounts, from Fort Hall to California. From the Snake he followed the well-known trappers' trails to the Humboldt, then continued over the route by which he had returned in the spring of 1834. In the Owens Valley, now a part of eastern California, he was obliged to abandon the wagons, and crossed the Sierra Nevada with pack animals.

The first wagons were probably taken across the Sierra Nevada by the Stevens party of 1843. This expedition is of great importance to trail history, for it definitely pioneered and opened the most difficult stretch of the California Trail. In many ways the group—composed of twenty-six men, eight women, and seventeen children—was better suited to such an adventure than any other early emigrant party. It was predominantly Irish and five, or possibly six, of the wagons belonged to an intermarried family group—the Murphys, Martins, and Millers. One of the other wagons was that of "Old Man" Hitchcock, a mountain man returning to the West with his widowed daughter and her four children. Another was that of Dr. Townsend, traveling with his wife and her seventeen-year-old brother, Moses Schallenberger—the chronicler of the expedition. Of the three remaining wagons, one belonged to Allen Montgomery and his wife; one to John Sullivan, traveling with his sister and two young brothers, and the other to Elisha Stevens. Caleb Greenwood, an oldtime beaver trapper accompanied by two half-breed sons, was taken along as guide and Indian interpreter. The rest of the party was made up of unattached young men, well mounted and probably leading pack animals.

Although the Murphy contingent certainly controlled the vote, unattached Elisha Stevens was elected captain. A slight, wiry man of about forty, he had earlier been connected with the fur trade of the Northwest and, though unfamiliar with the Oregon Trail, was a thorough frontiersman. He was cautious without being timid, a strict disciplinarian without being overbearing, and sufficiently foresighted to avoid trouble before it arose.

With all the wagons ox-drawn and a few milch cows trailing behind, the caravan set out from the west bank of the Missouri, opposite Council Bluff, on May 18, 1843. Under Elisha Stevens's firm but gentle leadership there was no discord or dissension in the party, and with the exception of normal hardships on such a journey, the long trek to Fort Hall was relatively uneventful.

The caravan reached Fort Hall on August 10, and stopped for several days to rest and graze the animals, then moved on down the Snake, and two days later turned southward up Raft River Valley. In his memoirs, Schallenberger made no reference to the wheel tracks of Walker's wagons which were, no doubt, still visible, and which the party must have been following, since Greenwood knew nothing of the route beyond Snake River. In any event, the Stevens party traveled by the same general route that Walker had taken to Hum-

Wagons on the California Trail. From Life on the Plains and Among the Diggings, *A. Delano. Courtesy of The New York Public Library, Rare Book Division.*

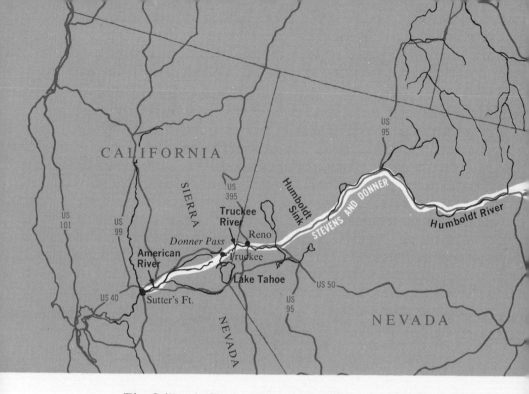

The California Trail: routes of the Stevens and Donner parties. Elisha Stevens's party, opening the most difficult stretch of the

boldt Sink, arriving there at the end of September. The summer of 1843 on the Nevada deserts must have been less dry than usual, for Schallenberger wrote that the grazing was good for the entire distance, and that the water, though brackish, was drinkable even at the sink.

It is not at all probable that the Stevens party followed Walker's exact trail all the way, since the deserts along a considerable part of the Humboldt are wide and greasewood-covered, making wheel tracks exceedingly easy to lose. It is even less probable that they discovered his trail leading southward from the sink. Otherwise, Stevens would doubtlessly have continued on the same course, rather than stopping a week to search out the way to California. The party was still undecided when a band of Paiute Indians came to the sink, among them their aged chief, whose name Greenwood understood to be Truckee. Actually, what he took to be the name was a Paiute

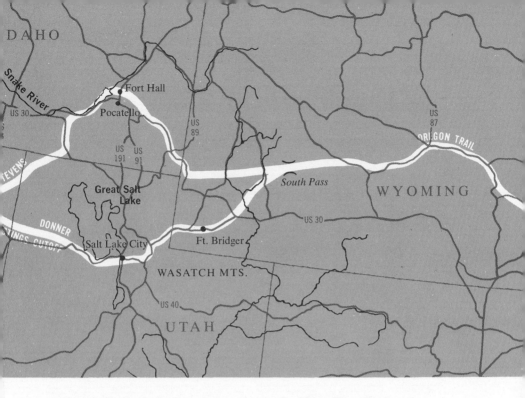

trail, probably took the first wagons across the Sierra Nevada.

word of agreement, meaning *all right* or *very well*. The chief—father of Winnemucca, who would be the scourge of white men in the Nevada deserts for more than twenty years—was affable, highly intelligent, and thoroughly acquainted with the deserts and mountains. He understood Greenwood's sign language perfectly, knew where Sutter's Fort was, and the best way to get there. Squatting, he drew a map on the ground. Two suns to the west there was a river flowing eastward from a great canyon in the mountains, and beyond the head of the canyon the streams flowed down to the white man's fort. Halfway to the river, water would be found at hot springs.

The start was made early on the morning of October 8, following the general route that is now Highway 40. The hot springs were not reached until midnight. Water was cooled in tubs for the suffering animals, but few would drink, and those that did sickened. Stevens ordered the caravan on through the night, and at two o'clock the next afternoon it reached the river, thirty-five miles east of present Reno. With no feed, water, or rest in thirty-two hours, the animals were at the point of exhaustion. Although the emigrants had suffered far less than their stock, the desert crossing must have seemed interminable to them, for Moses Schallenberger estimated the distance to be eighty miles. It was actually only forty, and this stretch of the trail is still known as Forty-Mile Desert.

Even though Stevens was anxious to push on, so as to cross the Sierra Nevada before winter set in, he stopped two days to let the animals graze and recuperate from the ordeal of the dry crossing. Unlike many captains who were to follow his trail during the next ten years, he gave as much attention to the welfare of the animals in his charge as to the humans. By doing so, he had brought the oxen through in better shape than when they left Missouri. Their bodies were lean and tough, and their unshod hoofs had become as hard as polished ebony.

Probably on the morning of October 12, the Stevens party started westward along the river they had named for old Truckee. Highway 40 now follows the general course of the river, the distance to the town of Truckee is less than seventy miles, and if it were not for passing through Sparks and Reno a tourist would easily make the drive in an hour and a half. It is true that the first thirty miles of roadway, along the hillsides of the lower canyon through the Virginia Mountains, is somewhat winding. But the run across Truckee Meadows, with Reno at the center, is almost level. West of the meadows the road enters the throat of the upper canyon, which narrows as it penetrates deeper into the Sierra. The hills become steeper, the roadway a bit snaky, and in places the cautious driver might slow down to forty miles an hour. If he is careless enough to enjoy the scenery as he drives, he may catch a glimpse of the clear mountain stream, brawling around great boulders as it winds and twists through the canyon below. But Highway 40 was not there in 1843, and no white man had ever followed the twisting, brawling Truckee.

In the lower canyon the Stevens party was often unable to travel more than two or three miles in a day. On precipitous hillsides the wagons had to be unloaded, and held with guy ropes to keep them from tipping over. To get through at all, the river often had to be crossed three or four times in a single day, and with each crossing the horn of the oxen's hoofs softened. Back on the rocky hillsides the softened hoofs wore down rapidly and oxen went lame. Sparing them as much as possible, Elisha Stevens pushed on. October was drawing toward its end, there had already been flurries of snow, and the summit of the Sierras must be crossed before winter set in.

Above the meadows the caravan was nearly stalled. Where the river flows northward along the present California-Nevada line, the canyon walls pinched in so close that the only possible passage for wagons was in the rocky bed of the stream. Men were obliged to wade in waist-deep icy water, straining at the wheels and lifting them over boulders. The oxen's feet had become so tender that the poor beasts would not take a step without goading. To lighten the wagons, everything possible was loaded onto the saddle horses, and the women and children scrambled along the margin of the river as best they could. The only feed for the animals was a few rushes growing by the stream, and with each day the stock grew thinner and weaker. Then the sky clouded over and a foot of snow fell.

It is believed that the Stevens party reached the present site of Truckee, California, on November 14, after thirty-two days of fighting their way less than seventy miles up the river. A mile farther on, the main stream turned abruptly to the south, and a branch continued to the west. The canyon to the south was steep and rugged, while that along the branch was wide enough to permit the passage of a wagon. Here Stevens split his party. The sky had not cleared since the snowfall, and another storm appeared to be coming on. Sutter's Fort could not be far away, but if the entire party took the wrong route and were snowbound there would be no chance of turning back or sending ahead for relief. Choosing four of the best hunters among the young men, and two of the younger women, Stevens mounted them on the strongest horses and sent them up the south canyon. They were to cross the summit, find the fort, and arrange for a rescue party if the expected storm struck.

The mounted party ascended Truckee River to the western shore of Lake Tahoe, found a pass through the high mountains, and discovered a stream flowing to the west—probably the Middle Fork of the American River. Living entirely upon game, fording the ice-cold stream time and again, and often forced to find a way around impassable gorges, they reached Sutter's Fort on December 10.

When the party was split, the wagon division followed the western branch of the Truckee two miles and a half. There they found a large lake, but beyond its farther end the canyon was blocked solidly by high mountains. Stevens moved the wagons along the north side of the lake for a short distance, then made camp where wood was plentiful and there was a little grazing for the cattle. Two days were spent in searching for a pass across the summit. A spot very close to that at which Highway 40 now crosses was finally chosen, but the oxen were too exhausted to pull loaded wagons up the steep mountainside. It was decided to abandon all but five wagons, and for the men to back-pack necessary bedding and the remaining provisions to the top of the pass.

Above the canyon floor the snow was two or more feet deep, and in places the mountain was so steep that an empty wagon could hardly be taken up. At one ledge near the summit the oxen had to be led up through a narrow defile, then a wagon dragged to the top with half a dozen yokes straining at chains while men hoisted from below. Five days of back-breaking labor were required to drag the wagons to the top of the 7189-foot pass, then Dr. Townsend became worried. He had invested most of his savings in broadcloth, silk, and other light fabrics which would bring high prices in California. If left in his abandoned wagon until spring, the goods would certainly be stolen by Indians, and he would be financially ruined.

Moses Schallenberger, Dr. Townsend's brother-in-law, offered to stay behind and guard the wagons until a relief party could be sent back from Sutter's Fort. He was an excellent hunter and was sure he would have no trouble in shooting plenty of game. Two other men, Foster and Montgomery, offered to stay with him. It was generally agreed that they would be safe enough, but Stevens insisted that two cows, too thin and footsore for hard travel, be left with them. They would supply a little milk, and could be butchered in the event of poor hunting. With the young men provided for, the wagon party moved westward from the summit. For three days they made their way along the route that is now Highway 40. Some twenty miles beyond the pass they were caught in a raging snowstorm. When the storm subsided, the seventeen younger men set out to find Sutter's Fort, leaving the two eldest with the women and children. They reached the fort on December 13, just as a rescue party was starting out, and those left at the wagons were soon brought in.

Back in the canyon Schallenberger and his two companions had barely time to build themselves a shack before they were caught in

Summit crossing of the Sierra Nevada, near Donner Lake.
From Beyond the Mississippi, *Albert D. Richardson.*

the same storm that marooned the wagon party. Snow piled three or
four feet deep, the cows could find no feed, and no game could be
hunted. For a few days the men made out with what few scraps of
food had been left in the wagons, then butchered the starving cows,
as much to put them out of their suffering as for meat. But there was
little meat on the cows, half-starved for more than a month, and no
game was astir in the deep snow.

One snowstorm followed another, no hunting could be done, and
by mid-December only one thin quarter of beef remained. Unless
help arrived before it was gone, or unless the men could get out on
snowshoes, it seemed certain that they would die of starvation. None
of them was experienced with snowshoes, but Foster and Montgomery fashioned three pairs from ox-bows and rawhide, while Schallenberger stripped and dried the meat. In their ignorance they bound
the snowshoes to their feet at both toe and heel, then set out for the

pass. At each step the clumsy shoes sank deep into the loose snow. Being secured at the heel, they had to be raised straight up, lifting snow as if they were shovels. Before the top of the pass was reached, Schallenberger became exhausted and was nearly crippled with leg cramps. The mature men could go on, but he could not. They had no choice but to give him the largest share of the dried meat and let him go back to the shack, hoping that a rescue party could get through before he starved to death. But Moses Schallenberger was too ingenious to starve. There were traps in one of the wagons, and fox and coyote tracks in the snow. Until he was rescued on February 26, 1844, he kept in good health on roasted foxes, but coyote meat was too strong to be stomached, even on the days when he had to go hungry.

Three years later the Donner party encountered exactly the same situation at the same place, but with far different results. The Donner tragedy, the most famous in American trail history, was brought about largely by the chicanery of Lansford Hastings. Ambitious, dishonest, and a clever propagandist, Hastings had arrived in California by sea in 1843, when the first surge of Oregon migration was at its crest. He was quick in observing the weakness of the Mexican Government, and equally quick in devising a scheme for turning it to his own advantage. Thousands of American immigrants were pouring into Oregon, but only a few trickling into California. If he could divert the tide he believed he could overthrow the Mexicans, set up an independent nation, and establish himself as ruler. In an effort to do so he published and distributed throughout the East his *Emigrants' Guide to Oregon and California*, extolling the glories of California and damning Oregon with faint praise. With practically no knowledge of the geography, and no investigation, he invented the Hastings Cutoff, and assured prospective emigrants that by taking it they could reach California quickly and easily. They would simply turn their wagons away from the Oregon Trail at Bridger's Fort, "bearing west southwest, to the Salt Lake; and thence continue down to the Bay of San Francisco."

The Donner brothers, well-to-do Illinois farmers in their early sixties, were among the thousands who became enthralled by Hastings's propaganda. They sold their farms, loaded the families and household furniture into specially built wagons, and set out for California in April, 1846. The spring travel over the trail was heavy, one caravan following another across the Kansas prairies. But no group stayed intact long after the outset. Wrangling broke out under the monotony of the plodding pace, and the most restless pulled out to join faster moving caravans. The Donners were in no hurry. They accepted Hastings's assurances as they accepted the Scripture—on faith and without rationalization—and were confident that by the cutoff route they could easily reach San Francisco Bay in early fall. In spite of warnings by oldtime frontiersmen that the cutoff was impractical and dangerous, they dropped back, letting the unbelievers surge ahead. Gradually they were joined by other Hastings converts.

Leisurely following at the tail end of the spring migration, the heterogeneous group of eighty-seven men, women, and children—leaderless, and united only by their unquestioning faith in Hastings's propaganda—arrived at Bridger's Fort on July 28. Still in no hurry, the Donner party rested until August 1, then set out to the southwest on an old trappers' trail leading into the Wasatch Mountains. The going was rough, but eight or ten miles a day were traveled until the caravan reached the Weber River, where the trail entered a narrow canyon, impassable to wagons. It was too late to turn back and take the established route, or winter would surely catch them before they could cross the Sierra Nevada. Baffled, and with their faith in Hastings completely shattered, the party began to panic. Blaming each other for their predicament, the men seized axes and crowbars, and frantically started hacking a roadway around the canyon. Gentle and kindly George Donner did his best to keep peace, but he was not a strong leader. Each day the panic increased and the discord erupted into feuds. Bickering and quarreling, the party fought its way through the Wasatch Mountains for more than a month, and reached Salt Lake in mid-September, completely disorganized.

Miraculously, only one human life was lost in crossing the Nevada deserts, but many of the wagons had to be abandoned, provisions ran low, and more than half the livestock was lost to drought, starvation, and Indian arrows. Still quarreling and disorganized, the Donner party reached the foot of the pass which would thereafter bear their name on the afternoon of November 3. It had begun to snow, but the men were tired, so decided to pitch camp and make the crossing next morning. By evening a howling blizzard was raging. It lasted several days, piling three feet of snow in the canyon, and when it ended the party discovered that its cattle had drifted away.

The Donner party snowbound in the Sierra Nevada. From
Beyond the Mississippi, *Albert D. Richardson.*

Only forty-seven of the Donner party survived, and the gruesome story of its resorting to cannibalism is too well-known to need repeating. Victims of chicanery, gullibility, panic, and weak leadership, they suffered an ordeal that is almost beyond belief, but news of their tragedy doubtlessly saved the lives of many who might have followed in their footsteps. By the time the last members of the party were rescued the American flag was flying over California, and within six months a stream of immigrants was pouring through the gateway known as Donner Pass.

THE MORMON MIGRATION

In April, 1847, Brigham Young led the first migration of Mormons westward from Winter Quarters, near Omaha, Nebraska. These people were seeking a Promised Land, but were not deluded into believing they might find a second Garden of Eden. Young had already had the land spied out, and chosen a narrow strip between Great Salt Lake and the Wasatch Mountains, a region so arid that Jim Bridger offered to pay a thousand dollars for the first bushel of corn raised on it. Young's purpose was to carve out of the wilderness a refuge for his people, so far from civilization that they would be safe from such persecution as they had suffered in Missouri and Illinois, and where they might prosper through hard work, industry, and frugality.

The preceding fall fifteen thousand Mormons had gathered at Winter Quarters, but a mass migration was impossible, since they had been stripped of all their property and most of their livestock when driven out of Illinois. The entire sect was destitute of funds, and there were neither wagons nor draft animals enough to transport half the people. The only hope was to send work battalions ahead to establish a foothold, while the rest remained to raise crops. Then groups would migrate as best they could when a place had been provided for them in the new Zion.

It was the advance battalion of 143 carefully selected men between the ages of thirty and fifty that Young led westward. The caravan, drawn by oxen, mules, and horses, consisted of seventy-three wagons and a leather ferryboat that was mounted on wheels. In addition, nineteen milch cows were taken along, and a crate of poultry hung from the tailboard of nearly every wagon.

Sad experience had taught the Mormons to stay clear of "Gentiles" as much as possible. To avoid the throng of emigrants on the Oregon Trail, Young led his caravan up the Platte Valley on the north side of the river, but the Mormons traveled in an entirely different manner from any others who had pioneered a new trail. Hard work was a part of their creed, and Young enforced it rigidly. Furthermore, he was preparing a way for his people who were to follow. He kept a road-building crew well out in front, cutting down gulch banks, bridging creeks where timber was available, and preparing camp sites. When buffalo country was reached, he set his men to jerking meat for the next winter, but allowed no more animals to be killed than necessary.

By traveling from dawn till dusk, the Mormon caravan outdistanced the spring migration before reaching Fort Laramie. A short distance below the fort it crossed to the south side of the river and continued along the established trail. At the regular crossing, near where Casper, Wyoming, now stands, the river was in flood. After swimming the livestock across, the wagons were ferried easily in the leather boat, bringing an idea into Brigham Young's ingenious mind: A horde of Gentiles was swarming up the trail, eager to reach California or Oregon as soon as possible. Rather than lose time in cutting logs and building rafts, many of them would pay fifty pounds of flour to have a wagon ferried across. He christened the boat *Revenue Cutter*, and left a dozen men to operate it. Until the spring rush had passed they were busy night and day, and the revenue they collected went far toward feeding the Mormon pioneers until a crop could be raised in the new land.

The Mormons were first after the Donner party to take the cutoff route from Fort Bridger, but their experiences were quite different. Beyond the Weber River Canyon they found that the panicked Donner party had hacked its way blindly. Camp was pitched, and a thorough survey of the mountains made, in which the route that

Mormons crossing a river en route to Utah.
From Harper's Magazine.

is now Highway 30S was discovered. The entire battalion set to work, and within less than a week had opened a clear passage to Salt Lake. On July 24 Brigham Young, desperately ill with mountain fever, was carried to the mouth of a canyon above present Salt Lake City. He scanned the arid land that sloped away toward the distant lake, cut off from the Great Plains by five hundred miles of rugged mountains, and from California by an equally wide barrier of burning deserts, then spoke his famous words, "This is the place."

By late August fifty acres had been plowed, irrigation canals were being dug to bring water from the mountains, a plot the size of a city block had been surrounded by a stout log stockade, and half a dozen cabins built. Under irrigation the land had proved fertile, so Young hurried messengers back to Winter Quarters. A work force of fifteen hundred young men and women were to take the trail the following spring, bringing all the wagons, livestock, household furniture, seed, and farming equipment that could be spared.

The caravan of 1848 was made up of five hundred and sixty wagons, leaving the Saints at Winter Quarters almost destitute of transport, but ingenious Brigham Young met the situation by having his people build themselves handcarts. During the next four years more than three thousand of these carts were pulled over the one-thousand-and-thirty-mile trail to Salt Lake City. With a man in the shafts, and women or children pushing from behind, a five-hundred-pound load could be carried, and thirty miles were often traveled in a day—more than double the average distance of a wagon train. One party dragged its carts fourteen hundred miles from Iowa City to Salt Lake in nine weeks, and suffered fewer deaths than most of the Gentiles' wagon parties. All the Saints were not so fortunate. In one company a sixth of the members died of starvation and frostbite, but the migration went on without a halt. By 1849 Salt Lake City had become a thriving community of five thousand inhabitants, surrounded by hundreds of fertile farms. Although there were two Mormons with James Marshall when he discovered gold at Sutter's Mill, Brigham Young would not permit his people to take any part in the California gold rush. Still, it was a godsend to them.

In the spring of 1849 the Overland Trail was so thronged with gold rushers that there was seldom a time when one party was not within sight of another. Anxious to be first in reaching the gold fields, many of these early Argonauts were too impatient to take the long California Trail by way of Fort Hall and Raft River, so followed the Mormon roadway from Bridger's Fort to Salt Lake City. To supplement their provisions before crossing the deserts, they would have paid high prices for any farm produce the Mormons could spare, but Young would not let his people traffic with them. Contact with the Gentiles had always led to resentment and persecution. He had brought the Saints into the wilderness to avoid it, and had no intention of letting the bars down. Most feared of all were the Missourians, but there were two among them who were trusted and admired. They were Colonel Alexander Doniphan and Ben Holladay. Doniphan had befriended the Mormons, saving many of their lives by warning them of impending attacks when they were driven out of Missouri, and Holladay had been his personal courier.

THE FREIGHTERS AND THE MAIL SUBSIDY

From early youth, Ben Holladay had been an astute, farsighted businessman. During the Mexican War he had made and saved several thousand dollars, operating sutler wagons with the Army of the West. At the close of the war he opened a trading post at Weston, Missouri, across the river from Fort Leavenworth, and it had prospered. Young Holladay was quick to recognize the opportunity presented by the Mormon migration and the gold rush. He reasoned that California, with its tremendous influx of population, must be badly in need of provisions. He believed the Mormons had those provisions but would not trade with the Gentiles, and that they themselves must be in need of clothing, utensils, tools, and other merchandise of civilization. Borrowing every dime he could raise, he bought fifty Conestoga wagons, loaded them with seventy thousand dollars' worth of the sort of merchandise most needed by the Mormons, and set off for Salt Lake City.

Brigham Young welcomed Holladay, not only as a trader but a friend, and accepted the entire caravan—merchandise, wagons, and draft animals—paying for it largely in cattle at six dollars a head and flour at a dollar a hundred pounds. Holladay arranged to use the wagons for three months, loaded his flour on them, and set out across the deserts and mountains for California, driving a herd of more than a thousand beef cattle. The trail across the Nevada deserts was already well marked by the skeletons of animals lost by the gold rushers. Driving so large a herd, and with little grazing for it, Holladay left many a marker along the barren trail, but his profit from the venture was fantastic. In the mining camps some of his cattle sold for as high as fifty cents a pound, and his flour for as much as twenty dollars a sack. The next year he doubled the size of his caravan, and the size of his profit. The Mormon trade remained Holladay's exclusively, but he soon had a rival for the transportation business of the rapidly expanding West.

The great overland freighting industry was born of the Army's inability to supply troops during the Mexican War. In the spring of 1848 James Brown was awarded a contract to haul a hundred tons of freight from Independence to Santa Fe at $11.75 per hundredweight. The War Department was so well pleased with his performance that he was awarded much larger contracts in 1849 and 1850. To finance the venture he formed a partnership with William Russell, a financier, promoter, and politician. Brown died soon after, and Russell organized the firm of Russell, Majors & Waddell. With headquarters at Leavenworth, the firm dominated the overland transportation business until the outbreak of the Civil War. By 1856 it had established freight stations from the Missouri River to the Pacific coast. Thereafter, there was seldom a time, except when the mountain passes were clogged with snow, that a dozen or more of its freighting caravans were not rolling along the route which had come to be known as the Central Overland Trail.

Although freighting constituted the larger part of the traffic over the central route, mail service had a far greater effect upon the development of overland transportation. It also resulted in opening a new California section of the Overland Trail. Until 1851 the only overland mail was that carried to Salt Lake City by Ben Holladay as an accommodation to the Mormons. But when California became a state its citizens demanded that the Federal Government furnish them regular overland mail service. Congress responded in a rather half-hearted manner, advertising for bids to supply monthly service. Holladay, who was already toying with the idea of establishing a stagecoach line, offered to supply mail service between the Missouri River and Salt Lake City for forty-five thousand dollars per year, but the contract was awarded to Samuel Woodson at about half the figure.

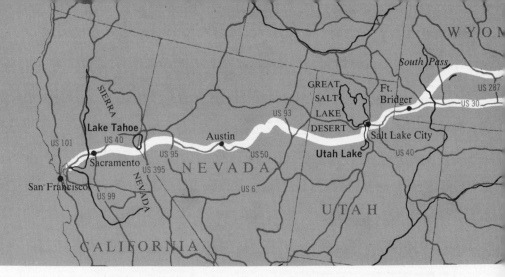

The California Trail: the Central Overland Stage and Pony Express
routes. The completion of first the telegraph and then the trans-

At the same time George Chorpenning was awarded a contract to
carry the mail between Salt Lake City and San Francisco at fourteen
thousand dollars per year.

Soon after the beginning of the gold rush the roundabout Raft
River section of the original California Trail was abandoned. In spite
of the eighty-mile waterless trek across the Great Salt Lake Desert,
the anxious Argonauts took the Mormon road from Fort Bridger to
Salt Lake City, then followed the route which is now Highway 40
to intersect the original trail at Wells, Nevada. To avoid the blistering salt flats and shorten the distance to San Francisco, Chorpenning
pioneered a new course for his mail route. It led south along the
Jordan River to Utah Lake, skirted the southern end of Great Salt
Lake Desert, and struck westward to the present location of Austin,
Nevada. From there to Sacramento his course was roughly that now
followed by Highway 50. Chorpenning's route soon became the
mainline for overland freighters, and later for stagecoach lines and
the Pony Express.

Both Woodson and Chorpenning expected to make excellent
profits on their contracts by hauling light freight and express along
with the mail sacks, but soon found that the subsidies were far too
small to cover the expenses of monthly service. They struggled

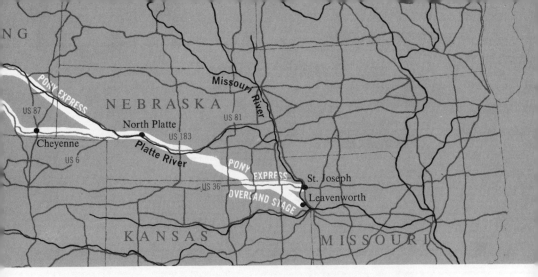

continental railroad put an end to these colorful but hardly profitable ventures.

along through the summer and fall of 1851, but when winter snows filled the mountain passes the service collapsed. Mail piled high on both sides of the Rockies and Sierra Nevada, and the Californians' demand for fast, dependable, weekly mail and passenger service became too vehement to be ignored by Congress. It advertised for new bids, the mail to be carried on fast passenger coaches. Ben Holladay submitted offers on both the eastern and western divisions, but was outbid on the former. He was awarded the contract between Salt Lake City and Sacramento at fifty thousand dollars per year, and invested an enormous sum in building relay stations and equipping the line, but it was a dismal failure. Great as the clamor for rapid transportation had been, there were few passengers, and the cost of manning and operating the line was tremendous. Although he had for several years been ambitious to establish a transcontinental stagecoach line, it soon became clear to him that such a venture could be successful only with a Government subsidy of at least a half-million dollars. Unlike most men who have made a bad investment, Holladay swallowed his loss and got out at the end of his first year.

For several years the California mail service was operated on a hit-or-miss basis, with subsidies increased each time a contractor went bankrupt. By 1856 John Hockaday was being paid one hundred

Waiting for letters at a station on the Overland Trail. From Beyond the Mississippi, *Albert D. Richardson.*

and ninety thousand dollars annually for carrying the mail from the Missouri River to Salt Lake City, and Chorpenning was receiving one hundred and thirty thousand dollars for carrying it over his old route to San Francisco, but the service was far from satisfactory. The mail, along with express and an occasional passenger was hauled in mule-drawn wagons. In summer it sometimes got through from the Missouri to California in as few as thirty-two days; in winter it was often as many as ninety, but still the contractors could not make expenses. Then, in 1857, Congress voted a subsidy of six hundred thousand dollars for semiweekly mail and passenger service, each trip to be made in twenty-five days or less. Both Holladay and his powerful rival, Russell, Majors & Waddell, entered bids for service by way of the Central Overland route, but the contract was awarded to Butterfield & Company.

When it was discovered that the Butterfield route lay entirely through the South, the North sent up a howl of protest, demanding that Congress also establish rapid mail and passenger service by way of the much shorter Central Overland route. In a spectacular bid to outdo Butterfield, William Russell immediately made an offer for his firm to provide daily stagecoach service at an annual subsidy of nine hundred thousand dollars. A bill to authorize the subsidy was presented to Congress, but was blocked by southern Senators on grounds that the northern Rockies and Sierra Nevada were impassable in winter.

Soon after the bill was blocked, gold was discovered in Colorado. Russell believed that Denver would boom as San Francisco had, and that a stagecoach line connecting it with the Missouri River would make fabulous profits. When his partners opposed the venture he formed a separate company, borrowed heavily, and made a huge investment in coaches, horses, relay stations, and equipment. But the line suffered tremendous losses from the beginning, and soon became hopelessly insolvent. Russell was a plunger and not always ethical in his financial manipulations, but Majors and Waddell were scrupulously honest—and extremely jealous of their reputations. Fearing that Russell's failure would reflect upon the freighting firm, they agreed to let it take over the bankrupt stagecoach line and pay off the debts.

Although Russell was in close contact with Washington and must have known that it was no more than wishful thinking, he assured his partners that the nine-hundred-thousand-dollar subsidy bill would not only pass the Senate but that he could secure the contract if Hockaday and Chorpenning were bought out and fast year-round stagecoach service established on the Central Overland route. He pointed out that the firm already had numerous freight depots along the route, and large numbers of idle oxen during the winter months. The depots would serve as relay stations, considerably reducing the cost of building a stage line. The idle oxen could be used on snowplows in the Rockies and Sierra Nevada, keeping the roads open for winter travel by both stagecoaches and freight caravans, and thus increasing the freighting profits.

Deluded by Russell's assurances, his partners agreed to the plan. Hockaday and Chorpenning were bought out, scores of additional relay stations built, the facilities of the defunct stage line transferred to the Central Overland route, and semiweekly service established to Sacramento. The cost of building the line was enormous. This on top of having bailed out Russell's bankrupt business left the great firm short of funds, but astute Ben Holladay, extraordinarily wealthy from his exclusive Mormon trade, was glad to lend his giant competitor whatever money it needed. All he asked was a fair rate of interest and a chattel mortgage.

With the fresh supply of cash Russell, Majors & Waddell bought additional coaches and horses, established camps to keep the mountain roads open in winter, and cut the running time between Leavenworth and Sacramento to twenty-five days or less. Within a year its service was fully equal to Butterfield's, but still no subsidy for the central route was voted by Congress, and the cost of operation was staggering. Time and again the firm found itself pressed for funds, but Ben Holladay was always glad to make a loan—for an additional chattel mortgage.

THE PONY EXPRESS

By the close of 1859 conditions in the United States had reached so critical a stage that civil war appeared inevitable. If it should come, California's wealth might well determine the outcome, and California was very doubtful. Although admitted to the Union as a free state, it might swing to the southern cause unless kept in contact with the North by far more rapid communication than could be supplied by stagecoach mail. Whether from patriotism or in hope that it would lead to the coveted mail subsidy, William Russell stepped forward with an astounding offer: By using swift saddle horses in short relays, his firm would supply semiweekly ten-day mail service between St. Joseph and San Francisco for five hundred dollars a round trip.

Russell's partners were appalled when he told them of his offer. The cost of building and equipping such a line might well be ruinous in their strained financial condition. Moreover, five hundred dollars a round trip would cover only a small fraction of the operating costs. But neither Majors nor Waddell felt that they could honorably repudiate the offer, even though no contract had been awarded. With another large loan from Holladay, eighty additional relay stations were built and supplied along the 1966-mile route. Four hundred of the fastest horses available were bought, and two hundred keepers and stablemen hired, together with eighty of the most courageous young frontier riders that could be found. To the booming of cannon and screaming of excited crowds, the first Pony Express riders dashed from opposite ends of the line at dusk on April 3, 1860.

Circumstances seemed to conspire against the Pony Express from the moment the first riders leaped into their saddles. The spring of 1860 was unusually cold and wet. Rain was falling in a downpour when, at 2:15 A.M. on April 4, Sam Hamilton galloped out of Sacramento with the St. Joseph mail mochila flung over his saddle. By dawn the rain had turned to snow, but Hamilton was sixty miles to the east, tossing the mochila to "Boston" Upson, high in the foothills of the Sierra Nevada. Twenty years old, five feet tall, and the son of

A relay station of the Pony Express. From Marvels of the New West, *William Thayer.*

a wealthy California newspaper publisher, Boston had roamed the Sierras from childhood, and knew them as no other white man did. His carrying of the first Pony mail over the summit is one of the most amazing feats in American frontier history.

Above the four-thousand-foot level a raging blizzard was blowing, and gales at more than sixty miles an hour piled snow fifteen to twenty feet deep. The trail was completely obliterated, and visibility reduced to less than a hundred feet, but Boston fought his way upwards from one isolated relay post to another. He made the last three miles to the summit relay post afoot, shouldering the mochila and leaving his pony bogged belly-deep in a snowdrift. Beyond the summit the blizzard was less severe, and at 2:18 in the afternoon he rode a staggering pony into Friday's Station on Lake Tahoe. In a storm that few men could have lived through, he had carried the first Pony mail fifty-five miles across the high hump of the Sierra Nevada in just eight hours, better time than the fastest stagecoaches could make in summer weather.

At the eastern end of the line the riders were less able to cope with the fast schedule. Rainfall was almost continuous, the Platte Valley a quagmire of deep mud, the nights dead black, and misfortune lurked in the darkness. One rider was caught in a buffalo stampede during a night thunderstorm. Another was delayed five hours while fighting off a wolf pack from a pony exhausted by the deep mud. A third rode into a relay post to find the stable empty and the keeper badly wounded by raiding Indians. With his pony already jaded, it took him half the night to reach the next post. The eastern boys fell twenty hours behind the schedule, but the desert riders more than made it up. At 3:55 on the afternoon of April 13, the first Pony Express mail reached St. Joseph. An hour and thirty-five minutes later a rider galloped his pony into Sacramento with the mochila from the East.

From the time of the Joe Walker massacre, the Paiute Indians had been the white man's unrelenting enemy. But there had been very little tribal organization, and attacks were confined to those of roving bands that skulked the trail along the Humboldt River. Then, in 1859, the richest silver deposit the world had ever known was discovered in the Washoe hills of western Nevada. These hills were covered with piñon pine, and were the winter headquarters of Chief Winnemucca and his Paiute tribesmen, who gathered from the deserts to subsist on piñon nuts. During the winter of 1859-60 a rabble of frenzied fortune seekers stampeded into the Washoes, overrunning the hills, fighting for a claim no larger than a blanket, chopping down the piñon pine, and killing any Indian who showed his head.

Although the Paiutes were the most primitive Indians on the continent, Winnemucca was an able and intelligent chief. In retaliation for the killings he organized his warriors, laid a clever ambush, and led a band of drunken prospectors into it. The cry of *massacre* was raised, the miners demanded that the Federal Government protect its citizens, and a troop of cavalry was rushed from California to annihilate the murderous Indians. But before the soldiers got across the mountains, Winnemucca and his tribesmen had disappeared into the deserts where no cavalry could follow. For more than a year they carried on so fierce a campaign that no caravan could cross the Nevada deserts without a military escort. The isolated Pony Express relay posts, strung at twenty-five to thirty mile intervals along the old Chorpenning mail route, became the chief target for raiding Paiutes. Howling like wolves, a band of a hundred or more would swoop down on a lonely post, killing keeper, hostler, and guards; pillaging, burning buildings and haystacks, and driving away the relay horses.

By the fall of 1860 more than half the Pony Express posts between Carson City and Utah Lake had been destroyed and Paiute ambushes set in every mountain pass along the trail. But except for one short period the mail went through. Never following exactly the same route twice in succession, and avoiding the regular mountain passes whenever possible, the riders made their way across the deserts as best they could, depending upon the speed of their superior mounts to outrun surprise attacks. But as more and more relay posts were destroyed the advantage of speed was lost, for a horse often had to be ridden a hundred miles to reach a remaining post. Many a rider was wounded by Indian arrows but, miraculously, only one was killed. The mail was often late, sometimes as much as a week, but no rider ever turned back, and only one refused to make his run.

That no Pony Express rider ever turned back stands as one of the finest examples of courage in American history. That Russell, Majors & Waddell never turned back should stand equally high as an example of patriotism. It well may be that William Russell's offer to provide California with ten-day mail service at the ridiculously low price of five hundred dollars a round trip was made solely in hope it would result in his firm being awarded the coveted contract. And it is certain that Majors and Waddell agreed to stand by the offer because they believed it necessary in order to uphold the honor of the firm. But if honor was ever involved, the firm was absolved of any obligation, either moral or legal, before the end of 1860, since legislation authorizing payment for the services had been blocked by southern Senators. Although Russell, Majors & Waddell faced almost certain ruin if the exorbitantly expensive service were continued, its need to the Union was becoming greater with every passing day. The firm went deeper into debt and kept the ponies running.

By February, 1861, war appeared to be a certainty, and California was leaning toward the Confederate cause. Its remaining loyal to the Union depended largely upon the policies set forth in Lincoln's inaugural address and speed in transmitting the address to Sacramento. At a cost of seventy-five thousand dollars Russell, Majors & Waddell prepared the Pony Express to make its supreme effort. Hundreds of extra men were hired, scores of temporary relay posts established, and a small army of guards, keepers, and hostlers sent into the Nevada desert. By Inauguration Day fast relay horses were posted at ten-mile intervals along the entire 1966-mile route, and the finest riders assigned to the most difficult sections of the trail.

"Pony Bob" Haslam was chosen for the most hazardous assignment; that of carrying the President's address 120 miles across Paiute-infested western Nevada. Heavily armed guards were stationed at all the relay posts, but it was impossible to give the riders any protection on the trail, and the Paiutes were on a rampage. Pony Bob had hoped to make his run under cover of darkness, but the mochila containing the address reached Smith's Creek soon after dawn. Within less than two minutes Haslam was galloping away to the west. With fresh horses at Mount Airy and Castle Rock, he made the fastest time ever ridden to Cold Spring. He was at first surprised, then worried, when no Indians tried to ambush him in either of the mountain passes. To the west of Cold Spring the trail led through a wide desert valley, thickly dotted with sage brush and greasewood. Since the Paiutes had left the passes, Pony Bob reasoned that they had probably set an ambush in the valley, but circling it would cost three or four hours. Without hesitation he spurred straight down the trail, reins around the saddle horn and a pistol in each hand.

A Pony Express rider. From Beyond the Mississippi, *Albert D. Richardson.*

As Haslam expected, war-painted Indians boiled out of the brush like a pack of rabid wolves, and arrows filled the air like straws in a hurricane. But this was no ordinary ambush. He had no sooner broken through the main body of the pack than he was surrounded by mounted warriors, several on stolen Pony Express horses, too swift to be outrun. His only chance lay in outdistancing the others, then picking off the Express ponies one by one. Haslam won through in a running battle of more than two miles, but an arrow from close range ripped through his mouth, fracturing his jaw and knocking out five teeth. Another lodged in his left arm at the shoulder, leaving it paralyzed and useless. At the next relay station he stopped only to have the arrow cut out of his arm, and to mumble, "Fetch me a clean rag to hold in my mouth; I'm going on through."

Pony Bob Haslam did go through. When he reached Fort Churchill his face was unrecognizable, and his arm swollen larger than his thigh, but he had brought Lincoln's address one hundred and twenty miles in eight hours and two minutes, and had changed mounts twelve times. Just seven days and seventeen hours after the address was telegraphed from Washington to St. Joseph, a Pony rider galloped it into Sacramento. No such feat of speed, endurance, and courage was ever before accomplished, but swift as the ponies had been they were not fast enough to keep up with the demands of the changing times. Their famous run was barely completed before telegraph lines were being strung from both ends of the trail. For seven months the ponies raced across the deserts and mountains, shuttling messages between the advancing lines of poles. In October, 1861, the lines met, the wires were joined, and the Pony Express had fulfilled its destiny.

9

Heyday of the Old Trails

IN ADDITION to the telegraph, it was imperative that California be bound to the Union by more rapid and frequent passenger service. A week after Lincoln's inauguration a contract with a one-million-dollar annual subsidy was authorized for daily stagecoach service over the central route, but it was too late to save Russell, Majors & Waddell. After pouring five hundred thousand dollars into the Pony Express, and losing an equal amount in operating its California stage line, the firm was too near bankruptcy to provide the necessary service. The contract was awarded to Butterfield and Company, with the proviso that its operations be transferred to the Central Overland route. A few months later the firm of Russell, Majors & Waddell was taken over by Ben Holladay, its largest creditor. Not long after, Butterfield sold out to Wells Fargo & Company.

During the Civil War freighting and stagecoaching on the Central Overland Trail reached its glorious peak. Denver, Salt Lake, and Virginia City were booming. Eastern Kansas and Nebraska were dotted with towns, and California was growing like a yearling colt. In 1863 alone, the Washoe hills poured out twenty million dollars in bullion. To haul supplies and equipment across the Sierras required two thousand men, five thousand wagons, and thirty thousand mules. From the Missouri to the Pacific a hundred or more great freight caravans were constantly on the trail and its numerous branches.

Double that number of stagecoaches sped over the well-worn thoroughfare night and day. Ben Holladay had become fabulously wealthy, and the competition fierce between him and Wells Fargo. For four years the two great rivals fought each other for the transcontinental passenger business, each trying to outdo the other in speed and the magnificence of their coaches.

Wells Fargo & Company often tried to buy out Holladay, but he would never sell. Then, in October, 1866, wily Ben suddenly changed his mind and sold out to his colossal rival for more than two million dollars. He was becoming skeptical. Ever since the outbreak of the Civil War there had been plans for a transcontinental railroad, but little progress had been made beyond the surveying of a route. The general belief, shared by the directors of Wells Fargo & Company, was that it would be at least ten years before tracks could be laid across the two highest mountain ranges on the continent. Ben Holladay disagreed. Scarcely twenty years before, the Sierra Nevada had been considered impassable to wagons, but thousands had crossed during the gold rush. With California and Oregon growing as they were, and with the Washoe hills yielding silver at the rate of twenty million dollars a year, the West needed railroads in a hurry, and the mountains could no more hold them back than they had held the Forty-Niners.

Ben Holladay had reasoned well. On May 10, 1869—less than three years from the time he sold out—the Central Pacific and Union Pacific rails were joined at Promontory Point, Utah, and as the golden spike was driven it sounded the death knell of overland stage-coaching. Within another quarter century most of the old trails of the old West would be little more than a memory, buried beneath the cinder beds of the greatest railway system on earth.

Bibliography

ALDRICH, LORENZO D. *A Journal to the Overland Route to California and the Gold Mines.* Dawson's Book Shop, 1950.

ALTROCCHI, JULIA. *The Old California Trail.* Caxton Press, 1945.

BAKELESS, JOHN. *The Eyes of Discovery.* J. B. Lippincott Company, 1950.

BANNING, WM. AND G. H. *Six Horses.* The Century Company, 1930.

BARKER, RUTH L. *Caballeros.* D. Appleton-Century Company, 1931.

BEMIS, SAMUEL F. *Diplomatic History of the United States.* Henry Holt & Company, Inc., 1953.

BERRY, DON. *A Majority of Scoundrels.* Harper & Brothers, 1961.

BILLINGTON, RAY. *Far Western Frontier.* Harper & Brothers, 1956.

BLAKER, ROSEN. *The Golden Conquistadores.* Bobbs-Merrill Company, 1960.

BOLTON, HERBERT E. *Outpost of Empire.* Alfred A. Knopf, Inc., 1931.

BOLTON, HERBERT E. *Padre on Horseback.* Sonora Press, 1932.

BOLTON, HERBERT E. *Rim of Christendom.* The Macmillan Company, 1936.

BROOKS, ELISHA. *A Pioneer Mother of California.* Harr Wagner Publishing Company, 1922.

BRYANT, EDWIN. *What I Saw in California.* Fine Arts Press, 1936.

CALIFORNIA HISTORICAL SOCIETY. *Russians in California.* California Historical Society.

CAUGHEY, JOHN. *History of the Pacific Coast.* John Caughey.

CLELAND, ROBERT. *California Pageant.* Alfred A. Knopf, Inc., 1946.

CLELAND, ROBERT. *From Wilderness to Empire.* Alfred A. Knopf, Inc., 1959.

CLELAND, ROBERT. *Pathfinders.* Powell Publishing Company, 1929.

COMAN, KATHERINE. *Economic Beginnings of the Far West.* The Macmillan Company, 1912.

CONKLING, ROSCOE AND MARGARET. *Butterfield Overland Mail 1857-1869.* Arthur H. Clark Company, 1947.

COOKE, PHILIP ST. G. *Conquest of New Mexico and California.* Bio Books, 1952.

CORLE, EDWIN. *The Gila.* Rinehart & Company, 1951.

CORLE, EDWIN. *The Royal Highway.* Bobbs-Merrill Company, 1949.

COY, OWEN C. *The Great Trek.* Powell Publishing Company, 1931.

DELANO, ALONZO. *Across the Plains and Among the Diggings.* Wilson-Erickson, Inc., 1936.

DELLENBAUGH, F. *Breaking the Wilderness.* G. P. Putnam's Sons, 1905.

DENIS, ALBERTA. *Spanish Alta California.* The Macmillan Company, 1927.

DE VOTO, BERNARD. *The Course of the Empire.* Houghton Mifflin Company, 1952.

DICK, EVERETT. *Vanguards of the Frontier.* Appleton-Century Company, Inc., 1941.

DILLON, R. *California Trail Herd.* Talisman Press, 1961.

DRIGGS, HOWARD. *Westward America.* G. P. Putnam's Sons, 1942.

DUFFUS, R. L. *Santa Fe Trail.* Longmans, Green & Company, 1930.

DUNBAR, SEYMOUR. *A History of Travel.* Bobbs-Merrill Company, 1915.

ECCLESTON, ROBERT. *Overland to California on the Southwest Trail in America.* University of California Press, 1950.

ELDRIDGE, ZOETH. *March of Portola—Discovery of S. F. Bay.* California Promotion Committee, 1909.

ENGLEBERT, OMAR. *Last of the Conquistadors.* Harcourt, Brace & Company, Inc., 1956.

FERGUSSON, ERNA. *New Mexico.* Alfred A. Knopf, Inc., 1951.

FERGUSSON, ERNA. *Our Southwest.* Alfred A. Knopf, Inc., 1952.

FOREMAN, GRANT. *Marcy and the Gold Seekers.* University of Oklahoma Press, 1939.

FOREMAN, GRANT. *Pathfinder in the Southwest.* Arthur H. Clark Company, 1926.

FULLER, GEORGE W. *History of the Pacific Northwest.* Alfred A. Knopf, Inc., 1931.

GARDINER, DOROTHY. *West of the River.* Thomas Y. Crowell Company, 1941.

GARRARD, LEWIS. *Wah-to-Yah and the Taos Trail.* University of Oklahoma Press, 1955.

GEIGER, VINCENT, AND BRYARLY, WAKEMAN. *Trail to California.* Yale University Press, 1959.

GHENT, WM. J. *Early Far West.* Longmans, Green & Company, 1931.

GOETSMANN, WM. *Army Exploration in American West 1803-63.* Yale University Press, 1959.

GOLDER, F. A. *March of the Mormon Battalion*. The Century Co., 1928.

GRIFFIN, J. S. *A Doctor Comes to California*. California Historical Society, 1943.

HAFEN, LEROY AND ANN. *The Old Spanish Trail*. Arthur H. Clark Company, 1955.

HAINES, FRANCIS. *Nez Perce*. University of Oklahoma Press, 1955.

HANCOCK, SAMUEL. *Narrative of Samuel Hancock*. Robert M. McBride & Company, 1927.

HARLOW, ALVIN. *Old Waybills*. The Century Company, 1934.

HARRIS, BENJAMIN. *Gila Trail*. University of Oklahoma Press, 1960.

HENRY, R. S. *Story of the Mexican War*. Bobbs-Merrill Company, 1950.

HOLBROOK, STEWART. *The Columbia*. Rinehart & Company, 1956.

HOLBROOK, STEWART. *Yankee Exodus*. The Macmillan Company, 1950.

HOLLON, W. EUGENE. *Great Days of Overland Stage*. American Heritage, VIII-6, 1957.

HOLLON, W. EUGENE. *Southwest—Old and New*. Alfred A. Knopf, Inc., 1961.

HORGAN, PAUL. *Great River*. Rinehart & Company, 1954.

JACOBS, MELVIN. *Winning Oregon*. Caxton Press, 1938.

JOHANSEN, DOROTHY O., AND GATES, CHARLES M. *Empire of the Columbia*. Harper & Brothers, 1957.

JOHNSTON, WM. G. *Overland to California*. Bio Books, 1948.

KELLER, GEORGE. *A Trip Across the Plains*. Biobooks, 1955.

LAUT, AGNES. *Overland Trail*. Frederick A. Stokes Co., 1929.

LAUT, AGNES. *Pilgrims on the Santa Fe*. Frederick A. Stokes Co., 1931.

LAVENDER, DAVID. *Bent's Fort*. Doubleday & Company, Inc., 1954.

LAVENDER, DAVID. *Land of Giants*. Doubleday & Company, Inc., 1958.

LIENHARD, HEINRICH. *From St. Louis to Sutter's Fort, 1846*. University of Oklahoma Press, 1961.

LOCKWOOD, FRANK C. *Pioneer Days in Arizona*. The Macmillan Company, 1932.

LUCIA, ELLIS. *Saga of Ben Holladay*. Hastings House Publishers, Inc., 1959.

LUMMIS, CHARLES F. *The Spanish Pioneers*. A. C. McClurg & Co., 1929.

MAYNARD, THEODORE. *The Long Road of Father Serra*. Appleton-Century-Crofts, Inc., 1954.

MONAGHAN, JAY. *The Overland Trail*. Bobbs-Merrill Company, 1947.

MORA, JO. *Californios*. Doubleday & Company, Inc., 1949.

MULDER AND MORTENSEN. *Among the Mormons*. Alfred A. Knopf, Inc., 1958.

MURPHY, BILL. *Pictorial History of California*. Fearon Publishers, 1958.

OGDEN, ADELE. *California Sea Otter Trade.* University of California Press, 1941.

OLDER, MRS. FREMONT. *California Missions and Their Romances.* Coward-McCann, Inc., 1938.

PADEN, IRENE. *Wake of the Prairie Schooner.* The Macmillan Company, 1943.

PARRISH, PHILIP H. *Before the Covered Wagon.* Metropolitan Press, 1931.

PATTIE, JAMES OHIO. *The Personal Narrative of James Ohio Pattie.* J. B. Lippincott Company, 1962.

PATTON, ANNALEONE D. *California Mormons.* Deseret Book Co., 1961.

PEATTIE, D. C. *Forward the Nation.* G. P. Putnam's Sons, 1942.

PERRIGO, LYNN I. *Our Spanish Southwest.* Banks, Upshaw & Co., 1960.

PHILLIPS, PAUL. *The Fur Trade.* University of Oklahoma Press, 1961.

RIEGEL, R. E. *America Moves West.* Henry Holt & Company, 1930.

SABIN, E. L. *Kit Carson Days.* Press of the Pioneers, Inc., 1935.

SANDOZ, MARI. *Love Song to the Plains.* Harper & Brothers, 1961.

SCHALLENBERGER, MOSES. *The Opening of the California Trail.* University of California Press, 1953.

STEWART, GEORGE. *Ordeal by Hunger.* Henry Holt & Company, Inc., 1936.

STONE, IRVING. *Immortal Wife.* Doubleday & Company, Inc., 1944.

STONE, IRVING. *Men to Match My Mountains.* Doubleday & Company, Inc., 1956.

TERRELL, JOHN U. *Journey into Darkness.* William Morrow & Company, Inc., 1962.

THOMPSON, R. A. *Fort Ross.* Biobooks, 1951.

VESTAL, STANLEY. *Old Santa Fe Trail.* Houghton Mifflin Company, 1939.

WARE, JOSEPH E. *Emigrant's Guide to California.* Princeton University Press, 1932.

WARREN, SIDNEY. *Farthest Frontier.* The Macmillan Company, 1949.

WATERS, FRANK. *The Colorado.* Rinehart & Company, Inc., 1946.

WELLMAN, PAUL. *Glory, God and Gold.* Doubleday & Company, Inc., 1954.

WILSON, RUFUS R. *Out of the West.* Press of the Pioneers, Inc., 1933.

WINTHER, OSCAR. *The Great Northwest.* Alfred A. Knopf, Inc., 1950.

WINTHER, OSCAR. *The Old Oregon Country.* Stanford University Press, 1950.

WISTAR, I. J. *Autobiography of Gen. Isaac J. Wistar.* Harper & Brothers, 1938.

WYMAN, W. D. *California Emigrant Letters.* Bookman Associates, Inc., 1952.

Index

traders, 182-186
  caravans of, 177-178, 180, 186-207,
    211-212, 218, 219, 255-256, 288-289,
    301-302
  fur, 183-185, 198, 221-227, 234
  horse, 176-180
  trading centers, 182, 207-212, 255-256,
    288
trails, beginnings of, 1-7
trappers, beaver, 185, 187, 191, 197-198,
  204, 209, 240, 242-248, 266, 270
  in Gila region, 33-40
  and Old Spanish trail, 161-174, 179,
    180
Truckee, Calif., 278, 279
Truckee River, 267, 273, 278-279
Tubac, Ariz., 27-28, 29, 32, 89
Tucson, Ariz., 75-76
  and Butterfield stage line, 102, 106-
    107
  routes to, 82-83, 89-90, 90-93
Tumacacori Mission, 27-28
Turner, Captain, 58
Tuzigoot pueblos, 13
Twin Falls, Idaho, 238, 254
Two Ocean Creek, 2

Umatilla River, 239
Union Pacific Railroad, 181, 302
United States Government:
  and California migration, 271-272
  and Santa Fe Trail survey, 193-194
  transportation legislation by, 94-100,
    289-294, 302
  and westward expansion, 40-41
United States highways, *see* High-
  way . . .
Upper (Alta) California, *see* California
Upson, "Boston," 295-296
Utah, 1, 262, 270, 286
  Old Spanish Trail in, 153, 155, 159-
    160, 173, 180
Utah Lake, 160, 161, 166, 290
Ute Indians, 153, 155-156, 157, 158-160,
  161, 173, 177, 179, 180, 182

Vancouver Island, 221-224
Velicatá Mission, 129-130
Verde River, 38
Verger, Father, 146, 147

Vigil, Juan, 216
Vila, Captain, 129, 138
Virginia City, Mont., 301
Virgin River, 161, 167, 169-170, 175,
  177
Vizcaíno, Sebastián, 125-126, 128, 131-
  133, 134, 138, 140-141

Waddell, William B., 289, 292-294,
  297-298, 301
wagon roads:
  establishment of, 67-80, 204
  contracts for, 95-100
wagon trains, *see* caravans
Wakara, Ute chief, 179, 180
Waldo, Bill, 201
Walker, Joseph, 33, 180, 198, 266-269,
  271, 274, 275-276, 296
Walker Pass, 268
Walker River, 267, 271
Walla Walla, Wash., 254, 260
War of 1812, 242
Ward, Johnny, 111-112
Warner's Ranch, 56, 79, 107
Wasatch, Chief, 161
Wasatch Mountains, 2, 6, 155, 172, 173,
  174, 283
Washoe hills, 296-297, 301, 302
Weaver, Paul (Pauline), 67, 68, 70,
  71, 73, 75, 76
Weber River, 283, 286
Weller, Senator, 95
Wells, Nevada, 266, 290
Wells Fargo & Company, 115, 301-302
West, prehistoric, 1-2
Western Emigration Society, 270
Weston, Mo., 288
Westport Landing (Kansas City), 212,
  261, 263
White River, 160
Whitman, Marcus and Narcissa, 257-
  260
Willamette River, 256-257
Williams, "Old Bill," 33, 179, 198
Wind River Mountains, 241-242
Winkler County, 84
Winnemucca, Chief, 277, 296-297
Wolfskill, William, 159, 161, 171-173
Woodson, Samuel, 289-290
Wyandotte, Kansas, 219
Wyeth, Jacob, Dr., 251

A NOTE ON MANUFACTURE

The text of this book was set in Linotype Janson, an old-style face originally cut by Nicholas Kis in about 1690. The book was composed by Ruttle, Shaw & Wetherill, printed by Cincinnati Litho Corporation, and bound by Vail-Ballou Press. It is printed in a deep brown ink on S. D. Warren Company's Eggshell Laid light-toned paper.

The typography and binding designs are by Laurel Wagner. Herbert Anthony drew the detail maps, and Charles Berger the endpapers. Research on the pictures and maps was performed by Rhoda Tripp.

DATE DUE

FEB 1 0 '70		
MR 7 '80		
DE 8 '80		
NO 15 '82		
NO 3 0 '82		
GAYLORD		PRINTED IN U.S.A.